MW00582854

LIT: LIFE IGNITION TOOLS

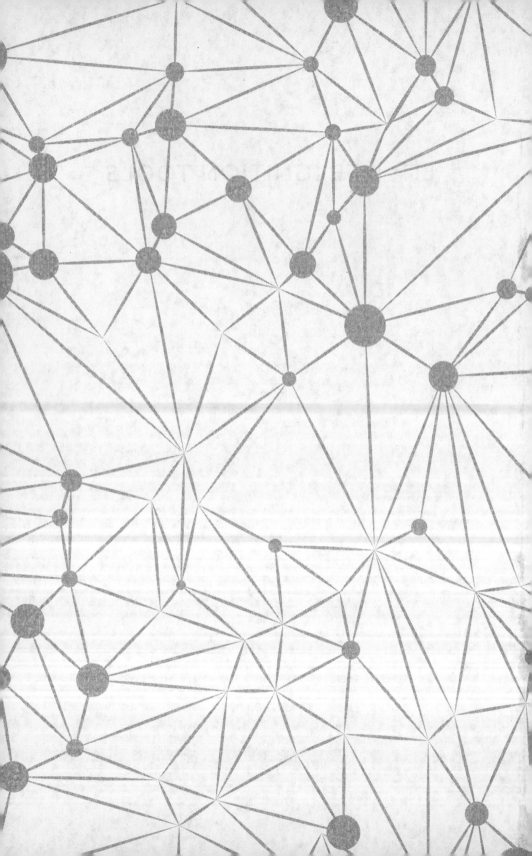

LIT

LIFE IGNITION TOOLS

Use Nature's Playbook to
Energize Your Brain,
Spark Ideas, and Ignite Action

JEFF KARP

WITH TERESA BARKER

_WM_

WILLIAM MORROW
An Imprint of HarperCollinsPublishers

Illustration on page xxxviii by Mao Miyamoto Medical Media, Inc.

HarperCollins books may be purchased for educational, business, or sales promotional use. For information, please email the Special Markets Department at SPsales@harpercollins.com.

FIRST EDITION

Designed by Bonni Leon-Berman

Library of Congress Cataloging-in-Publication Data has been applied for.

ISBN 978-0-06-301073-4

24 25 26 27 28 LBC 5 4 3 2 1

Dedicated to the late Nitamabit/Nii Gaani Aki Inini (Dr. Elder Dave Courchene), Anishinaabe Nation, in honor of his service to the People and Mother Earth and his work in fulfillment of the dream and vision of the Turtle Lodge to awaken, nurture, and strengthen the spirit in all Peoples.

CONTENTS

Introduction: One Boy's Journey to LIT — ix

Get the Ball Rolling! Lower the Activation Energy — xxxv

Flip the Switch: What's Holding You Back? 1
Intercept routine patterns to make simple, deliberate changes.

Live for the Questions: Swap Caution for Curiosity
and the Deeper Dig.. 22
Tap the vitality of inquiry.

Get Bothered: Wake Up to What You Want...............................41
Identify the "Why?" that motivates you.

Be an Active Opportunist: Scout Ideas, Insights,
and Inspiration Everywhere 57
Train your brain to seek diverse experiences and seize opportunities.

Pinch Your Brain: Attention Is Your Superpower........................... 77
Interrupt mind drift and the pull of distractions with intentional tugs.

Get Hooked on Movement: It's the Key to
Evolutionary Success... 97
Take any small step—in anything—to activate fresh energy.

Fall in Love with Practice: Savor the Joys of the
Brawny Brain 119
Enjoy the rewards of repetition and the joy of incremental improvements.

Do New, Do Different: Invite Surprise and Serendipity 136
Play with nuance and novelty to generate new possibilities.

Focus Beyond Failure: Tee Up Energy for Renewed Action 151
Use the emotional charge of failure to fine-tune where you channel your purposeful efforts.

Be Human: Be Humble 166
Let awe be your access point for inspiration and your capacity for greater good.

Press "Pause": Protect Time to Be and Behold 183
Prioritize time for unhurried play, solitude, and silence to recharge your spirit.

Hug Nature: Revitalize Your Roots 203
Embrace your place in the natural ecosystem and connect with life's powerful resources to flourish.

Light the World: Create a Daring, Caring Culture 227
Stay present to your deepest desire for a good life and a world that empowers all to thrive.

Afterword: The Answers Are in Questions   255
Acknowledgments   257
Notes   259
Bibliography   279
Index   283

INTRODUCTION

One Boy's Journey to LIT

The universe is full of magical things
patiently waiting for our wits to grow sharper.
—EDEN PHILLPOTTS

As citizens of the twenty-first century, we often feel the world is spinning out of control, or at least out of *our* control. Catastrophe and dysfunction loom large in our minds. Anxiety and depression have been declared public health epidemics. Sometimes the ability to direct our lives seems so far out of our grasp that we just surrender. Unable to focus the way we want to or resist the distractions and demands of the moment, we release ourselves to the torrent and simply react—to horrific news, to flame-throwing tweets or texts, to advertising and influencers, and to the omnipresent pull of media and social media algorithms with their own agendas. And I say this as an optimist who believes that humans have fundamentally good qualities and do care about other creatures (including one another) and about the health of the planet. Even so, at times it seems impossible to act with intention and create the lives we truly want to lead. But I'm optimistic for two reasons. One is that we're waking up to our place at this moment in time and to our potential as problem solvers on a planetary scale. Science, newly coupled with Indigenous knowledge and deep expertise, continues to generate new evidence of the complex interconnections of life on this planet. With our emerging awareness of our role in the ecosystem and the complexities that arise from our choices, which are often damaging, we can see the need for fresh, innovative thinking. We can no longer act as though we don't know what's going on or what's at stake, accepting cultural norms that ignore consequences, muddle our intuitive senses, and immobilize us.

We're also increasingly aware that whatever our circumstances, we want our lives to have meaning and purpose. We want our relationships and work to be fulfilling. We want some happiness in the mix. And we know that we can't wait for someone else to make that happen. We've got to do it for ourselves.

Best of all, neuroscience tells us that our brains are up to the task. Plastic and malleable, hungry for the right challenge, our brain is capable of creativity, new knowledge acquisition, and growth, even as we age. This much we own and can control. It's our evolutionary inheritance, nature's playbook. We can choose to activate the neural networks that shake our brain awake, flip the switch to enliven our senses, and stimulate our thought processes beyond what we may have imagined possible.

Where to start? How do we filter out the noise and distraction, overcome inertia and other obstacles to design the lives we want? How can we regain some control and switch on our innate abilities to focus on what matters most, while still living amid the cacophony of modern life?

The best people to teach us how to cope may be the very people who've struggled the most with attention and learning challenges. Many have refined the skills necessary to thrive in a world filled with constant stimulation, distraction, and stress.

How do I know this? Because I'm one of them.

MY JOURNEY TO LIT

As a professor at Harvard Medical School and MIT, I am very lucky; I get to learn from and collaborate with some of the most innovative minds in the world of medicine, science, and technology. But I was not "supposed" to be here. No one would have predicted this for me.

When I was a kid in elementary school in rural Canada, I had the attention span of a fruit fly, and I struggled to keep up. Reading, writing, classroom discussion, and teachers' instruction—I couldn't make sense of any of it. It wasn't just that I was distractible and my brain didn't process things in a conventional way; my mind felt completely open to just existing in the world, in a constant mind meld with the universe. For me, it felt weird to isolate and define things, to pin down ideas and limit learning to what seemed to me to be fragments of information. If new knowledge was constantly making old ideas obsolete, to me it made more sense to assume that everything is in a constant state of change—not only the world around us but our understanding of it. To my mind, school felt more like a museum than a workshop. It took a ton of effort for me to narrow my focus so stuff could enter, stick, and stay.

And I was an anxious kid. I couldn't relax and just be myself, feel okay as "the quirky kid," because I felt like something worse than that: an alien, a human anomaly. I realized early on that there were many things I was "supposed" to do, but none of them came naturally or seemed logical. More troubling still was that much of it didn't feel like the right thing to do; it felt actively wrong. When a teacher asked me a question, whether on a test or in class, I typically found the question confusing, often unanswerable. The "right" answer seemed like just one of many possibilities. (This plagues me to this day and makes me less than helpful to my kids with their homework.) So most of my school years were an exercise in trying to figure out, interpret, and fit others' expectations.

As a kindergartener, each day I walked up the steps of the older brick building, past the principal's office, down the hall, and into my classroom. There was the typical large square carpeted area for story time, as well as lots of books and interactive toys. Like most young children, I was curious and filled with energy. I could not sit still. Everything excited me. I wanted to explore, roam, see, and touch. It was impossible for me to sit in a chair for hours and listen. "Pretend your bottom is glued to your chair," my kindergarten teacher encouraged. *Okay,* I thought. *I can do that!* I wrapped my fingers around the bottom of my seat, held it against my rear, stood, and waddled around the room as my classmates giggled. The teacher sent me to the principal's office. I got to know the principal pretty well that year.

By second grade, it seemed as if my classmates possessed a superpower that allowed them to decipher the strange letters on the pages of books. But my mind couldn't make sense of them, and I didn't understand how the other students were sounding those letters out and using them to form words. My mother tried phonics, flash cards, everything, but as the school year came to a close, my teacher recommended that I repeat the grade.

Desperate to help me, my mother enrolled me in a summer school for children with learning disabilities. There I received one-on-one attention. Teachers built on my strengths, and I thrived. At the end of the summer, a private educational consultant recommended that I return to my regular school, advancing with my peers to grade three, with access to a quiet resource room.

But my third-grade teacher didn't see the promise that my summer schoolteachers had seen. That teacher assigned a label to me that would follow me for much of my school life: troublemaker. At one point when we had to take a test, she put blinders—an upright folding panel—on my desk and said, "There—you can't look elsewhere, you don't have any distractions"—and then she got out her stopwatch and timed me, which made me anxious. She did that in front of the class, and everyone made fun of me, following her lead. I was teased a lot.

One day I noticed another student struggling with math problems. I wanted to help, so I walked over to try to show him how to do the work. The teacher quipped, "Well, isn't that like the blind leading the blind?" I was confused. What did it mean for a blind person to lead a blind person? I wasn't blind! Why had she said that?

That night, I asked my mother. She sat me down on the edge of her bed, took a breath, and said, "Your teacher is a jerk. But you still have to respect her. You have to do your best."

I tried to follow her advice, and occasionally I excelled. I entered speech competitions—and I won. My mother took me for lessons in computer programming. After the first session, the teacher met Mom at the door and said, "No need to bring him back. He already understands more than I do."

But many skills, especially memorization, eluded me. (To this day I forget what I was thinking just a moment ago, and often I need to read the same thing twenty times before it sinks in.) I was always distracted, and because I consistently struggled to understand, my slow pace reduced the potential rewards even more and crushed my confidence.

I was a puzzle for my teachers, a misfit in the conventional academic sense, and a total outcast socially. Year after year, many teachers gave up on me. One teacher called me a "lazy con artist." Another told me, "You'll never make it in the real world." In fourth grade, my report card was a line of Cs and Ds. It was the same for grade five, then grade six. I was so discouraged. Had it not been for my tenacious mother and my seventh-grade homeroom and science teacher, Lyle Couch, I might have given up. Mr. Couch focused on my unique strengths and encouraged me.

That was also the year that my mother stepped around the school's chain of command and made the case directly to the school board. A formal assessment had identified me as "communications disabled"—I had difficulty extracting information from one medium (e.g., from the blackboard or a book), then assimilating and comprehending the information so I could answer a question or transfer the information into another medium (e.g., notebook or workbook). The board accepted the diagnosis of a learning disability and approved established accommodations for time and testing that had been denied me for so long.

Today, with society's much greater understanding of ADHD, part of my eventual diagnosis, there are evidence-based approaches for building self-regulation skills designed for kids (and adults). But at that time and in that place, the only option was to wing it.

Over the years, I slowly gained motivation and became more persistent. I didn't know it at the time, but my evolution as a learner mirrored the two fundamental concepts of how neurons change and grow—how they learn—that the neuroscientist Eric Kandel would someday identify as the basis that sea slugs and humans have in common for learning and memory: habituation and sensitization in response to repeated exposure to stimuli. (And slugs have only 20,000 neurons, compared to the estimated 86 billion to 100 billion or so in humans, not counting the estimated 100 trillion to 1,000 trillion synapses that connect them!) Habituation means that we become less reactive to stimuli, as you might to traffic noise outside your window. Sensitization means that our reaction is stronger, as happens when, for instance, a sound or a smell or even the thought of something becomes a trigger.

Living my own experiment, I learned to make use of both. I discovered some basic ways to work with my brain to habituate to some stimuli (ordinary things that distracted me) and sensitize (sharpen my attention) to others to be able to reel in my wandering mind and redirect the synaptic messaging with intention. At one point, in the room where I studied there was a pinball machine next to me and a TV behind me. I learned to ignore both and used playing the pinball machine as a reward for finishing my homework.

Over time I became hyperaware of how to intentionally hijack processes in my brain this way to be less reactive or more sharply focused as needed. The result: I was able to focus on what seemed most purposeful, then follow through and maximize impact as opportunities opened up. I tinkered and fine-tuned until I learned how to use these powerful tools to tap into the heightened state of awareness and deep engagement that I call *lit*.

I call it *lit* for two reasons. First, "lit" aptly describes how the flash of inspiration feels—as if a bright light just flipped on in the dark. Or a spark has set your thinking ablaze. When you've had an epiphany, been awestruck, or simply been superexcited, you've felt that spark. Second, "lit" is how these moments appear to the scientists who study them. Inside the brain (and in the gut as well), engaged states activate neurons. In the brain, this triggers an increase in cerebral blood flow that neuroscientists can see when they use functional magnetic resonance imaging (fMRI). On a monitor, this oxygenated blood lights up an otherwise gray image of the brain with yellow-orange hot spots of activity. Emerging science shows that this neural activation is associated not only with particular cognitive activity or emotions such as fear and anger but also with love, awe, happiness, fun, and "peak states," or flow.

My take on it is that *lit* is a life force, an energy that thrums through nature and the cosmos—and each of us. It drives the connection and curiosity that are innate in (though not exclusive to) our species, programmed into our DNA, the circuitry for a sense of wonder or "oneness," which we see so abundantly expressed in infants and young children. As we leave our lavishly *lit* baby years behind us, we have to make an effort to unlock and tap into that energy flow. Surprisingly, we can do so easily through our life experiences. As in all journeys, there are challenges to overcome, obstacles or circumstances that can dim the *lit* connection. But they can be overcome. It's through the adventures of life that we engage and are able to fully activate *lit*. And all it takes is the smallest flicker of a spark for ignition.

That *lit* spark is the brain's mechanism for tapping into the vital transformative energy that activates our senses and thought processes. In *lit* mode, we engage at the highest level of our abilities. We not only develop the mental muscles to stay focused, we also build the confidence and the dexterity to riff off of new information on the fly. We're more likely to use our critical thinking skills, which can keep us from blindly accepting what we're told, or told to believe, especially when our intuition says otherwise. We find it easier to connect with people, are more alive to the possibilities all around us, and are better able to capitalize upon them. In a stream of ever-replenishing energy, we're constantly learning, growing, creating, and iterating. We're building our capacity while doing our best work.

As I honed strategies that enabled me to activate my brain this way at will, I identified a dozen that were simple to use and never failed to open my thinking in just the way that was needed, whatever that was. Whether it was to direct my attention or disrupt it, sharpen my focus or broaden it, do something stimulating or quiet my mind, these Life Ignition Tools (LIT) worked for me, and then for others as I shared them.

Discovering that I could engage that *lit* state at will changed my relationship to obstacles of all kinds. In physics, inertia is a property of matter, the passive resistance to change in speed or direction. Unless an outside force intervenes, an object at rest will stay that way; an object in motion continues. Gravity and friction slow a rolling ball; a swift kick accelerates it. Metaphorically, *lit* is the swift kick that breaks through inertia and gets the ball rolling. In my experience, whether the inertia is due to outside resistance, habit, apathy, or just a lull that's lingered too long, through the years and to this day, when I'm in this brain state, nothing can stop me. I'm *lit*.

Once I learned how to work with my neuroatypical, voraciously curious, but chaotic brain, I discovered infinite opportunity to question, create, and innovate as a bioengineer and entrepreneur on a global scale and help others do the same. These LIT tools took me from being a confused and frustrated kid, sidelined in that special ed classroom in rural Canada, to becoming a bioengineer and medical innovator elected a fellow of the National Academy of Inventors, the Royal Society of Chemistry, the American Institute for Medical and Biological Engineering's College of Fellows, the Biomedical Engineering Society, and the Canadian Academy of Engineering. As a professor I've trained more than two hundred people, many of whom are now professors at institutions around the world and innovators in industry; published 130 peer-reviewed papers with more than thirty thousand citations; and obtained more than a hundred issued or pending national and international patents. The tools also helped me cofound twelve companies with products on the market or in development. And finally, they've been instrumental in creating a productive, supportive, and dynamic high-energy environment in my lab, which recently morphed from Karp Lab to the Center for Accelerated Medical Innovation.

LIT worked for this kid who appeared to show no promise and the young man who remained frustrated and discouraged for many years. I delivered the commencement speech at my high school in 2011 and was the first inductee into the school's hall of honor (along with two prior students who are members of an iconic Canadian rock band, I Mother Earth), the very school system where many of my teachers once held out so little hope for my future success.

Though I still struggle every day in various ways, I'm grateful to be able to say that these LIT tools enabled me to meet and far exceed those dismal early expectations. But I am most excited about what the tools have done for others. Members of the lab have gone on to start labs of their own or launch other enterprises that continually demonstrate the immeasurable impact of their work in the world as they set out to make it better, advancing their fields and improving the lives of millions of people. You'll meet some of them in the pages ahead.

If we want breakthroughs in science and medicine, if we want successful, disruptive innovations on all fronts to support healthier communities, and if we want to cut through the noise and focus on what is most important, we must learn how to use all of the tools in nature's playbook, our evolutionary arsenal. We must shake up our thinking—not just now and then but on a daily basis. In practice, LIT tools make it possible for us to take anything we're hardwired for—including undesirable or unhelpful behaviors and habits—and with intention channel the energy in them to create a positive outcome. It's easier than you might think because the more you do it, the greater the rewards, the momentum, and your impact for good. You're never too old to charge your brain this way, and most definitely no one is ever too young. In fact, LIT tools can be lifesavers for kids, as they were for me.

MINING YOUR NEURODIVERSITY

Some people assume that they don't have what it takes to be highly creative and focused or to maintain a high level of productivity, discipline, and engagement. All too often, people believe this lie because of messages they received at an early age. Type "famous people who failed" into any search engine, and you'll quickly learn that educators considered Albert Einstein to be a poor student and that Thomas Edison was "addled" and not worthwhile to keep in school. Walt Disney was once fired because his boss thought he "lacked imagination and had no good ideas." One of Oprah Winfrey's employers told her she was "unfit for television news."

And those are just the stories that someone thought to chronicle. Countless others remain untold of people who were once considered failures, underachievers, slow learners, different, lacking, unmotivated, but then went on to achieve great things. I'm sure you know some in your own life. We now know that many students struggle because they learn in different ways than most of their peers do, or they've been told that they aren't good at math or reading and they believe they can never learn. The result is that "we are educating people out of their creative capacities," noted Ken Robinson, the late British author, speaker, and international adviser on education and the arts, in his talk "Do Schools Kill Creativity?," one of the most-watched speeches in TED Talks history. Political pressures have only made matters worse, steadily narrowing content and instruction that would develop students' critical thinking skills. This includes understanding that they are capable learners, diverse in many ways, each with the inborn potential to be a valuable contributor.

Perhaps surprisingly, it takes as little as *one hour* to teach children that their intellectual abilities can be developed with effort. Once they are taught this important truth, their grades improve significantly, according to the National Study of Learning Mindsets. Many young people need a mentor, an extra nudge. There is no single pathway to knowledge.

Society itself, and our desire as a social species to fit in and feel we belong, can work against creativity and critical thinking as well. Much about the environments into which we're born and in which we're raised, educated, and inducted into work life is the product of cultural forces beyond our immediate control, and they can be painfully slow to change. One reason schools are a lightning rod for criticism is that they are the arena in which pedagogy, politics, and public opinion—diverse and often divisive—suck the air out of the room for children—and for many of their inspiring teachers. After all, human neurodiversity isn't limited to the quirky mind. Neurodiversity represents the range of *all* minds, all children. Each of us—including you—is somewhere different on that vast continuum. That's why what we call genius actually manifests itself in so many different forms, across the range of human endeavor and the full human family, not just the celebrated few. Invaluable potential goes untapped simply because we fail to recognize it.

Temple Grandin, the scientist and author known globally for her work in animal behavior and her life experience as someone with autism, described the particular focus and intensity that she was able to bring to complex challenges in her work and life. "People with autism see the simple," she told me as we talked about how she had been drawn into her career in science and the opportunity to make complex issues regarding animal behavior more accessible to more people. As an education activist, she has pressed for greater attention to the value of neurodiversity, in particular visual learning, warning that education practices that fail these learners fail our society. "Today, we want our students to be well rounded; we should think about making sure that the education we provide is as well," she wrote in an essay for the *New York Times*. Certain characteristics and skill sets of divergent thinking are "critical for innovation and invention" and are "essential to finding real-world solutions to society's many problems."

Like Grandin, others have discovered that their uncommon qualities of mind, treated as deficits in some contexts, can turn out to be their strongest assets. Biodiversity and the contribution of every single species is an evolutionary strength of life on Earth. The value of diversity in the way our brains interpret the world applies to all of us. Diversity makes the collective smarts smarter.

"All children start their school careers with sparkling imaginations, fertile minds, and a willingness to take risks with what they think," Robinson once said. In his book *The Element: How Finding Your Passion Changes Everything*, he writes that "The key is not to standardize education, but to personalize it, to build achievement on discovering the individual talents of each child, to put students in an environment where they want to learn and where they can naturally discover their true passions."

When school becomes a learning factory where efficiency drives the engine—of curriculum, instruction, testing, and evaluation—it shortchanges everyone. This is especially true for children trapped in the margins, but anywhere diversity is sidelined, that catalyst for creativity is lost to us all.

As we work for systemic change that can be slow in coming, we need to focus on creating a life strategy for ourselves and all children that will unlock our capabilities. We can take steps ourselves to cultivate curiosity, creativity, and active engagement with the world. Robinson likened it to mining: "Human resources are like natural resources; they're often buried deep. You have to go looking for them; they're not just lying around on the surface. You have to create the circumstances where they show themselves." In our conversation, Grandin talked about the need to create environments that stretch children as learners, provide them with choices and consequences, and show confidence in their capacity to unleash their potential. "You've got to stretch these kids," she said. "You don't chuck 'em in the deep end of the pool." We all need that stretch to enliven our learning and our lives.

ENERGY TRANSFER, THE "IT" IN *LIT*

As I explored in search of a scientific explanation or a foundational understanding of the *lit* mind state, I heard various ideas from scientists, psychologists, philosophers, activists, and others. Like the parable of the blind men and the elephant, each touched on an essential truth about the *lit* phenomenon, as viewed through their own lens of expertise or experience. But for me, the unifying principle that pulls all of them together is the simple idea of energy.

As a scientist, I'm admittedly keen on the concept of energy transfer as a way to understand how things work, whether it's a feat of engineering, a natural ecosystem, a marriage, or the contagious power of inspiration. Plants use photosynthesis to transform energy from the sun into energy for their own growth, and eventually ours, as we consume the energy stored in the food we eat. But it doesn't stop there; every transfer of energy leads to another. The energy we consume sustains us, then changes into action as we go about our work and lives, interacting with one another and our environment. With every interaction, we transfer energy—we set energy in motion. The process of energy transfer is intrinsic in nature, which includes us.

We are essentially energetic beings. Energy fields are in constant play in the human body, in our heart, brain, skin, liver, intestine, and all our atomic components. Every reaction we have, whether to our environment, to other people and things they say or do, or to our own thoughts, changes the movement of atoms in our bodies and thus changes the energy fields within us and the energy we generate and transfer outward. When we say we feel "energized" to do something, whether to work toward a goal or see a friend, it's not just a feeling or mood; it's a physiological fact. So when I talk about *lit* as an energized brain state igniting fresh potential, the energy transfer is as real as photosynthesis or kicking a ball.

We routinely transfer emotional energy to others via what we say or how we say it. Even spirituality, in whatever way we experience it, involves a transfer of energy from a source that uplifts us to the way we express that when we, in turn, support or encourage others. Inspiration, love, even grief are forms of energy transformation. Science has yet to be able to explain how, but somehow, all of these energies intersect and synergize. The energetic spark at their intersection—the *lit* spark—becomes a catalyst in the dynamic system powering the Earth and energizing its diverse web of life. No matter how our circumstances may dull the connection, we all have that spark nestled deep inside.

> *Everything in life is vibration.*
> —ALBERT EINSTEIN

In recent years, neuroscience has lifted the lid on the innate capacities of the brain to change and grow with our conscious intention. It turns out that we can, at will, tap into a kind of peak experience or optimal mind state and tweak our brain to sustain it, expand it, and act on it. We can do this not only when we're engaged in something we enjoy but, perhaps more important, when we're not—when we're stuck or feeling drained or discouraged. These are precisely the moments that can become crucible points for growth, change, and innovation. Imagine being able to engage as fully as you wish or transform (or simply improve) your experience of any circumstance at will. We can. Each of us is born *lit*. There is nothing here that your brain isn't already hardwired to do—or can't learn how to do.

SURVIVAL OF THE *LIT*-EST

The story of evolution tends to be presented as a long look in the rearview mirror at the journey out of the primordial swamp and the trudge across time. It is a story of adaptation versus the threat of extinction for those species that couldn't adapt to their changing environment. (Don't think of them as evolutionary slackers or failures in a natural sense; more and more it is the case that they cannot overcome our own species' disastrous impact on their habitats.) Among survivors, we aren't necessarily better than the others so much as differently adapted for certain kinds of success. We don't take the prize for evolutionary longevity; plenty of insect, plant, and animal species have been around longer. And many can fly, run, swim, see, and hear far beyond anything we can do. If anything, we are late in recognizing the diverse and highly sophisticated forms of intelligence in animals, plants, and all species, the "immense world," as the science journalist Ed Yong put it in his book by that title, which James Bridle described as "planetary intelligence" in his book *Ways of Being: Animals, Plants, Machines: The Search for a Planetary Intelligence.* "Until very recently, humankind was understood to be the sole possessor of intelligence. It was the quality that made us unique among many life forms—indeed, the most useful definition of intelligence might have been 'what humans do.' This is no longer the case," he wrote, adding that "we are just starting to open the door to an understanding of an entirely different form of intelligence; indeed, of many different intelligences."

What does set us apart is that the human brain has evolved as a remarkable processing network that continually reconfigures itself to integrate new information, a process called plasticity. "Microscopic parts of your neurons change gradually every day," notes the neuroscientist Lisa Feldman Barrett, who writes extensively about brain plasticity and the neurobiology of emotions. "Branch-like dendrites become bushier, and their associated neural connections become more efficient. Little by little, your brain becomes tuned and pruned as you interact with others."

This rapid and robust remodeling of brain circuitry, in response to new experiences, information, and insights, gives us the capacity for creative expression, strategic planning, and problem solving that has taken us to the moon and back, produced great works of art, and made it possible for us to develop natural healing remedies and practices as well as treat and heal ourselves with advanced drugs, implants, and surgical techniques and reduce the spread of diseases. This evolutionary advantage has enabled us to adapt to changes in our environment, as well as intentionally and quickly shape our environment to suit us—something that other species can't so easily do.

Add to that our capacity for storytelling and how we adapt and change the stories we tell ourselves. The narratives we craft about ourselves and our world, both personally and collectively, shape our beliefs and behavior and the way we perceive the world and define what matters most to us. We act on our desires and values, creating and revising realities around those narratives, and our brain adapts to those new environments. Holding that mirror up to myself, for example, earlier in my career, for many years, I worked all hours, disappeared into distractions, and was a no-show for my family in many ways. The story I told myself was that I was an incredible multitasker, frantically but effectively balancing work and family. When events finally shook me awake, I saw the lie in that story. I decided to change my priorities and commit to making a family-centered life a reality. Changing my narrative didn't just shift the superficial triage of expectations I'd developed over the years; it shifted the way I experienced my family, myself, and my work, and that helped me start to make choices that aligned my behavior with my intentions. I discovered that the more I acted on those intentions, the more natural and energizing the thought process and follow-through became. Changing the story changed my brain. Changing the narrative on a societal scale works the same way. As members of communities of any size, when we reframe the stories we tell ourselves and focus our attention and energy on solving problems, not just learning to live with them, our brains are equipped to adapt and advance our efforts in fresh, new ways.

What strikes me is how diversity, adaptability, synergies, and relationships collectively represent the processes that power nature to thrive through evolution. The way mushrooms and other fungi pass essential environmental information and nutrients along to trees is just one example in a truly infinite world of them. Nature's diversity presents all kinds of ways to adapt through synergistic relationships, so when it gets knocked down it has ways to get back up. That doesn't mean that nature can always restore what's been lost or irreparably damaged but that the systems and processes reliably activate for adaptation and growth.

The beauty of using nature's playbook as our own is not just to go into nature, enjoy the scenery, or close your eyes and expect that great things will happen (though they might). In a practical sense, immersing ourselves in nature encourages our brain to engage not only with how it looks or feels to us but with the intrinsic processes of nature that favor our health and survival. LIT tools train our attention on these entry points for experiences that enable us to open our senses to the adaptive and interconnected processes that so beautifully and powerfully energize everything—including us. We can create that experience for ourselves. And as the science of epigenetics shows, our experiences can lastingly influence our genetic expression—which genes are switched on and which aren't—making intentional experiences and changes by choice the closest we can come to having a hand in nature's evolutionary process.

Seeing the brain as an adaptable network that interacts with our environment and experience also enables us to see that the environment that our brains interact with these days—the environment that we have "humanized"—is messing with our ability to adapt.

I'm reminded of Walt Disney's Carousel of Progress at the Magic Kingdom, a massive rotating theater stage featuring lifelike mechanized characters representing a "typical" American family celebrating the joys of life with the advent of electricity and advances in technology through the twentieth century. The exhibit, created for the 1964 World's Fair, has been updated over the years to reflect new waves of technological innovation transforming our lives. What struck me about the exhibit when I sat in the rotating theater, first as a kid in the 1980s and then with my own children in the early 2000s, was the idealized depiction of this passion for progress. It was all about supposed innovation, with no consideration of adverse consequences. There was something cringeworthy in the larger story it unwittingly told about the impact of this drive for a singular kind of progress, detached from and devoid of any relationship with nature—with no sense of us as part of a natural ecosystem. It celebrated human culture as the primary environment, reducing our ambitions as a species to designing our lives separate from nature, but in so doing, separating us from the best of our natural selves.

That's been the dominant narrative for much of the world—much of the human portion of it, at least—and as a result, we've created a largely manufactured environment, a construct for convenience, consumerism, and hypercompetitiveness that threaten our existence, while leaving us increasingly disconnected from nature and our essential interconnectedness. In effect, the drive for more, better, and easier, though improving life in many external ways, has hindered the internal workings of our minds. Our appetite for the online life and digital devices, for consumer goods and conveniences, so dominates our lives now that for all practical purposes the digital environment and consumer culture have become our habitat. The economy has become our ecosystem. We've become habituated in this manufactured environment to respond to marketing cues, often ignoring nature's cues on our behalf. This human-made ecosystem, propelled by technological innovations, has evolved much more quickly than our brains have developed the capacity to recognize the threats it poses to us. Disconnected from nature, we've become unmoored from the primal relationship that since the beginning of time has been a trustworthy source of cues for our survival.

At some point on our way up and out of the primordial swamp, through eons of evolution when the human brain evolved from primitive drives necessary for sheer survival in a hostile environment to more sophisticated capabilities, we used our smarts to alter our environment in ways that, it turns out, work against our health, our future, and the future of the planet itself. There's nothing inherently wrong with exciting technology, expansive opportunities and conveniences, or efficiencies that free us up for better things. The catch is that the part of our brain that still operates on Stone Age reflexes—quick to act but less prepared to think through consequences or plan ahead—has scrambled the circuitry that our digital-age brain needs in order to adapt and create a favorable future. Our ingenuity now threatens our survival.

"Our evolution obviously has not kept up with the technological evolution, where one occurs in hundreds of thousands if not millions of years and the other occurs in a heartbeat, and as a result we're ill prepared to live in this world," James Doty, a neurosurgeon, professor, and founder of the Center for Compassion and Altruism Research and Education at Stanford University, told me. "As a result, all the mechanisms that were helpful when we lived in the not-modern world only aggravate our situation and increase stress, anxiety, and depression."

So it's time we traded the rearview mirror on evolution for one that opens the view forward for a clear-eyed look at the environment we've created for ourselves and the planet, and consider whether our wisest choice is to adapt to that manufactured environment or change it.

THE LEB DIMMER SWITCH

In contrast to those of our earliest ancestors, our lives have become relatively easier, less demanding, safer, and more secure. But the brain still prefers the simplest, most energy-efficient option of well-honed mechanisms and habits. Neuroscientists describe an "energy-saving" mode that the brain uses to reduce energy consumption by reducing information processing. (Generating electrical and chemical signals for processing is energy intensive!) If we'd had to think through all the essential processes our brain bundles for efficient operation, we'd never have survived. But the more we rely on this energy-saving maintenance mode—which I call low-energy brain, or LEB—the more our brain settles into patterns of routine responses.

Convenience, rewards, and digital distractions designed to hijack our attention and hold it with sensory hits are like candy to the brain. Quick fixes easily become habit forming even when they are misaligned with our intentions and even when we know it and want to change. These habits are hard to break precisely because they target and hijack the brain's reward system to promote LEB.

Spend too much time in LEB mode, and as the brain opts for habitual responses, we risk losing the capacity for engaged, purposeful action as the brain prunes lesser-used synapses, the communication links between neurons. In effect, these fading connections act like a dimmer switch on the energy our brain needs for more complex, creative, and stimulating thought processes—*lit*!

> *What you're getting in this low-power mode is more of a low-resolution image of the world.*
> —ZAHID PADAMSEY, NEUROSCIENTIST

Studies of mastery provide a surprising insight. When scientists use fMRI scans to study what happens in the brain as someone masters a new skill, they can actually see the lights in the frontal cortex go out. As novices attempt a new task, their frontal lobes ignite with activity that glows yellow-orange on the image. They're thinking deeply about every step of what they are learning. But when experts are asked to perform the same task, their frontal lobes show more gray than yellow. They don't need to put the same kind of mental energy into a task they already know. Instead, they rely on habits stored in other areas of the brain. Even during childhood, the most prolific time for brain growth, if a lot of time is spent on one kind of activity—whether it's soccer or video games—the brain's penchant for pruning means that early specialization can come at a cost to the broader network of neural connections designed to generate the most robust, well-rounded growth.

LEB skews toward what is easiest or quickest even in matters that merit more from us. For example, relationships, the sense of belonging and contributing to something larger than ourselves, making a difference with our lives, and doing what we can to make the world a better place—these areas need energy and attention to thrive. Because LEB prizes efficiency above all else, it rides the brake on our motivation to step beyond our well-worn habits. It limits our ability to connect with others in fulfilling relationships that grow with time. It prevents us from looking beyond ourselves to tap inspiration from nature and each other, and it weakens our natural inclination to look inward for greater self-awareness and a rich inner life. There is also the hardwired tendency for our brain to assume that what it first learns, or hears repeatedly, is true.

This puts us at a disadvantage in the flood of misinformation, disinformation, and sophisticated propaganda that has become commonplace in social media, notes Nathan Walter, a professor of communication studies at Northwestern University, and others who study the effects of misinformation and why it's so hard to correct. We are navigating this new world, he says, "but the vessel that we use, our brain, is very old."

LEB has gotten us stuck in some patterns that no longer serve us well. In our personal lives and as a global community, so much of our tension and conflict is the legacy of generations of LEB driving human behavior: the inertia of everyday life or worse, bias and prejudice, self-interest, greed, and power grabs—default behaviors that are long overdue for an overhaul.

When LEB starts to dominate society on a large scale, things can become dangerous. We live in a society in which we are buried beneath overwhelming amounts of information and disinformation. Companies such as Amazon, Apple, and Instagram invest billions of dollars to exploit our LEB behaviors because they make more money that way. Online social networks have tapped into the same technology used in slot machines—rewarding us with "likes" in variable bursts that are specifically designed to hijack our brains and get us hooked. The pace of response time lures us to stay on the networks longer as we keep checking for social feedback. We all know the effort it takes to stop ourselves from "just checking" the endless feeds and enticing distractions. It feels so much easier to just keep scrolling than to stop and figure out what to do instead. Platforms evolve and branding changes as users migrate from Facebook, Snapchat, Instagram, and TikTok to more secretive platforms promoting conspiracy theories and violence, but their strategies and objectives remain the same: to cultivate and exploit LEB behaviors.

Without higher-energy thinking, we do what the big corporate players and politicians want us to do. We reach for junk food instead of the good stuff, even when we know the difference. We press the "buy" button of a distant online retailer instead of buying locally to support the merchants who support our communities. We accept one talking head's take on world events instead of reading several sources—especially responsible, fact-based ones—to form our own opinions. We become a society of people who mindlessly scroll (or troll) social media instead of opting for more meaningful interactions. LEB puts the brakes on the innovative thinking we need to solve complex problems or see new possibilities; confronting challenge, it immediately tips into well-trodden paths, nudging us to reach for the same tools and approaches over and over again.

The more time we spend consuming and interacting this way, the more our brains become habituated to, and dependent upon, those brief "hits" or superficial connection. The more we come to look forward to likes, the more conditioned we become to need them and the more energy it takes to break their grip on our attention. This LEB feedback loop becomes a kind of mental gravity that holds us down, an obstacle to *lit*. In the process, we let others define what is important to us to make intentional decisions. Some habits serve us well, of course. Mastery frees our attention to learn new skills, dream, innovate, and improve—but *only if* we consciously and continuously nudge ourselves to do so. LIT tools enable us to jump the gap (as the spark in a spark plug does) from LEB to *lit* and fully engage the malleable network that reconfigures in an instant.

Rudolph Tanzi, M.D., Ph.D., a scientist whose pioneering work on Alzheimer's disease and other mysteries of neuroscience continues to break new ground, says that the story of the evolving human brain is entering a new and critical evolutionary chapter. He suggests that our limbic system, the brain's emotion central, is evolving from the primarily instinctive fight-or-flight response driven by our primitive brain stem to a more nuanced response and feedback loop characterized by emotional awareness and higher thinking. "There's a huge evolutionary vector right now away from selfishness to self-awareness," he told me, referring to the way our thoughts, actions, and experiences shape our genetic expression and, as our genetic inheritance, shape our development, health, and well-being. "The old brain is selfishness, the new brain is self-awareness. We live in the middle and it's always a choice you have to make: Am I going to be self-aware and know what my brain is doing right now, or am I just going to be a servant to my brain stem that instinctively whips me around and makes me do whatever I want while I just live with fear and desire and these inhibitions every day? That's a choice we make every day."

ENERGY ACTIVATED BY INTENTION

The *lit* mind state is hardwired in each of us, always accessible. Once we learn how to use it with intention, we can do so at any time and in any situation. The LIT tools you'll find in this book ignite the energy to fire up any aspect of our lives. You can use them in the short term to energize the moment or in the long term to strategize your way to creating the life you want. In nature, energy changes from one form to another and from stored or potential energy to energy in action. Similarly, you can think of *lit* as:

- A natural energy flow that is in continuous exchange within the ecosystem and within you, yours to tap at any time
- A naturally heightened brain state, fluid and evolving, characterized by active curiosity, creative and intellectual arousal, and focused emotional engagement
- A process innate to us and a system of principles and LIT tools you can engage in specific, practical ways to ignite the process and keep it going

But the most important thing is to not get lost in thought about it. Rather, take any simple step to *act on it*. Start anywhere. To use these LIT tools, follow your curiosity or just pick a tool randomly to start the day and use in whatever moments arise for you. The more often you use them, the more natural *lit* will become for you.

The best part is, LIT tools are easy and habit forming. Over time, you'll discover that the *lit* spark stays kindled. In the brain, the energy transfer that lights up your neurons becomes autocatalytic—the more you do it, the easier it is to ignite because the neural pathways are established and buzzing. Unlike the habits that hijack our brain and dim the energy for creativity and curiosity, *lit* energizes those pathways, takes us off autopilot, and helps us stay alert, present, and fully engaged. You could say that *lit* uses the principles of persuasive design—the hook-and-hold rewards that the brain craves—but instead of profit-driven marketers driving your choices, you're in charge, channeling your energy to what matters most to you. That might be to brainstorm an idea, fire up your creativity, deepen your everyday experience, or change something in your life—or the world.

EVOLUTION ACCELERATES INNOVATION

At our lab, the *lit* process and LIT tools now inform just about everything we do. Our purpose is to find new ways to save lives and improve the quality of life for everyone—and do it as quickly and rigorously as we can. We take on challenges in the realms of drug delivery, medical devices, diagnostics, and regenerative medicine. We aim to innovate on a global scale. Every time we make an advance, we take a step back and ask: How could this be even bigger? How can we do more to help more people? How can we take what we've learned and make a massive difference?

We use LIT tools to stimulate creativity and excitement during meetings, presentations, decision making, casual conversations. We even include goof-off time as a *lit* strategy. (See "Press 'Pause,'" page 183.) Whether we discover something there that applies directly to our task or not, the energy transfer from nature delivers a wealth of new ideas, energy, and tools to help us solve problems. When you feel limited in your thinking, that's when you are destined to fail. Turning to nature in whatever way you can opens up completely new angles of thinking.

This process has been critical to our development of innovative medical solutions. In addition to a surgical glue inspired by slugs and sand-castle worms, we've used the same nature-forward creative process to develop a diagnostic for cancer based on the tentacles of jellyfish; surgical staples based on the quills of porcupine; and a tiny needle bed with swellable tips for diagnostic sampling of tissue fluid based on the snout of a spiny-headed worm. These bioinspired solutions—drawing from nature for ideas that trigger our thinking in fresh ways—are no coinci-dence. We routinely turn to the most successful researchers of all time, evolution and nature, purposefully looking for ways to see problems and solutions differently, and think more creatively about possibilities.

In the early years after I launched the lab, I called it the Laboratory for Accelerated Medical Innovation. No easy acronym there and too long to remember, but that was the mission from the start—to accelerate innovation. What I didn't realize at the time was that the process we developed to accelerate medical innovations could work for anyone, in any circumstances, to jump-start energy, focus, and action. That's why I wrote this book.

GREAT MINDS GET *LIT*

When I first started thinking about writing *LIT,* I wondered if I was alone in my experience. Would my focus on process and the tools to ignite innovation translate universally to other people? As a scientist, engineer, and inventor, after seeing how these coping tools that I de-veloped over time to deal with my learning differences worked for me, I wanted to share them. But first, because I'm always wanting to improve on something that works, I was curious to see if some commonalities ex-isted for other people and if there was a way to build on those strategies. That led me to a diverse array of people who've achieved personal and social impact of different kinds, whom I'll introduce you to in this book. I wanted to understand what tools other people use to break free from their own version of LEB when they could easily rest on past accom-plishments and expertise. I wanted to find out:

- How others found and cultivated what was important to them (their passion)
- How they optimized their effort and maximized their impact
- How they remained committed to purpose (rather than driven by productivity)
- How they kept dreams or aspirations alive despite setbacks

- How they kept learning, growing, and evolving beyond earlier accomplishments
- How they experienced nature as an aspect of their life
- How they thought about their own lives and the inspirational, almost magical aspects of their stories, and their thought-provoking and sometimes curious insights

As I talked with various people, they shared their stories and recommended other people to talk with. I could hardly stop to write the book because the interviews were always stimulating and fascinating—*lit*!

I discovered that, like me, some of them had struggled with a range of neurodiverse conditions or other issues. Dyslexia, bipolar disorder, autism, attention deficit disorder, and other problems had challenged them during their formative years. Others had been encouraged from early childhood to follow their passions, and they'd learned to access inner resources as mental tools early in life. Turns out, great minds really don't think alike. They are diverse, motivated in different ways, vulnerable, and imperfect like the rest of us. But one common quality they shared was how they learned from many sources and experiences, how they made decisions, how they consciously chose to spend their time, energy, and attention. They've cracked the code on what it takes to continually energize their thinking *and* act on it. Those strategies are core elements in the LIT toolbox, and I hope that in these stories you will find similarities and inspiration to spark your own *lit* journey.

Rudolph Tanzi grew up listening to his mother, a medical transcriptionist, tell stories about patients and their struggles. It made him curious, fueling his interest in medical research. He spoke of a simple process he uses, whether before addressing a congressional subcommittee on a matter of science, joining a TV talk show host to talk about his books, or stepping onstage to jam on keyboards with Joe Perry of Aerosmith: he reminds himself of his preparation and purpose. "Your job is not to impress," he tells himself. "It's not to win. It's not to show how good you are. Your job is to use your preparation *to serve*."

I agree. This book is my way of passing on to you what I have learned from the many sources that have inspired me and from my own experience. As you read and consider the strategies, I ask just one favor: use these strategies to serve—your family, your friends, your coworkers, your community, and your world. The big issues and big questions confronting us today, the problems we must solve if we are to survive, call for our most passionate and enlightened high-energy brain thinking. So does our personal search for a meaningful, even joyful life.

Our human potential is so much greater than mere efficiency or even comfort, but we can lose sight of that when the conversation around us is more about productivity than purpose, more about compliance than creative and critical thinking, more about *me* than *us*. This pattern of not questioning assumptions ultimately limits our ability to channel our energy for the greatest impact and greatest good—which can be our greatest source of satisfaction. LEB is a dimmer switch on our greatest potential.

We can't foresee how humans will fare in geological time. We are only capturing a snapshot in our evolution, and future humans could look and live very differently than we do today. But evolution as a process of improvement can be a useful model for our own individual development in the space of a lifetime. One thing is certain: we don't have to settle for watching the lights go out. We've still got the same amazing brain that nature gave us to problem solve our way forward. We all have a repertoire of tools we use to express ourselves. It's up to us to refine and evolve those tools over time to be the most effective versions of ourselves.

Get inspired → learn → act and evolve. Use the LIT tools in this book to activate and cultivate your brain's plasticity and your own (and society's) evolutionary potential.

The world needs people who can see problems and possibilities from fresh angles.

The world needs you.

It's time to get *lit*!

GET THE BALL ROLLING!

Lower the Activation Energy

Let's get real about the many LIT tools advocated in this book. You might find the idea of igniting the energy, excitement, creativity, and passion locked in your brain to be inviting at first, then daunting. It may sound great, but it may also sound like work. That's because it is—for your brain. Any intentional action is an effort for your brain because it's easier to act on autopilot—all the more so when you try to shift from an established pattern to a new one. However, as you stick with even small changes, over time your brain will rewire itself, and as it does, the mental energy required to do a new thing will diminish. At some point, the new thing will become the established thing, more automatic and requiring much less effort. The beauty of turning LIT tools into habits of thinking is that they become easier to use—they come to mind more readily—and inject fresh energy into your thinking. As I mentioned earlier, just changing the story we tell ourselves can be enough to trigger brain-based changes that will launch the rest.

No matter where you start with the LIT tools ahead and what your goals or intentions may be, the one universal step that will jump-start anything else you do is this: lower the activation energy. In science, activation energy is defined as the minimum energy necessary to trigger the reaction that will put everything else into play. A spark plug provides a spark of electricity that ignites a fuel/air mixture for combustion that makes a car go. Enzymes, which are natural catalysts, speed up chemical reactions in the body without themselves being consumed or permanently altered by the reaction. They remain to catalyze the same reaction repeatedly. All of these provide the boost that lowers the activation energy. LIT tools work the same way.

In daily life, the lower the activation energy needed for us to take the first step toward any goal, the more likely we are to start and to follow through. It might be something as simple as leaving our running shoes by the door if we want to go running or keep a routine going. Just seeing the shoes there brings it to the forefront of our mind, lowering the amount of mental effort we need to put into going for a run.

Activation energy constantly influences our everyday choices. Watching a show you like or eating a few cookies from that package of your favorites? Shopping online or continually scrolling social media? These have a low activation energy, because you already gravitate toward them, especially media use, as everything about the technology and user experience is meticulously designed to entice us and hook and hold our attention. How about cleaning out the closet you've avoided for six months or hauling yourself to the gym on an off day? Just not feeling it? For something that's already unappealing to you, the activation energy is higher because you've got to overcome inertia or resistance. Often, we actually have the energy to do all of these things but our lack of motivation makes the activation energy needed feel high. Lowering the activation energy level boosts the "willingness of the mind," to borrow from Robin Wall Kimmerer.

The more energy it takes for us to get started toward a goal, the harder it feels or slower it goes. Both can be discouraging, which, added to the effort required, makes us even less likely to start or continue an activity. When I was a kid struggling in school, it wasn't just the content of the material or even my learning differences that I had to overcome; the shame and anxiety I felt were an even bigger obstacle at times. You can eventually learn a piece of information; it's harder to overcome shame and manage anxiety. Any goal I set for myself came with that high activation energy and seemed insurmountable. LIT tools helped with that by changing the way I thought about things—changing my thought processes—including how I thought about myself and how I could take small steps that would lead to meaningful improvements.

LIT tools essentially cue the brain to cut through inertia to initiate action. Whatever the first step may be, it always becomes easier when you find ways to reduce the activation energy.

Here are four *lit* strategies that will effectively lower activation energy as you engage with any of the tools ahead:

- **MINIMIZE OBSTACLES.** First, identify the sources of resistance for you, then change what you can or ask others for help to do so.
- **MAXIMIZE REWARDS.** These can be anything that gets you excited, brings you joy, energizes you, calms you or quiets your mind, or gives you a feeling of accomplishment.
- **MAKE THE MOST OF MOMENTUM.** Take advantage of what I call the velocity of intention to boost momentum. Once you become aware of your intention and then start acting on it, that builds momentum and the velocity increases. It's easier to pick up speed when you are already moving. So tap the energy of a conducive environment or motivated others around you; they're a motivational accelerant. Consciously cultivate a habit of action over inaction and intentional actions over habitual ones.
- **PACE YOURSELF.** Think of everything as a pendulum swing or the way biorhythms affect your energy levels, metabolism, attention, mood, and every other aspect of your physical and mental functioning. Depending on where you are in that pendulum swing or cycle, you can lower the activation energy in different ways and use LIT tools to alter your trajectory.

In other words, motivation, momentum, and proper timing can reduce activation energy.

••

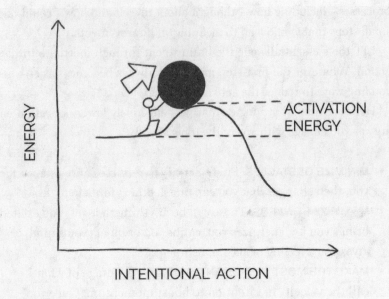

Get the ball rolling, and lower the activation energy.

Activation energy is the amount of purposeful energy it takes to get something started and then to continue with it. In the figure above, activation energy is the effort required to push the ball to the top of the hill, where the last nudge sends it over the top and down the other side. In any effort, once you get the ball rolling, momentum works in your favor and the next steps become easier. You can break larger goals into smaller steps, then lower the activation energy for each one.

Nature works in our favor, first with neurochemical rewards that act as incentives and second with rhythms we can attune ourselves to for optimal timing. We are all endowed with cells that produce neurochemicals (dopamine, serotonin, oxytocin, endorphins, and others) that facilitate pleasurable sensations (or the promise of them) and experiences that we want to repeat over and over again. They can boost our motivation, attention, and mood. Studies have found that exploring a new environment or having novel experiences improves memory by boosting dopamine levels, lowering the threshold for learning. These rewards drive our motivation to work for things, investing effort that we might otherwise not. They help us more deeply engage with others and the broader world and maximize our ability to learn and make intentional decisions. Most important, they energize us for action. Every LIT tool engages this reward system in different ways, but the process starts with making that first step easier—and then each step that follows. Marketers and others exploit our brain's reward systems for their own purposes, creating dopamine-rich environments that spur us to action in ways that profit them. But we, too, by our choices, can cultivate or tap into dopamine-rich environments—creativity, curiosity, and meaningful relationships—and recruit our brain's reward system to serve our intentions.

For our social species, even the simplest connection—for example, working collaboratively on a task with someone else or singing or dancing with others—can prompt your neurons to light up and sync up, according to studies. Ask someone to join you in reaching a challenging goal and use that boost of energy transfer to lower the activation energy to start and stick with it. The feeling that we're on the same wavelength with others—scientists call it synchrony—may be literally true. Researchers think it may be a sign that certain chemical and electrical signaling in the brain involved with cognitive processing—what enables us to comprehend our environment, communicate, and learn—can sync with others in a shared experience. It makes sense to me: we are made of matter, and all matter is made of molecules; all molecules have energy and vibrate in constant motion, and anything we do or think involves neuronal synchronization. Amazingly, we can connect to others through activating the same regions of our brains in synchrony to bring a surge in positivity for our mental health.

Think of it as social bonding and you can see it in the way people in relationships, or from diverse walks of life or expertise, come together with a deep sense of shared values. I see this in the lab where, in spite of the expansive diversity among us, we are deeply synchronized on core intentions—working together to do important work and solve problems.

We can also tap into natural rhythms to optimize energy and our brain's reward system. Notice the rhythms that support flourishing in all living things and adapt that intuitive timing for your own benefit.

Our genes are programmed to synchronize our biology to our environment, and our circadian rhythms affect us much more than sleep does. Each organ in the body (e.g., heart, lungs, liver, muscles, kidneys, eyes) has a circadian rhythm that helps you adapt to environmental changes. These rhythms, and their effect on our mood, also affect what we find exciting or pleasurable at any given time and the amount of energy we have for engaging. That in turn affects how our reward system responds, so "right timing" takes advantage of the rhythms and rewards in an upswing, reducing the activation energy needed to engage.

Finally, nature holds the deep circuitry of our embodied intelligence—the complex, evolutionary "smarts" derived from our species' constant interplay with our environment and a multitude of sensory experiences, some of which are beyond our conscious awareness. The concept of intelligence has already evolved far beyond earlier beliefs that it resided in the brain alone. We now recognize the powerful mind-body interconnectivity and to some degree have extended that understanding to include the interconnectivity of mind, body, and spirit. All that's left to do is recognize that each of those domains is grounded in nature; the natural world is the source from which the rest emerges and the circuitry through which those energies must travel to be fully realized. Ultimately, nature itself is the linchpin, the essential, fully integrated circuitry enabling what I consider to be our fully engaged embodied intelligence.

Note mood and energy level, and identify sources of resistance.

Minimize obstacles.

Maximize rewards and positive feedback.

Maximize momentum—and GO!

Each LIT tool chapter ahead includes tips—which act like sparks or enzymes—to help you lower the activation energy needed to start and stay engaged in an activity. In the lab a core problem-solving principle is radical simplicity, which for us means taking the complexities of the science and the processes needed to bring solutions into practical use, identifying what's essential, and finding the simplest way to do it.

For a quick start with any LIT tool, radical simplicity works for you as you:

- Tap into brain chemistry to immediately generate rewarding effects
- Use intentional novelty to excite your brain
- Cultivate a habit of action over inaction and intentional over habitual action
- Let purpose and intuition empower you
- Dial down the inner naysayer
- Let nature give you an energizing lift

Carrying out a tiny bit of *lit* action in the morning sets the stage for the rest of the day. It can be this simple: If when I get into the car, I let pass the impulse to play a podcast or music and opt instead for a quiet awareness of the moment—even if that's just to recognize any friction that occupies my mind—that one intentional step starts a less distracted day, and the rest of the day will flow from that. If I pause to say good morning or acknowledge someone instead of hurrying past, the feeling of social connection, however brief, has *lit* energy. Simpler still, taking a moment to awaken my senses to something in the natural world—the sky out the window, the plant on the sill, my dogs, or even something in myself—engages nature for a more grounded day. The goal isn't to battle yourself throughout the day or shame yourself for not doing something more. It is just about taking a single small step forward and then going with the flow for a while and seeing what that brings.

Every day we have the opportunity to figure out what we want and what we need to do—what's driving us that day, that moment. Maybe it's a job choice or relationship considerations. Maybe it's something as simple as whether you're going to eat French fries or steamed broccoli. Exercise or let it slide? How can you be in the right mindset to make choices that will resonate in a way you can feel good about and excited to resume where you left off? We all want to reap the benefits that come from our best thinking. Lowering the activation energy kick-starts every LIT tool in the chapters that follow. Knowing that you have direct access to your own thought process, are you ready to tinker with it?

FLIP THE SWITCH

What's Holding You Back?

Intercept routine patterns to
make simple, deliberate changes.

*We have to be willing to let go of "that's just the way it is,"
even if just for a moment, to consider the possibility that
there isn't a way it is or a way it isn't. There is the way we
choose to act and what we choose to make of circumstances.*

—LYNNE TWIST, GLOBAL ENVIRONMENTAL ACTIVIST

Joyce Roché constantly feared she would be found out. The dread would
tighten its grip every time she was singled out for recognition, promoted,
or achieved something impressive. Which happened a lot.

For more than twenty-five years in corporate America, Roché was
recognized as an incisive strategist and leader, a trailblazer, serving as
the president and chief operating officer of Carson Products Company
and vice president of global marketing at Avon Products, where she was
the first African American woman vice president and first vice president
of global marketing. *Fortune* magazine featured her on its cover.

But, as Roché recalls, "just about every new accomplishment came
with the stultifying doubt that I did not deserve the success and that
sooner or later I would be discovered as an impostor, as 'unfit' for my
post, and that sooner or later 'they'll find you out.'" She is now able to
take a long look back at what amounted to decades of stellar success

and secret fear. It wasn't until years later, when she did a deep dive on the subject to write a book she hoped would help others, that she would learn from experts in the field that this chronic dread and self-doubt afflicts many high-achieving individuals, especially young women and, within that group, especially women of color, and that there was a name for it: impostor syndrome.

Two *aha* moments ultimately helped Roché flip the switch on the power she gave the impostor narrative and see herself in a truer light. "The first time I remember becoming fully aware of my abilities and competencies was when I was faced with the possibility of being over-looked for a promotion I knew I was qualified for," she explained. "Senior management felt more comfortable with a white male colleague, and so to advocate for myself I had to compare my abilities and accomplish-ments to those of the 'heir apparent' and of another male peer. At that point, I recognized the full extent of my experience and my value to the company."

The second *aha* moment came after almost nineteen years with Avon, when she realized that she'd hit the glass ceiling there and to ad-vance into senior management, she would likely have to leave the com-pany. "At that point, I suddenly felt a level of comfort in who I was and what I had achieved," she said. "All the success and recognition I had received over the years seemed to have sunk in without my noticing. I now believed in my abilities and management skill enough to step out to find the opportunity I felt I was ready to take on." Roché became a celebrated trailblazer in the corporate realm, but perhaps her greatest success would be the day she left it to follow her heart and step into the CEO role of Girls Inc., a nonprofit she felt passionate about that works directly with girls to develop their skills to navigate economic, gender, and social barriers. She wondered whether it would be the right move for her, recognizing that she'd be new to nonprofit leadership. But her deep connection to purpose vanquished the old voice of self-doubt.

Impostor syndrome became part of the workplace lexicon in the late 1970s, referring to the self-doubt that many women described as an ob-stacle on their career paths. But variations on the theme are a plague on all our houses, afflicting many people: new parents, striving teens, anxious college students, restless midlifers, and any other of us who at one time or another feel boxed in by our own insecurities or anxious expectations. In a review of studies of impostor syndrome, half of the included studies that reported finding a gender effect found no difference in the rates of men and women suffering from impostor syndrome. I've struggled with insecurities and anxiety, too. But over the years, I've recognized, especially as a mentor, how often we consider but hesitate to take a step or a risk and bet on our capacity to learn and grow. We link our identities and self-worth to external sources of validation—work outcomes, popularity, status, or others' approval—and in doing so mute the more important internal sources of strength over insecurities. We invest our insecurities with the power to limit not only our own potential but the broader potential to solve the pressing problems that beset the world.

Flipping the switch is *lit* in a holistic way, acting on the seemingly small or everyday things that keep us from stepping into the full potential of the moment. Taking the step. Taking the risk. Betting on ourselves. It can be as simple as recognizing when we might be more intentional, then figuring out: How can I lower the activation energy to take a step forward and actually do that?

"People get caught up in so many things that are completely distracting from the true nature of reality," says neurosurgeon James Doty, the founder and director of the Center for Compassion and Altruism Research and Education, an affiliate of the Wu Tsai Neurosciences Institute at Stanford University. "The thing that we know is that your internal mentation has a profound effect on your external world. If you accept that and you create the best internal world you can make for yourself, then that has a huge amount of power on the world."

ACCEPT BARRIERS OR BUILD BRIDGES?

As a child, I was always fascinated by how things work. "Things" included everything, not necessarily just machines. "Why?" was my constant refrain. I wondered why and how the boundaries that define how we lead our lives had been created, and by whom. Perhaps because of my own challenges in school, I wondered who had decided what we were supposed to study in school. I wondered why traffic lights are the way they are, and sidewalks, and people leaving for and coming back from work at regular times, and why weekends are two days, and why roads have specific widths, and why smoking on airplanes was once deemed safe—you get the picture. I also wondered why I couldn't say just what was on my mind when it mattered—why humans need to filter what we say even when it needs to be said. I would try to track those things back to their origins. That constant inquisition tried the patience of most of the adults in my life, maybe even my mother at times.

As time went on, I realized that essentially everything decided by humans is in some way arbitrary. How we live is based on individuals like us who come together and synergize with other individuals, create momentum, and build support; then things happen. Decisions are made. Rules are set. Lines are drawn. Further, I realized that many things are not fully optimized—they're not as good as they could be. Or should be. Who decides—for all of us—that something is good enough? Why not make it better?

Humans generally orient themselves to social and intellectual structures, norms that guide their choices. Structure can be helpful. But at some point those frames of reference, arbitrary as many of them are, can become unquestioned boundaries on our thinking. This has become increasingly so, and increasingly concerning, as social media, as well as online content driven by algorithms and created by AI tools, become ubiquitous. Whether naturally occurring or manufactured, these structures narrow our perception of the world we see or even imagine and shrink our sense of agency and possibility. As we know, LEB leans toward the familiar, the structured patterns, always preferring the less effortful "way things are" over possible change. Neuroscience suggests that neurochemical processes in the brain-based reward systems and our preference for continuity may further resist change that requires us to abandon a strong belief or conviction.

When we not only stick to beliefs despite evidence that we're wrong but dig in even more (a phenomenon called belief perseverance), our brain may lock out change unless we make a conscious effort to be open to learning and changing how we think. Just look around. There was a time when many people believed that women couldn't be engineers, lawyers, doctors, and astronauts. Men couldn't be nurses or primary caregivers for children or hold other jobs that had traditionally been assigned to women. But that's the point: those were assigned roles, based not on someone's genuine human potential but on beliefs, biases, and toxic traditions that imposed boundaries on what seemed possible. That's the power of a twisted norm to hold sway.

Whether in a lab discussion about how to innovate or in our daily life and relationships, the boundaries we accept on our thinking make it hard to see a fuller range of possibilities. The less we question the limits of conventional thinking, the less capable we feel of doing so, and possibility shrinks to fit.

ADAM RIPPON: LET YOUR DREAMS INSPIRE

Adam Rippon, a 2018 Olympic bronze medalist in the figure skating team event and the first openly gay athlete in his sport to compete in the Olympics, said he had felt compelled to come out three years earlier rather than wait until he retired, to help empower others to live authentically and pursue their dreams. "When you're comfortable with who you are, you almost get this superpower where you know that you can kind of do anything. And when you have that superpower, then you have that self-empowerment—it's incredible." Coming out, he said, had given him "the confidence to do crazy things and push myself in a way that I never did before, because I wasn't afraid what other people would think of me."

Everyone faces challenges pursuing their dreams, and everyone's struggle is different, he noted, but aligning with your highest aspirations frees up energy for the effort. "It's important to not really put a limit on what you think is possible. When you put a limit [on yourself], then you think that's the max of anything possible and it's hard to push past that. But when there's no limit, the possibilities are endless and you end up pushing yourself a lot further than you even thought was possible."

*When you become comfortable with uncertainty, infinite
possibilities open up in your life.*
—ECKHART TOLLE

To be *lit*, then, we need to shed our blinkered perspective and constantly seek a fresh perspective, the alternative—even if surprising—view of problems, ideas, and all that we think we know, including about our own potential. We can break through pervasive mental boundaries. We think of them as solid lines, but more often they are dotted lines, easier to redraw than we might think. Life repeatedly offers these opportunities, but we often miss them. For example, we can be less reactive to other people and pause to respond more thoughtfully. We can take ownership of our choices instead of blaming others and accept more gracefully when others choose something different from what we prefer. We can stay present and attentive to the people we're with instead of routinely cutting away to check our phones or multitask. We can practice compassion toward ourselves and others. On the face of it, that's a choice of behavior. In the brain itself, that's the process of neuroplasticity: how neurons grow, change, and reorganize for continued growth, strengthening new connections and expanding neural pathways.

In LEB mode, our brain perceives new information through old filters, processes it through familiar pathways, and reaches predictable conclusions. We limit our understanding to the perceived boundaries of what we already know, or variations of it, and it all becomes part of a story we've accepted without question. In effect, we shine a penlight on something and mistake that pinpoint view for the full picture, whereas if we turned the room light on or let the sunshine in, we would illuminate a much broader perspective. LEB manifests itself in countless ways that hold us back or work against our greater success. We misjudge situations and people, often to our detriment as well as theirs. We accept limiting beliefs, then make important decisions based on them. How can we break free from all that, break open a closed mindset or repetitive thought process? We are hardwired for habit, yes, but we can flip the switch on old patterns, tackle something new, and learn and grow throughout our life. Nature is on our side.

THINK ABOUT HOW YOU THINK

How was it possible for Joyce Roché to harbor such crushing self-doubt for so long in her career, when all evidence showed her to be not just qualified but excellent in her field? Reassurances from friends and colleagues didn't silence the inner naysayer, she says, although they were a valued source of encouragement. Over time, she told me, she used self-awareness and an objective process to calm herself and manage her fears. She developed the practice of analyzing a situation with a basic accounting of her strengths and her weaknesses, along with a recognition of external obstacles not of her making. The process enabled her to deconstruct her thinking and remove the obstacles to engaging in a more measured, authentic way.

How do you think? Once you begin to observe your thoughts, as Roché did, you will discover all sorts of ways to hack the system that weren't accessible to you before. It's like discovering shortcuts on your computer keyboard.

I was lucky to have that question come up at a critical time fairly early in my life, but only because my thought processes had gotten me into so much trouble in school. By the time my struggles in school sank to a low point in about fifth grade, I'd been written off as a loser by most of my teachers—and I believed them. Then my mom signed me up for extra help in after-school sessions at a learning center in the community. There the tutors would ask me to answer a bunch of questions, and after I gave my answer, they'd ask me about my reasoning. They'd ask, "Well, how did you think about that?" It was interesting because that simple question—How did you think about that?—immediately turned me inward to consider my thought processes.

Being coached to reflect on my thinking process, especially so early in life, helped me develop some self-awareness and recognition when my thinking was slack or stuck in overdrive. With practice, it became easier to use that mental toggle switch to shift from stumped and frustrated to curious about why I was stuck, then examine my thinking, find a way to work around it, and forge ahead. This is something anyone can learn to do at any age and in any circumstance.

That new skill soon sparked my curiosity about other people's thought processes. I was endlessly fascinated by the differences in the way we think about things and how those differences shape our understanding and behavior. For example, when you're asked a question, your answer depends completely on how you interpret it. And for a lot of questions, there's not a single interpretation. Through understanding different ways of approaching questions and new information, I became able to think more critically about problems and learned to engage others in that conversation.

Fast-forward to today. One thing that defines what we do at the lab—that really distinguishes our work—is how we think about problems: how we define them, how we design a structure for exploration and experimentation, and how we anticipate the next levels we'll need to address.

My research focuses on medical technologies, but not in a conventional way. For example, there's no specific disease or technology focus. We're not an *X* lab or a *Y* lab or any specific focus-oriented type of lab. Early on in my professorship, I was told I would need to focus our work more—define the "brand" more tightly—because otherwise no one would understand what we were doing. But I knew that my passion was more expansive than that, and our mission, too: to focus on the *process of medical problem solving* as it applies to potentially almost any problem. Questions are integral to this process. At every step, the question that drives the discussion—the one that helps us flip the switch in our thinking to problem solve—is: "How did you get to that answer?" We can think deeply about how we think about problems, question our thinking, and connect it to the core of a problem. In the lab, if someone asks why we did *X* experiment and the answer is "To learn *Y*," we can then ask, "Well, how will knowing *Y* help us to improve the functional response we're looking for? What is the connection?" If there is no connection, our approach may need to be revised.

What does this look like in the lab? Typically, by the time we take on a project, some conventional approaches tried by others have failed. *To change the outcome, we have to revise the thinking.* The conventional process is often linear: finding one solution to a problem, then turning to the one that presents itself next. This procedure is logical but narrow, because to translate a medical innovation from the lab into therapeutic use, many more steps must be considered beyond the science itself. Any device or therapy must be tested extensively before it is moved forward to human clinical trials, then become readily producible, packaged, marketed, distributed, patented, and supported long term. All of these issues must be addressed before the science can become broadly useful. Even before that, the parameters of a project or problem have been heavily influenced by what others—from scientists to funding committees—have thought possible. We can't advance projects unless someone funds us, and often that funding is for a relatively narrow scope of research.

To change the outcome, we had to revise how we thought about every aspect of the problem and defined our objective.

A *lit* life calls on you to change some long-standing habits, explore, inquire, rethink your assumptions about a lot of things—okay, rethink *all* assumptions—reframe how you think about failure and success, and do a deep inward dive to find what matters most to you. To flip the switch means to (1) challenge assumptions, (2) find intention, and (3) focus on action.

I'm inspired by the story of my collaborator Ali Tavakkoli, a bariatric surgeon at Brigham and Women's Hospital in Boston who is also the chief of the Division of General and GI Surgery. Tavakkoli saw how gastric bypass—a surgical treatment for obesity—helped people with type 2 diabetes. But many patients weren't willing to consider surgery, and there was no other medical option that had as significant a benefit for most patients.

In conventional gastric bypass surgery, the stomach and small intestine are restructured to change the way they absorb and digest food. Traditionally, a surgeon, such as Tavakkoli, would logically come up with a surgical approach. In this instance, though, he imagined a nonsurgical approach: "surgery" in a pill! He came to us to see if we could develop a pill that would form a coating on the intestine in the same region that is isolated from food by gastric bypass. And could we make it "transient," so that it would provide the therapeutic benefit precisely when needed, but without the permanent side effects of surgery?

The short answer is yes, and the radically simple innovation has the potential to transform treatment of type 2 diabetic patients. Tavakkoli saw an opportunity to develop another option with diabetic patients in mind, and his expertise in bariatric surgery and his inclination to constantly ask "Why?" led to a breakthrough idea: an orally deliverable noninvasive approach to do the same thing. Tavakkoli didn't have the materials science expertise to develop and prototype the technology, but he did have models to test its feasibility in his laboratory. Instead of letting the idea fade into the abyss because he lacked a particular expertise, he reached out to someone who did, a seasoned biomaterials expert, to help, and that person eventually connected him with us.

"What stands in the way becomes the way," Marcus Aurelius wrote in *Meditations,* and the idea that obstacles can become an impetus to action, focusing our energies to overcome them, is a core Buddhist teaching as well. But before we can focus our energy that way, we have to figure out what stands in the way. For me as a kid, my lack of clarity about my learning disability was a formidable obstacle not only in the school setting but also in my and my parents' efforts to do something about it. With a diagnosis, we were able to tap the appropriate resources, and my efforts produced some initial and surprising progress.

Far too often the obstacle lies in our thoughts about ourselves: *I'm not experienced enough. . . . I can't just change course at this point. . . . I'll never succeed.* Progress can stall for a variety of reasons, and it's on us to get over the initial punched-in-the-face feeling and restart the process. Maybe we're missing information or expertise. Perhaps we need some guidance, the right mentor, or a more supportive environment. We have a choice: Will we sideline ourselves, or will we use these points of resistance as inflection points toward personal evolution?

Thinking about how you think and analyzing your thought processes can help you identify the root of a problem so you can take steps to do something about it. Otherwise, you may change a strategy or tactic but the source of resistance just wells up in a new place.

Practical impediments generally give way to practical solutions when you focus your attention on them. To use a garden metaphor, you find a stone under your spade and dig it out. Sometimes you don't have to dig too deeply to discover that it's your own inner dialogue, the negative self-talk that you cultivate, that's getting in your way.

JAMES DOTY:
COMPASSION TRANSFORMS THE ROOTS OF RESISTANCE

Survival instincts are hardwired in the brain, but negative beliefs about ourselves are not, says James Doty, the neurosurgeon and compassion researcher. They're imported from negative influences in our external environment, such as judgmental feedback from others in our formative years or cultural messaging that undermines our confidence. When that's what we "learn" about ourselves, we internalize it as true in the same way that we know water is wet and fire is hot. In effect, self-doubt makes our environment feel threatening and triggers the alarm in our brain.

"So we have created these negative dialogues in our head, and when you do that, the negative dialogue becomes your reality," says Doty. "If you say 'I can't,' then, by definition, you cannot. And that is a thing that many, many people carry with them every day. It's not, in my opinion, simply a matter of ignoring it. It's a matter of changing it."

Cultivating compassion for yourself can flip the switch, Doty says, because, as research shows, with intention you can change the dialogue from negativity to self-affirmation. You can cultivate the understanding that you're worthy and acknowledge you deserve love. You can acknowledge that your "shadow self" has aspects that you dislike and wish would go away. "And when you accept that, you change that dialogue," he says. "That's when your vision changes of the outside world, and when you see the true nature of reality, you move from this rumination, beating yourself up, to looking out and actually seeing that every human being is suffering. That you're not alone. That everyone deserves love. Everyone deserves affirmation. Everyone deserves to be cared for. That . . . then changes your perspective of the world."

The inner critic doesn't exist in the present moment. It depends on endless rumination over the past. We wouldn't rent the same bad movie 250 times, but we do that in our own mind.
—JAN CHOZEN BAYS, PHYSICIAN, ZEN PRIEST, AND CO-ABBOT OF GREAT VOW ZEN MONASTERY

Doty's own painful childhood provided early experiences that he later drew upon as a scientist focused on the effects of compassion. As he shared in his book *Into the Magic Shop: A Neurosurgeon's Quest to Discover the Mysteries of the Brain and the Secrets of the Heart,* as a young boy he was in a bad way when he first encountered the shopkeeper at the magic shop. His family circumstances were hard, and he felt terrible about both his life and himself. As time passed, the life lessons the shopkeeper shared began to change something within him.

His home environment didn't change, but in the supportive environment of that affirming shopkeeper, something shifted inside him. "Nothing in my personal circumstance changed with my time with this woman in the magic shop—nothing. I went back to the exact same environment. But what did change was how I looked at the world." He points out that the human capacity of nonverbal communication to intuit people's emotional states from facial expressions, voice intonation, body habits, even smell is quite acute as an evolutionary asset, with powerful practical impacts on our everyday interactions. "When an individual carries this burden of anger, hostility, despair, hopelessness, people sense that. And often that results in them shying away from another person or helping another person. So when I changed how I looked at the world, that changed how the world looked at me. And that then allowed me to transform my life."

Too many kids are living their label.
—TEMPLE GRANDIN

Joyce Roché's epiphany was a long time in the making, and she respects the journey it entailed, recognizing it now as a process through which she not only managed to disempower the nay-saying inner voice she had struggled so long to overcome but also found her heart and passion. Flipping the switch meant creating what she calls the voice of her "authentic, essential self."

"Show up for life as your whole self," she says. "Your essence is what makes you who you are. Find the quiet place inside where you feel safe to be yourself. From that place, work to clarify your own values and then ask whether the people around you share those values. Build connections with those people who do." Connecting with that spiritual essence was a critical element in her ability to conquer the impostor syndrome. So were the practical steps she took to act on her intentions and eventually make the move to Girls Inc.

Roché had made lists and been journaling as personal reflection for years at that point and had what amounted to a thorough inventory of "who I was and what I'd accomplished," she says. She began by reviewing those lists "to remind me of the journey that had gotten me where I was." Then she expanded the inventory. "I was painfully honest with myself about what I was and wasn't good at. I pushed myself to distinguish between the things I liked and those I really didn't like but I pretended to. And most important, I thought about what I truly valued in my life."

Reflecting that way, she realized that her objectives had changed. Proving herself, as she'd felt compelled to do before, was "no longer the objective . . . what I wanted was another [kind of] challenge, and everything else—location, industry—was wide open. Suddenly, I could see myself leaving the corporate world and devoting myself to a social mission that was important to me."

Every time Roché was able to ground herself in her journey, her values, her strengths and weaknesses, and her track record of performance, she saw that she was good at what she did and was able to flip the switch in her thinking. She could see new possibilities and free herself to invest her energy meaningfully in challenging new environments, where she thrived. Being aware of your thought processes and how they lead to your actions can help you pinpoint what is most important to you and be more intentional about how you're living your life.

Ultimately, Roché was able to turn her career toward what she now felt as a calling: to help girls and women find their voice and use it with confidence. In her time as CEO of Girls Inc., she was able to advance an organization that worked with girls to counteract negative cultural messages that suggest limited expectations and "open the lens to the possibility of what they could be." With her book *The Empress Has No Clothes: Conquering Self-Doubt to Embrace Success* she brought the issue of impostor syndrome into the open and stirred up a broader conversation that remains relevant today. She hopes that stories such as hers and tools for action can help others flip the switch in their own lives even sooner than she did.

SUSAN HOCKFIELD: ANSWERING THE CALL TO SERVICE

Sometimes the impetus for change comes suddenly, unbidden, a proverbial fork in the road that you weren't expecting. Susan Hockfield, the president of MIT for eight years—the first female president—and earlier, at Yale University, provost and dean of the Graduate School of Arts and Sciences, was always passionate about science but had never envisioned herself in a leadership role—until she was asked by Yale president Richard Levin to serve as dean. She reflected on it anew and in conversation with her husband. In that process, she awakened to a new awareness of others' service in creating the environment and opportunities that had been open to her.

"I'm a scientist, but I did not plan to lead in the academy," she recalls.

When the president of the university asked me to step into this role, my first response, of course, was "No, I'm a scientist." It was actually a very, very important moment of growth for me. I went home and talked to my husband about it. I gasped at my selfishness. Because I had not realized until that point that a lot of people had invested their time and effort in creating an environment that would allow me to discover my calling. And I thought, How terrible for me not to have realized that and not to recognize that there is not just a calling [to science], there is a call to service. And it was as if all of a sudden that switch got shifted, and I said, "Ah, time for me to step up." I did it with commitment, and I felt it was an enormous privilege.

It was not a calling the way that being a scientist was a calling but a call to service. I had never understood just how powerful that can be. Having your heart tuned to hear other kinds of calls over the course of your career is very important. I think stepping up to the call to service, stepping up to the responsibilities that rest on your shoulder, means you've accepted a responsibility for others, and human society relies on these kinds of organizing principles. And if we abdicate that responsibility, how will our societies cohere, how will our world cohere? The idea that you can actually reach for something that is beyond you right now—we celebrate that motivation in athletics, but we rarely translate that into other things. It's about inspiring exploration, it's people thinking about themselves beyond where they are today.

As a mentor and in his approach to his own life, Reginald "Reggie" Shuford urges authenticity to align our lives from the inside out. In the 2019 Martin Luther King, Jr. Leadership Development Institute commencement address, he encouraged the graduates to "Go the way your blood beats." He stated:

Oscar Wilde famously said: "Be yourself; everyone else is already taken." "Go the way your blood beats" means be true to your authentic self. At the end of the day, trying to be otherwise is futile, a waste of time and a fool's errand. You are exactly who you were intended to be. Embrace who you are. The sooner you do that, the quicker you can get on with living the life you were meant

to live. For me, early on, I tried to minimize my differences, fit
in with the crowd, and attract very little attention to myself. I
believe that is fairly common among young people. In time, you
will likely come to appreciate that what makes you different and
unique may be your superpower. Once you quit struggling trying
to be someone else, accept who you are and use that energy in a
positive way, your impact increases.

A CONSCIOUS CADENCE VERSUS
THE URGENCY OF NOW

In nature, homeostasis is a dynamic equilibrium, a self-regulating process for balance, from individual organisms to complex systems. Sudden
shifts (meteors that hit the Earth, fires, floods) can create imbalances as
the equilibrium shifts. Nature responds to fill the voids, and generally
the new growth happens at a slow, steady cadence. Life works much the
same way for each of us, and timing affects our efforts at new growth or
change throughout life.

As in all processes in the natural world, timing is a factor that can
give you an edge as you consider how and when to adjust your pace as
you change course or adapt in new ways throughout life. I call this a
conscious cadence.

If you're in a contemplative mood, you can take advantage of your
inward focus to reflect through inner dialogue. If you're outwardly engaged with work colleagues or family commitments, it may be the ideal
opportunity to observe how you engage, or how others engage with you,
with the intention of gaining insight from your outer-world experience.

In my early years in graduate school, or even earlier, I'd see people
ahead of me who seemed to have a strategy for everything: how they
asked questions, how they conducted themselves, how they figured out a
purpose to focus on in their research, how to filter out ideas to find ones
that can maximize impact, how to assess their impact. Up until that
time, the strategy I had was to follow my curiosity. But now suddenly
I was exposed to people who were proficient in many skills that I just

didn't have: presentation and communication skills, procuring funding, time management, and the list went on.

Most of all, I wanted to have a life strategy. I was frustrated that nothing was happening or seemed to be happening; that I wasn't developing a strategy and I didn't know how to get there. I now realize that it's the energy we invest all along that catalyzes the manifestation, the outcome. Over a longer period of time I was able to reflect on that period and realized I had been developing a strategy; I just hadn't recognized it. The life goals I wanted so badly to achieve and struggled to make happen eventually did manifest themselves, some only recently. It wasn't on the timeline I had hoped, always in a rush to make things happen faster. But there is a cadence to life that is intrinsic to each of us and throughout nature.

We often get carried away with fast timescales, the on-demand part of our lives, the urgency of now, and it keeps us from seeing the slow changes that are shaping us and our path. Look at a tree near where you live, and day by day, week by week, it looks about the same size. But a couple years later you'll suddenly realize that it has grown. An inner voice of cadence calls us to slow down, to pause, consider what we're investing ourselves in, and acknowledge when our energy is disconnected from what we really want to be saying or doing.

The education system (and many jobs) require us to do things on timelines—assignments, test dates, arbitrary deadlines—that are misaligned with our natural rhythms, but it doesn't have to be this way for personal growth and evolution. While we may feel pressured to quickly evolve, there is no deadline by which we must "accomplish" an understanding of our own life's rhythms. The process is ongoing, often incremental, and progress can be, too, when we bring intention to it.

When people tell me about their memorable pivots in life, it is inevitably against the backdrop of what came before. Perhaps it was a long period in which they had tried to convince themselves that what they were experiencing, however empty or unsatisfying, was normal and somehow fixable. They hadn't paused to dig deeply for the cause and consider the possibility that they needed to make a meaningful change, not a quick fix. As Roché described it: too much action and not enough pausing. For some, their situation wasn't objectively bad at all, and pursuing something different was risky. In either case, the farther they continued down that path, the more procrastination and inertia set in, making it all the harder to imagine that they could change. The activation energy for big change seemed too high. Eventually, something happened that added impetus, and that boost of momentum lowered the activation energy needed for a simple step that ignited the rest.

At twenty-nine, Gabe DeRita had a lucrative job in software sales in San Francisco, a condominium near the beach, and a circle of friends. It was the good life, a successful one by all appearances and by the conventional measures he'd come to embrace. Nonetheless, he had a nagging sense that something was wrong. "I just thought I was doing what I needed to do—I had this sense of checking all the boxes," he told me. As he was riding home on his bicycle one evening, a starkly different picture suddenly came to him like a vision. "I had this very clear sense of my future diminishing, that if I kept going on the path I was on, I would just burn out and die this slow death by a thousand cuts. I was turning thirty that next year and had a sense that my youth was leaving me. I didn't feel a sense of meaning or purpose. I had always thought I would travel the world by bicycle, and suddenly, it just came together: if I deferred this dream again, I might not ever get the chance to get it back."

In the days ahead, he began to rethink the assumptions he'd long held about what made a successful life, a pastiche of priorities he'd accepted but that had begun to feel less and less authentic. Over the next several months, he disengaged from the job and comfortable life he'd known, sold his belongings, and set out to ride his bicycle around the world.

"From day one, it was immediately clear I had made the right choice," he says. Over the next eighteen months, he traveled the world solo, much of the journey by bicycle. The people he met and his experiences on unfamiliar and often challenging terrain profoundly changed his orientation to life. He encountered the Japanese concept of *ikigai*, living with a sense of purpose and fulfillment, and brought those principles and method to his inner journey, cultivating habits and practices to support a life with greater purpose. Modest changes at first—daily meditation, more mindful food choices, and an active gratitude practice, for example—set him on a new path.

*Act. There's magic in beginning. I say that to young people
all the time. They've said to me, "I hear your passion.
I have that passion. I just don't know what direction to
go in." And I say, just take a step anywhere. You'll never
regret it. Let's say you change your mind. Let's say you
apply to go to carpentry school for the summer, and two
weeks into it, you hate it. It's not your thing. That's okay,
you know. Don't drop out too early, but take a step.
Just don't sit back and do nothing.*

—DIANA NYAD, BROADCAST JOURNALIST AND
WORLD-RECORD ENDURANCE SWIMMER

Notice your inner desire for possibility.

Take stock of what is working and what is holding you back.

Recognize new ways of thinking and other possibilities.

Take a deliberate step forward to actively engage.

LIVE *LIT* TO THE CORE

Flipping the switch is really about flipping a personal evolutionary switch, consciously choosing new possibilities beyond the immediate benefit or predictability of routine. We're all confronted with choices, decisions to make, problems to solve, circumstances that hold us back from achieving our goals or discovering new ones. We all need to balance work and personal commitments. Manage our finances. Plan child care or field the big questions that come with parenting or the flare-ups that arise in relationships with family or friends. Weigh decisions about where we live, what we eat, the communities we build, and the values we embrace.

Humans are endowed with the ability to break free from habitual responses to profoundly shape their brain wiring and gene expression. The mechanism of epigenetic change lies in how we interact with our environment and experience, which is said to "flip the switch" on gene expression. When we do so with intention, we constantly update our neural connections and strengthen pathways that actively cultivate our brain's plasticity and evolutionary potential. We engage nature's basic process for evolutionary success.

It might seem a long way from Roché's pivot from career to calling to DeRita's solo sojourn to Tavakkoli's innovative gastrointestinal surgery in a pill to the limitless possibilities that await you. But there is a shared path—and you can choose to take it by flipping the switch in your thinking. As Tom Rath, a researcher for more than two decades on the subject of activating our potential, has said, "People have several times more potential for growth when they invest energy in developing their strengths instead of correcting their deficiencies."

It's time to make what is likely the single soundest investment of your life: invest in your own potential.

Imagine

Step away for a moment from whatever you've told yourself (or others have told you) about what you should be doing with your life, and brainstorm other possibilities with yourself.

Take a page from Joyce Roché's journaling strategy to reflect on your thinking about yourself and your circumstances, and take stock of the strengths and interests you'd like to be central in your thinking about yourself and your future. My wife, Jessica, a Pilates instructor, offers this simple exercise—using just your imagination:

> Visualize that you have a pair of glasses and the ability to change the lenses as often as you want. Whenever something bothers you, be aware that this is merely your interpretation based on the "lenses" through which you are looking. When you have the

patience to acquire new lenses for your glasses, a whole new world opens up and a different story unfolds.

Whether you prefer an analytical approach or creative one, explore your thinking and the evidence all around in the natural world to discover:

- **PATTERNS.** Notice repetitive patterns that tend to send you down familiar paths in your decision making about work or life choices. These may be beliefs you hold about yourself or others or fears that hold you in place and discourage you from imagining something different. Experiment stepping free from them, even if just momentarily, to disrupt the pattern and open a fresh space from which to act with more intention and drift through your days and life a little less. Notice patterns in nature that repeat, serving structure or purpose, and those that are transient, reflecting spontaneity and change, too, as the natural "order" of things. Over the course of evolution, patterns always change in nature as the environment changes. Learning from nature, we can find inspiration to revisit old patterns as most will need updating at some point.
- **POTENTIAL.** Recognize that there is potential wherever you create space for change. Tinker with small changes to carve out time to pursue your interests or explore new ones that might hold the potential for you to grow. Notice how potential is a fundamental feature of nature, from a single seed to vast systems that keep everything going.
- **POSSIBILITIES.** Recognize that there are new ways to think about how you think and lower the activation energy to act on your intentions. Try infusing fresh inspirational energy into your day by grabbing lunch or coffee with new people who might help change your mindset or simply refresh your thinking. Notice how nature itself is a constant reminder of the dynamic interplay of elements.

LIVE FOR
THE QUESTIONS

Swap Caution for Curiosity
and the Deeper Dig

Tap the vitality of inquiry.

Those moments in our lives when a new question rises up
in us, stops us in our tracks, are pivot points. They are
openings for discovery and new possibility to break in.
—KRISTA TIPPETT, JOURNALIST AND AUTHOR;

FOUNDER, *ON BEING* PROJECT

Several years ago, I found myself thinking about salamanders, and specifically about their tails. When a salamander loses its tail, it grows back
within just a few weeks. Many other animals possess this ability: star-
fish and octopi can regrow their arms, zebrafish can regenerate their fins
and hearts.

It made me wonder: Can we trigger the same response in humans?
That question led me, my primary mentor, Robert Langer, and one of
our mentees, Xiaolei Yin, on a multiyear quest for an answer. One of
the answers led to a potential treatment for multiple sclerosis (MS) by
activating the body's regenerative potential and has promise for many
applications.

Research and innovation in the lab are most often rooted in solutions suggested by some aspect of the natural world. Nature is a touchstone in our creative process, and the uplift of energy powers us not only to find answers but also, and first, to generate fresh questions. We observe and inquire. We learned that porcupine quills can easily penetrate into tissue but are difficult to remove. How could that knowledge help us design better surgical staples? What allows spiders to walk on their webs without getting stuck while their prey is fatally trapped, and how can that understanding help us design medical tape that will adhere to a newborn's tender skin but can be removed without pain? Nature has answers to questions we haven't even learned to ask yet. Evolution has created a vast range of tough, long-surviving capabilities that often point the way to medical progress for us human beings. It's up to us to dig, but first we must determine the questions that can define the problem to be solved and lead us to the answers we seek.

We've learned in the lab that in the high-stakes world of innovation there needs to be a lot more emphasis on questions than on answers. Every success and failure we've had can be traced back to the questions we asked, or didn't ask, earlier in the process.

One of the most notable setbacks I ever had in my professional life turned on a question we'd never thought to ask. It was in a seminal moment early in the launch of the lab with a new technology we developed. We thought the technology had the potential to transform medical treatment for a host of diseases and improve quality of life for millions of people around the globe. The project dead-ended abruptly one afternoon when I met with a potential investor.

In brief, stem cells were infused into a patient's bloodstream. The cells would be programmed to travel to specific sites around the body to treat such conditions as inflammatory bowel disease, arthritis, or osteoporosis.

But the prospective investor pointed out that the therapy was "too complicated" to fund. Our team had not even considered what would have to happen to bring our ideas into the medical marketplace. It was the question none of us had asked: How will this treatment reach patients? The science was exciting, but we'd never considered how to move it into clinical use.

In that uniquely specific task, moving medical science into practical application, everything rides on the quality of the questions we ask to define and solve a problem. That includes the scope of those questions, as we learned. And sometimes you can follow a promising path, asking all the pressing questions, only to meet the challenge of "the missing piece" that becomes apparent only when, for instance, a clinical trial fails because a piece of basic research, often related to human biology, has yet to be discovered.

We were disappointed that our stem cell–targeting idea failed to secure funding because it was too complex. But we had it in our power to see that our solutions wouldn't dead-end that way again. Moving forward, we wouldn't just assume that somebody out there would determine how to manufacture, package, and distribute a therapy. We would investigate it—own every part of the problem to be solved—and bring in new lab partners with the needed areas of expertise to solve the bench-to-bedside challenge together.

We would ask more and better questions.

To ask the hard question is simple.
—W. H. AUDEN

Questions—some of them intentionally random—became part of our exploratory process with physicians, scientists, and others as we researched every facet of a problem we set out to solve. That meant conducting layers of exploratory inquiry to investigate the clinical problem, the science problem, the patent problem, the manufacturing problem, the regulatory problem, the practical use problem, the investment problem, and the go-to-market problem. I'm always looking for usable information, the kind of practical knowledge that you won't find in a research paper or textbook. I also question my questions: Why am I asking this question? Where does it lead? What might we be missing? In problem solving, there are so many different angles that can be explored, and the majority of them will lead to a dead end. The questioning itself becomes a sleuthing exercise, the questions tools to try to generate unique insights that will lead to a solution.

After the investor dashed our hopes for the stem cell therapy, I had to ask myself why I had overlooked the steps needed for implementation, which now seemed obvious. The reason was that throughout its history, academic research has focused mainly on basic science. Researchers generally lack formal training in how to use their findings to make and distribute products. They typically know little about patents, regulatory steps, manufacturing processes, trials, and patient-related needs. In those early days, I was no exception. Today, these questions are as central to the lab's process as the therapeutic approaches we develop.

The takeaway for any of us in any circumstance is to challenge ourselves to think beyond—to understand the unquestioned assumptions and beliefs that may be limiting our thinking. You don't have to prove them wrong; just question them to dig deeper and search further. Rigorous questions are at the heart of scientific inquiry, but you don't have to be a scientist to love asking questions and cultivating them in everyday ways. Questions of curiosity. Problem-solving questions. Basic skills questions. Questions about our purpose as human beings and the meaning of life.

Questions are like excavation equipment: versatile tools for action. Questions can cut like a backhoe through old assumptions, or like an archaeologist's trowel and brush that uncover buried artifacts or gems, or like the sculptor's chisel that releases a masterpiece from a slab of marble. Or think of a Swiss Army knife, the everything tool: a sharp question can pry the lid open on a conversation, cut to the core of a matter, tighten the screws of a loose concept. You can use a question to accelerate a conversation or slow it down to allow time for reflection. I like to think of *lit* questions in the larger sense as fire starters, lowering activation energy and generating the spark for dialogue, exploration, critical and creative thinking, and curiosity. These metaphors are excessive, perhaps, but the point is to underscore this aspect of questions as tools for action, much as we think of other tools as having power and purpose.

Questioning takes the familiar and makes it mysterious again, thus removing the comfort of "knowing."
—JULIA BRODSKY, EDUCATOR AND EDUCATION RESEARCHER

ARE YOU READY TO QUESTION YOUR OWN PROCESS?

Decisions we made in the past still influence us, and too often we accept them without questioning whether they still apply. We get confused by what the possibilities are and what we think is possible based on our experiences and environment at the present moment. So we need to question not only our current assumptions but also how these might stem from a historical assumption that bears reexamination.

In the lab, for example, in 2014 we published a highly cited opinion piece in the journal *Nature Biotechnology* in which we reported that an assumption associated with a particular type of stem cell was wrong; that stem cell type had been assumed to have no innate immune response when transplanted from one person to another. But we had found data in the literature that refuted the point. So we dug into the question and found conference presentations from years before when this assumption had been imprinted into the scientific literature.

What do we accept as true that may be based on an inaccurate or now-outdated historical precedent? What are we doing in this moment that is constrained by a factor we can remove by questioning its assumptions?

We're born curious, and asking "Why?" comes naturally; just listen to any preschooler. But the skill to craft a stimulating, strategic question is not innate. It can be learned, and it's something like an extreme sport for the brain, both challenging and exhilarating. The more you work with your own process, the more you will develop the skills and the confidence to question.

One technique is to study how people you admire ask useful questions. What part of their approach could you adapt for yourself? For me, asking that transformed my life. Early in my college career, I was determined to overcome my childhood struggle to master some basic academic skills. I wanted to ask better questions. To learn how to do so, I did something very geeky: I started to write down all the questions people asked at the end of lectures, looking for patterns. I found a few important ones. I'll stick to the scientific example, but each of these main points is applicable to any context. The best questions—the high-yield ones—arose when they drilled down in these ways:

- **THEY ILLUMINATED IMPORTANT ASSUMPTIONS THAT WERE MADE WITHOUT SUBSTANTIAL SUPPORT.** Scientists in training often will assume that the methodology they are using, which they read on a company website or in someone else's work, should work if they follow the procedures, so they don't check to see if it really works before they try it in their own experiment. I realized that it is important to ask initial questions, such as "How do you know your assay or the kit you're using is actually working properly?"
- **THEY EXPOSED FLAWS OR DISTORTIONS.** In science, this might include overstated conclusions, alternate conclusions, and missing control groups that, if included, might have narrowed the interpretation of the results—for example, when researchers perform experiments in salt water (buffered saline), get a great result, and make a strong, broad conclusion but don't test in more complex biological fluids that contain lots of proteins, which could change the answer.
- **THEY CHALLENGED HOW WE MONITOR PROGRESS, MAKE DECISIONS, AND IDENTIFY ISSUES AND OPPORTUNITIES.** Sometimes researchers use the wrong statistics to compare things, which biases whether a result is statistically different or not. Often when we use the wrong statistical approach, we may find a difference between two groups that does not actually exist!
- **THEY DISTINGUISHED BETWEEN RESULTS THAT WERE INTERESTING AND RESULTS THAT MATTERED.** In other words, they distinguished between those considered interesting because they showed a difference, and those that are important because the difference could matter to a patient or to potential applications beyond what was envisioned. A difference may be interesting, but a difference that matters—that's what all of us want.

That awareness helped me learn to develop questions that dive toward the target, whether satisfying my own curiosity or finding the best solution to a problem. It also made me determined to create an environment for others, eventually in my own lab, where we resist the rush for answers and solutions and instead press ourselves to ask better questions. Our major quest is to define the problem we aim to solve and the highest possible measure of success—which we then aim to exceed.

In the lab, one of the most important questions is "What bar do we need to exceed to get people excited?" In other words, what's the best result anyone has ever achieved, and how much further must we go to make a significant positive impact? What's the threshold for impact we must surpass? This is hard to define because it requires having a detailed understanding of the best results achieved by others.

I always remember what my mentor, Bob Langer, said about high-yield questions: it takes just as much time to work on an important problem as on a less pressing problem. Whether we succeed depends on the questions we ask that define the problems we want to solve. The better the questions asked, the greater the potential to make new and impactful discoveries.

INQUIRY TURNED INWARD

The questions we ask hold the power for change, whether in a lab or in your life. Inquiry turned inward, the examined life, has us consciously explore what is most meaningful to us and how to live aligned with those values. Because our lives are ultimately intertwined with all others and within the natural world as a shared habitat, the questions we ask can begin to shape our desire to serve life beyond ourselves alone.

As a practical matter, self-inquiry helps us recognize the rhythms and dimensions that are part of our biological nature and at the same time figure out how we can experiment to adapt, change our mindset, evolve our perceptions to better serve us. It's a lifelong practice. There is no discrete atomic truth about anything, just layers upon layers of fractals and interconnections that may be revealed over time—or you can just get on with the dig. Asking questions helps us figure out what we like about where we are—wherever we may be on life's continuum—and what we'd like to change or see evolve. The more we interact with others, hear diverse voices and perspectives, and listen to our own mind, the better we'll be able to question and evolve with intention.

We seek meaning in life and in our work, and the questions we ask ourselves can open fresh ways to think about that: What is meaningful in the moment? What's meaningful today but might change over time? What is meaningful in a more lasting way? Engaging in a process for self-inquiry helped me learn more about myself. I was able to examine my priorities and shift my attention to my relationships, especially with my family, to understand what was most fulfilling at its core. When I recognized the deep well of energy, comfort, or peace of mind that my family is to me, it deepened my sense of purpose.

> *If you never question things, your life ends up being limited by other people's imaginations. Take the time to think and dream, to question and reconsider. It is better to be limited by what you can dream for yourself than by where you fit in someone else's dream.*
>
> —JAMES CLEAR, *ATOMIC HABITS*

CURIOSITY IGNITES INQUIRY AND DISCOVERY

Pressed to identify his strategy for success, the geneticist and molecular biologist Phillip Sharp, who shared the 1993 Nobel Prize in Physiology or Medicine for the discovery of split genes and RNA splicing, says simply, "I've taken prudent risks, and I've been curious about the world." That's a bit of an understatement when you consider the results. Among other things, Sharp's work advanced our understanding of messenger RNA (mRNA) biology, which was a precursor of the mRNA-based vaccines used against Covid.

In a field where curiosity is a given, Sharp is hailed for asking questions with uncommon courage and creativity. It was his characteristic curiosity and persistent inquiry that led to his grappling with what he calls "the most fundamental questions of the day" about human biology that led to his discovery of split genes, an aspect of cell structure that enables engineered gene splicing to create mature mRNA. The discovery, made by Sharp and independently by the British biochemist and molecular biologist Richard J. Roberts, who shared the prize, changed the scientific understanding of cell structure, catalyzing new medical research on the development of cancer and other diseases. In what may take the prize as the most impactful postscript to a Nobel Prize winner's career, the discovery of RNA splicing during the 1970s paved the way for the development of mRNA vaccines against Covid decades later.

Sharp's description of his process and motivation is matter-of-fact: "All of these processes come out of life journeys and particular personality traits. I've always been someone who needs people but is comfortable being alone and is comfortable letting my mind wander in a somewhat undisciplined way." Just calmly sitting and pondering the best question to ask can energize a moment of an entire field. Slow, clear, and deliberate thinking can help us turn questions into keys to the world's biggest locks. "I knew our biological science was just at the precipice of being able to address those questions," he said, and a "wishful, sort of dreamy kind of thinking" led him to conclude, "there almost has to be something unknown in this critical process."

> Use questions to cultivate curiosity to unlock intuitive interest.
>
> Discover what excites you most to learn or explore.
>
> Embrace the energy of engagement.
>
> Press forward with new questions to explore what's most meaningful to you.

For any of us, curiosity kindles questions and questions rekindle curiosity. It is a *lit* loop that is as important to the toddler's question "Why?" as it is to the Nobel Prize league. With new ways to study the brain and brain-based behavior, researchers have begun to take a closer look at curiosity and the benefits of an inquiring mind. Studies suggest that curiosity, often described simply as a strong desire to learn or know something, is a cognitive state—"information seeking"—and is fully wired into the brain's thought processes—and reward system.

Neuroscience and education research tell us that when you feel curious, the pleasure, reward, and memory centers of the brain all light up, stimulating the brain for deep learning and discovery, as well as social connection. (Fun, too, as evidenced in a game of trivia or crossword puzzle.) Neural circuits respond to information as an intrinsic reward, whether the quest is motivated by interest or by deprivation, an information gap that we seek to fill. Even when the information itself may have little practical value or we anticipate that it may disappoint us or have negative consequences, the "seductive lure of curiosity" keeps us questing for more of everything! This is especially so if the information is novel, surprising, or counterintuitive or in some other way contradicts your beliefs about or understanding of something. That's one reason scrolling online feels so addictive and misinformation is so sticky and hard to ignore. In "The Future Belongs to the Curious: Towards Automatic Understanding and Recognition of Curiosity in Children," the authors stated that expressing curiosity has a generally positive emotional energy, making curiosity appealing, and that "attentiveness, exploration and happiness are the most frequently co-occurring affective states with curiosity."

Other research suggests we are born to be wowed. One study involving infants showed that they "created stronger associations between sounds/words and visual objects in a context where object movements violated the expected laws of physics."

If curiosity is such a good thing, so much so that it activates the brain for learning and registers in the brain's reward system, and if questions act as curiosity's voice, how is it that asking questions can also make us queasy, nervous, and hesitant? Because curiosity is emotionally arousing; if you're self-conscious about exposing what you don't know or worry about how you'll be judged for asking, your anxiety can squelch your curiosity and inquiry. For kids, negative reactions from teachers, parents, or peers can shut them down. In adult life, too, hostility to or shaming over questions has a chilling effect that can limit the kind of free and open discussion that leads to innovative ideas.

To find enchantment, you follow the lines of your curiosity.
—KATHERINE MAY, AUTHOR OF *ENCHANTMENT: AWAKENING WONDER*
IN AN ANXIOUS AGE

May-Britt Moser, a Norwegian psychologist and neuroscientist who shared the 2014 Nobel Prize in Physiology or Medicine, told me that in her experience seemingly "stupid" questions asked in her lab sometimes turn out to be the most interesting ones. At the very least, discussion validates the person who asked the question and encourages them and others to take risks.

The founding director of the Centre for Neural Computation and co-director of the Kavli Institute for Systems Neuroscience, Moser says that in settings such as hers, where the premium is on asking productive, high-yield questions, she believes that all questions—even the sometimes annoying ones—have value. I see the same in my lab. Even a question that triggers a predictable, knee-jerk reaction often creates some energy that sparks a spirited discussion. I ask that kind of question myself sometimes in a discussion. Someone might respond, "No way, that's just not possible," and I ask "Why not?" As they present their argument, I get to hear the reasoning from a fresh perspective—theirs—which can reveal unquestioned assumptions or a unique insight worth pursuing.

So if the lesson you've learned somewhere along the way is *don't ask*, don't buy it. The world needs your questions. Given the complexity of the challenges we face today, the world especially needs your good-faith, thought-provoking expressions of curiosity—your *lit* questions. Rather than shut down our "crazy ideas" or hesitate to ask questions that could break the ice and stimulate conversation, we need to learn to trust our instinct for inquiry—for curiosity and exploration—nurture it, and give it a voice throughout our life. Set fear aside, and rather than avoiding asking the big uncomfortable questions, purposefully seek to engage with them. The very act of reflection, through internal dialogue or shared discussion, stimulates the brain for deep learning and discovery, social connection, and intuitive and spiritual experience.

With all there is to gain, why stop short of that?

*You have to really be courageous about your instincts
and your ideas, because otherwise you'll just knuckle
under . . . and then things that might have
been memorable will be lost.*

—FRANCIS FORD COPPOLA

THE BRIDGE FROM *ASKING* TO *ACTING*

Our questions can kindle change, from those that lead to personal insights to those that can eventually shape public policy. When Vivek Murthy was appointed as surgeon general of the United States in 2014 (he was reappointed in 2021), a major concern was the nation's escalating opioid addiction crisis. As a physician, he knew firsthand the complexity and extent of the issue, and his goal was to change how opioid addiction was addressed. The criteria for diagnosis and treatment were important, but the response also needed to include community compassion and motivation to fight the problem. He started by launching a listening tour, traveling the country to ask what concerned people most about health matters. His main question: "How can I help?"

The result was the first report of its kind from the federal government recognizing the scale of addiction and substance use and misuse disorders as a public health crisis. "I see myself outside the box looking in, and it's not that I think rules don't apply to me, but . . . I question the rules a lot," Murthy said. "I question the status quo and say, 'Well, I don't think it *has* to be that way, I think we can do it a different way.'" In his 2020 book, *Together: The Healing Power of Human Connection in a Sometimes Lonely World,* Murthy reframed public health issues through a holistic lens that he has used to transform the conversation about issues touching on every aspect of contemporary life. As surgeon general he continues to push the boundaries of what constitutes our health. Long attentive to mental health as fundamental to public health, he flagged the escalating mental health crisis among youths in a 2021 report describing the silent pandemic growing in the shadow of the Covid crisis.

The nation's overwhelmed mental health system had failed to meet the needs of young people as well as adults. It is failing still. In subsequent reports and media interviews he has illuminated, as health concerns, issues ranging from racism and economic inequality to the dangers of misinformation and polarization. He sees human connection as the common denominator in health and "as a powerful and essential source of healing for all of us," he says.

Asking questions builds human connections. Listening to learn deepens them.

The question Murthy suggests to drive meaningful action: "How do we rebuild connection and community at a time where we have seen that fundamental underpinning of society deteriorate over the last several decades?"

Or consider the question that Gerhard Gründer, a German psychiatrist and psychotherapist, poses in his recent book *How Do We Want to Live? We Decide Ourselves About Our Future*. His question bears repeating: How do we want to live?

> *In return for these spectacular gifts of the Earth,*
> *say to yourself: "What am I going to do about that?*
> *What is my accountability in return for*
> *everything I've been given?"*
> —ROBIN WALL KIMMERER

ASK THE BIG QUESTIONS FOR A LARGER LIFE

During the Covid shutdown period, I decided that I needed to rekindle my relationships. Knowing that my ADHD was swinging me in all kinds of directions, I sought out skills that I could use to be more intentional with my time and decisions, a new strategy in my toolbox. Certain things were staring me in the face. For example, my sister has always been incredible at maintaining relationships with intentional effort. They're a huge priority for her—maintaining a village. I could work on doing that.

Meditation, another way to observe how my mind works, became part of that. I'm still experimenting with different meditation practices, but in addition to discovering a relaxing inner calm that I was surprised I had in me, I discovered that sometimes new and different questions would arise that kept me engaged in the meditation process rather than distracted from it. One such question was: How is this meditation interacting with my mind or body? Becoming aware of that interaction—thought patterns, physical sensations, and the mind-body experience in a meditative state—helps me observe what's on my mind, what is driving my thinking, and where it's taking me.

From our most intimate quandaries to those global in scope, our questions define the problems we want to solve. They're how we identify what is most important to us and develop strategies to achieve what matters most to us. The moral and ethical dilemmas of the day call for fresh thinking, smarter questions, and more energetic pursuit of solutions. The pandemic forced difficult questions that continue to resonate as we face the prospect of future global health crises: On what basis should the government assign priority access to vaccines? As cases spiked and hospital resources were stretched thin, questions arose about rationing care: Which patients should be put on ventilators or even be admitted to the overcrowded hospitals?

In the lab, high-yield questions lead to innovative solutions. We can bring the same to our own lives and our communities. We need to understand our core personal values, hopes, and aspirations, not simply to achieve our life goals but to find the courage to ask new and provocative questions of ourselves. For example, new questions are needed to challenge historic inequities. In global funding for urgent biodiversity projects, fights over who picks up the tab are slowing efforts to get the work started. We must work with the reality that, as one report noted, "the consumption habits of wealthy nations are among the key drivers of biodiversity loss, while poorer nations are often home to areas rich in biodiversity, but have fewer means to conserve them."

I think the first question is, "What am I optimizing for?"
You need to be clear about that. There are a lot of goals and
outcomes and results in life that we inherit from the people
around us.

—JAMES CLEAR, *ATOMIC HABITS*

Another pressing example: the historic narratives of communities and whole nations are only beginning to be questioned, reexamined, retold, and expanded to finally incorporate the fuller stories that reflect their true diversity, notes Lisa Sasaki, the interim director of the Smithsonian American Women's History Museum and former director of the Smithsonian Asian Pacific American Center. The challenge to each of us is to question those traditional storylines rather than just accept them as a factual and balanced accounting, she says. "A lot of people assume that they know history in this very linear way and that it's factual. What they tend to forget is that there's an intermediary in there, which is who gets to record history, who remembers history, and who shares it with you so that you understand that that is your history."

That narrative constantly evolves with the way we each interpret the story with ourselves at the center of it, plus an element of random connections the mind makes, often unconsciously. As an American of Japanese heritage, Sasaki offers an example from her own multigenerational family. Anti-Asian racism has been a reality for generations in America. Nonetheless, her grandmother, whose life experience differs from her own in significant ways, "would have a completely different set of reactions to the same histories that technically we both share. She'd be interpreting it differently, based on her experiences that she had. So as a result, history and identity are incredibly fluid. You layer on top of that this idea of oppression and inequity and the fact that, as a result of power structures, most of the time we definitely don't have a say—that fluidity changes whose history gets told becomes a pretty big deal.

"That's already changing the information that people are receiving, and that's a first step," she notes. "What we have to do now is acknowledge that we need to question: Who is telling our history? Who is recording it, and who is getting to speak? And how we interpret it is based on the experiences that we ourselves are having."

Hard questions about historic and systemic inequities have gained a greater voice in the public dialogue, and those questions (and debate) have generated a flood of documentation of historic events that had never been openly and honestly addressed. Knowing this to be true, the question is no longer whether the problem exists; it is what we'll do with the awareness.

The call to action is, in part, a call to question, more urgently than ever, not only who or what was responsible for the past but what part we'll take in the future. What can we do going forward? Imagine it as propagation, how we spread or promote an idea or attitude. An important question any of us can ask is: "What am I doing or what have I done that has propagated inequities or negativity?" How have my actions or my silence allowed something to continue when it needs to stop? That could be in the context of racism, sexism, lies and misinformation, or everyday gossip or meanness. We need to be aware of our habits and assumptions, any that we accept without challenge or test, and be open to revising them over time based on new experiences, new information—and new intentions.

Henry David Thoreau asked, "Could a greater miracle take place than for us to look through each other's eyes for an instant?" That might sound like an invitation to empathy, but I hear it as a call for curiosity and questions. Cultivate your curiosity about another human being and their experiences, and more meaningful questions will flow naturally. Rather than avoid the big or uncomfortable questions, use them to engage, to learn, and to advance the conversations for responsible action.

When you're a student, you're judged by how well you answer questions. . . . But in life, you're judged by how good your questions are. You want . . . to transition from giving good answers to asking good questions.

—ROBERT LANGER

INTERRUPT YOUR AUTOPILOT ON INCLINATIONS AND BOUNDARIES

Sometimes the simplest questions we ask of ourselves can obliterate obstacles we didn't even realize were there. Preferences and inclinations, assumed boundaries—some of our own making, some the legacy of others' opinions that we've never questioned—can yield to the simple question: "Why not?" The conditions we've accepted as givens can be largely invisible to us but are more changeable than we think if we recognize that they exist, question them, and experiment to see how we might change them to match our intentions.

To borrow from *The Power of Habit* author Charles Duhigg's description of the habit loop (cue, routine, reward): What's the cue, what's the routine (the inclination or boundary), and what's the reward that reinforces it? In any given instance, what is there that makes us more or less inclined to follow old patterns? Simply asking yourself the question can interrupt the inclination and open your mind to possibility.

I had every reason to decline the opportunity for an extraordinary speaking engagement about ten years ago. My long history of difficulty memorizing anything, plus anxiety about public speaking with new material and unfamiliar formats generally and the hundreds of hours it would take to prepare a new talk, made me reluctant. I didn't even have to revisit that uncomfortable detail; I'd already created the shortcut in my brain that instantly hopped to know whenever those neurons tingled. Coincidentally, a timing conflict with a work trip abroad gave me an out, so rather than try to reschedule that trip or rethink my old hang-ups, I just said no to the high-profile talk. The fates were not so easily appeased. The event organizers encouraged me to reconsider. They underscored the potential to reach a worldwide audience and the confluence of circumstances on their end that made the timing for me to appear in that annual program optimal. When I asked my colleague abroad for advice, their excitement was instant and unconditional; they would reschedule my trip there. So I thought about it, under deadline pressure for a quick reply, and naturally came to the rhetorical question we all ask with a shrug: "Well, why not?" And I said yes.

Once I was committed to making the speech, every part of me re-aligned to make it happen. In a frustrating moment with memorization, the answer to "Why not?" rushed to mind, all the self-shaming reasons I'd avoided that kind of thing for so long. But now I could see how those habits of avoidance (euphemistically relabeled as preferences) and boundaries that had kept me from venturing forward had stayed in place largely unchallenged. So finally, it was my chance: a big opportunity, motivation and momentum high. The activation energy had dropped enough for me to commit—a perfect time to follow through, give it my best shot, and at least shake up the old pattern. It turned out to be a phenomenal experience (aka "my most memorable failure," which I share in "Focus Beyond Failure" on page 151) and a breakthrough to literally a world of opportunity that awaited.

To use *lit* energy to your advantage, interrupt the autopilot of inclination and simply question it. Any of the LIT tools can serve to redirect your focus and energy, but asking a question takes advantage of the brain's natural response to disruption and novelty. Asking a question gives you the opportunity to act more from intention than inclination.

Imagine that this energy available to you works something like the magnetic force we see when charged particles attract or repel one another. If you want to interrupt that pull, you can make conscious choices that will support you. Reflect on the inclinations or arbitrary boundaries you currently impose on yourself. Pick something fairly simple and accessible—perhaps the music you listen to, your social circles, or your media use—and try choosing something new that you'd like to try. Give it a chance, and see what you think. If social media or online binge scrolling has been a magnetic pull for you, enlist some conscious choices to interrupt the pattern, even if just for one day as a start, or manage more closely the time you spend online or the places you go.

The goal is not to change all patterns; it is to recognize the patterns in your thoughts, choices, and actions and simply start with a question that will help you see more clearly where these inclinations are taking you. Use questions as the oar you can slip into the water to pause and leverage the moment to serve your highest purpose.

Cultivate Your Inquiring Mind

Surround yourself with energetic people who ask questions that are substantive, insightful, even inspiring, and make a point of working or studying with them—first, because others' questions stimulate our brain and catalyze our thinking. Using the LIT tools, we can metabolize those questions into action. Second, because other people provide valuable models for honing our own skills to generate more high-octane questions. To sharpen your skills:

- Practice shaping questions—and asking them. For instance, yes-or-no questions don't generate discussion; try asking how or why—or why not—to explore the counterintuitive.
- Use the questioning process to illuminate your curiosity, discover blind spots, or just enjoy interesting conversations. Observe the questions that pop into your mind and what other thoughts they inspire. For me that heightens the excitement and positive emotions around learning.
- Find the energy for—and in—small talk. I used to think that small talk was not useful and my attitude was, why are we doing it? Then I realized that it's a way to open up energy channels between two people. Questions work the same way: they open up the flow of energy, information, emotion, knowledge. You're asking for, inviting that energy transfer. Questions can help us stay focused when our attention might otherwise wander, perhaps staying engaged in a conversation by giving someone our fuller attention and showing interest with our questions, deepening relationships.
- Use current events or personal experiences as cues to reflect on some of the big questions.

GET BOTHERED

Wake Up to What You Want

Identify the "Why?" that motivates you.

The best thing we can do is engage.
Engage in your own life, in your neighborhood.
—DIANA NYAD

James Ankrum was adrift. He might not have appeared that way, grounded as he was in academic accomplishments and having been offered an opportunity to join a joint Harvard/MIT doctoral program. But it was, I learned later, a low point for him. The first in his family to graduate from college, he had recently earned a master's degree in engineering design at Cambridge University, funded by a Churchill Scholarship, which was awarded to only fifteen individuals each year, but had returned home to the United States after his father had died and decided to stay in the United States to sort out his next steps. He had the general idea of working on improved medical therapies, or maybe developing new tools to accelerate beneficial biotech discoveries, but no clear idea of the direction he wanted to go in with any of it. In a hard-charging environment where his peers were already racing down the field, Ankrum felt as though he'd been left at the starting gate.

He had asked himself the obvious question over and over: What do I want to do? The range of promising options was dizzying, full of potential, but every time he thought about them, he felt flat. Something was missing. The program commitment deadline was looming, and he needed to make a choice. Finally, it was the missing piece that got his attention, bothered him. Naturally, he wanted to feel excited about launching into something new. The sudden recognition of what he wanted most—to feel excited about what he stood to learn from his project—helped him shift his question. Instead of asking himself what he wanted to *do,* he asked what would be most exciting to *learn,* and the answer was suddenly clear. He was intensely curious about biology but lacked biological expertise. Now was the time to get that expertise, and he was in the perfect place to do so.

Changing his question opened an entirely different vision of his options. That became possible only when he paid attention to what was bothering him and then acted on it. He had no experience in biology, but that was what he wanted to learn, rather than focus solely on building his current strengths. He took a course that I taught where we initially met, and he learned to pipette for the first time. I saw a spark in James—a kind of magnetic curiosity and passion for learning—and asked him toward the end of the term if he'd be interested in joining my lab. He agreed to come aboard, and I immediately placed him on a stem cell project. With no experience in our research methods, it would be sink or swim, and at first it wasn't clear which it would be. He was superpassionate about learning, but he struggled a lot.

"Going into it, I'd never held a pipette or cultured cells of any kind," Ankrum says. That initial introductory class had been his first introduction to cell-based research, and he had felt like a fish out of water. But he kept at it. "I'd always wanted to work on projects that do more than generate new knowledge. I wanted to work on solutions that move toward therapies or toward new tools that will accelerate future discoveries." For five years, he worked on both cell-based therapies and medical adhesives and went through phases of experiments failing one after another—or working perfectly. Scientific research has a high failure rate; it comes with the field, and failure bothers any of us. But for Ankrum, being bothered by the high failure rate in research didn't prompt him to leave; it motivated him to diversify his efforts. He added another project to address his bothered awareness, that of his need for diversity in his projects to feel motivated.

"I found it helpful to always have my hand in two projects, as chances were something would always be working and give me that bit of satisfaction that progress provides to keep me pushing on the project," he noted. When he used that bothered energy to follow his curiosity, it kept his excitement (and patience with the process) continuously kindled. By using strategies that kept his purpose and passion aligned, he stayed on fire.

PAIN POINTS AS TRACTION FOR ACTION

In my line of work, when we go to solve a problem, we always ask, "What are the pain points?" In business and marketing—and psychology, too—"pain points" refers to the "painful" motivating factors that drive us to act. What specific fear or desire bothers you enough for you to change a behavior or buy a product? In other words, what's the problem you want to solve? In medical science, pain points aren't metaphorical; they are the aspects of human suffering that we seek to cure or alleviate: disease, injury, pain, and impairment. In my lab, we set out not only to create something new and effective but to do it in a way that can make the greatest positive impact. What gets us bothered serves as a touchstone that keeps us motivated and driven with a sense of urgency to solve a problem. Once we are in touch with that desire, the energy we devote to a project can ignite a spark for others and build momentum for problem solving on a wider scale.

Ordinarily in life, we try to avoid or push away things that bother us, but if we question ourselves instead, turning our attention to the source of the pain point, we can pause, reflect on it, and go a layer deeper: Why does this bother me? How could I tap this energy to do something about it? To serve my intentions? Instead of avoiding something that bothers us, we can go right to it and look for a spark to act on our intention.

In the lab, there is a specific and concrete pain point for any problem we set out to solve. The force of a pain point is pure, palpable energy. It's what keeps us pressing on our process to push the inquiry deeper, reframe the problem, and refine our focus to create something new that will move most quickly and effectively out into the world. As I've mentioned, that's the power we tap with the question we always ask in lab meetings at every step of the problem-solving process: What is the bar we must exceed to get people excited? To get other researchers excited, investors excited, the public excited? This is how we define targets. The "So what?" question always gets a good workout, spurring us to surpass whatever we've come up with thus far. It's superexciting when you start to realize that you are making progress and on the right track. You are more likely to go all in. It's a way to gain momentum.

Bryan Laulicht, who has a background in biophysics and medical science, initiated a project to reduce injury in children who swallowed button batteries, those small disc-shaped batteries that contain lithium, zinc, silver, or manganese and power many cameras, key fobs, remote controls, musical greeting cards, thermometers, and watches. Lodged in a child's throat, a battery can burn through the esophagus in less than two hours. This happens to an average 3,500 children each year in the United States alone, and the incidence has been increasing, with dozens of child fatalities and even more cases where kids suffer permanent damage.

One of Bryan's friends read an article about the increased incidence of injuries from ingested button batteries in children and told him about it, and the problem pulled on him in a personal way. "I often think, what if that happened to a member of my family?" he says. "And I typically come back to that when things get tough—it's worth doing because it could help someone I care about or who others care deeply about."

To make a better battery, we developed a scalable technology to inactivate the battery when wet, so there is no chance of a current damaging the tissue. The new technology doesn't compromise battery performance.

For Laulicht, an emotional touchstone keeps motivation high. Anyone can use an emotional connection this way to keep motivation strong. Your pain point carries the source of urgency for you, your strongest motivation to act on your intention. Maybe you've become aware of a habit or robotic pattern that bothers you and you want to change. Maybe the pain point is about something you want to be or don't want to be or something you want to do or don't want to do. Perhaps it's a goal that you want to reach. Your pain point might motivate you to find a new job, repair a relationship, or take active steps to solve a problem in your community. In a broader sense, pain points are what move us from not caring to caring, from inaction to action. The energy we then devote to solving the problem can ignite a spark for others and build momentum for problem solving on a wider scale.

> *Nature will send a message to you, maybe a mild message, and if you don't get it, it'll come again, increasing in force or pain. Pain is a really good teacher, the master teacher. If you have pain, you do everything that you can to try to get rid of that pain. Pain from a spiritual sense is a messenger to say, "Well, maybe you need to think about something, maybe you need to change. Maybe you're not following what you were intended to be, what destiny intended. Maybe you're doing something that is an opposite of what you were intended to do." To me, it's a time of reflection, for all of us to consider: Are we really being true instruments of that higher power of influence, that higher spiritual law that has a higher and greater understanding?*
> —DR. ELDER DAVE COURCHENE, ANISHINAABE NATION

When motivation lags, it can help to identify a pain point—create one, if need be—to up the ante and help you feel that there's more at stake, win or lose. It doesn't have to be complicated. The pressure to follow through can nudge you to take the next step—to act on your intention—to avoid the consequences of not doing so. For example, if you want to go to the gym but never do, find a partner so that now if you don't go, you've stood someone else up. That's a pain point.

Often the backstory behind innovation, particularly in medical science, lies in someone's proximity to the struggle or suffering they want to relieve, such as a family history of cancer, a grandparent with Alzheimer's disease, a friend failing in school because his family lost everything and became homeless, or a personal experience of tragedy or hardship and what it took to forge through it. All sorts of determined, motivated people describe aspects of their life experience that drove them to a sense of calling, a passion to create something different, something better for themselves or others. The same is true as we look to solve some of the most intractable problems confronting us today, from environmental problems to systemic racism and social injustice.

Reading, research, studies, and lab work can provide one kind of intelligence and even motivation, but boots-on-the-ground proximity taps into a deeper energy source. Whatever the sphere we're working in, we need to keep sight of the need, keep in touch with the reason to care.

When I asked Bishop Mariann Budde how a social justice activist like herself stays so fully engaged when progress can be slow, arduous, and often discouraging, she quoted Bryan Stevenson, the criminal justice reformer, and his famously succinct advice for those who are committed to the work: "Stay proximate." She keeps his words close in mind. "How do I make sure that I don't lose focus and intention as a leader and as a citizen? If you want to do this work over the long haul, and if you want to make a real difference, you have to stay proximate to the people who are suffering the most. If you are in relationship with people who are bearing the brunt of our inequity, and a *real* relationship, it's a lot harder to walk away than if it's an issue that you're fighting or working for, and I know that to be true."

Sometimes a moment, an occasion, an issue, circumstance,
or situation calls one into leadership. I always spoke up,
making space for the voices of the disenfranchised.
—REGINALD "REGGIE" SHUFORD, EXECUTIVE DIRECTOR, NORTH
CAROLINA JUSTICE CENTER

START ANYWHERE: PURPOSE FINDS PASSION; PASSION FUELS PURPOSE AND JOY

So often the advice to "follow your passion" presupposes that we magically know what it is and that the way is clear and straightforward. It may be true for a rare few, but not for most people. It certainly wasn't obvious to me as a kid. I liked to build things, sure, but nothing about my Lego creations or the robot I constructed from the cardboard cores of paper towel rolls suggested a future in engineering. I was also lucky to live near some woods. I roamed there, but with no precocious passion for nature beyond the creek-stomping adventures of a free-range kid. No one would ever have imagined that I'd be a scientist someday, much less a bioengineer translating nature's wisdom into medical therapies.

In adult life, sometimes free range can feel like free fall, especially when your peers seem to have found their path, discovered their passion. Or maybe you thought you had, too, but then something happens that yanks it out from under you.

Diana Nyad, the famed long-distance endurance swimmer, author, and playwright, told us that as a child she'd had intense interests, but swimming wasn't the singular one. She loved to read books and watch movies about driven athletes, but her signature intensity came from a surprising place for a child: a sense of mortality and the need to get serious about life fast. She hadn't known much about her extended family, but when she learned at about age ten that her grandparents had both lived into their mideighties, she did the math. Given their life spans and her age, she wrote in a school essay, "That means I have seventy-some years left. I'd better get busy if I want to be a doctor and an athlete and go help a lot of people and speak all the languages of the world."

That ambition might seem outsized for one so young, she admits, "but the point was, there was a recognition and a pulse of needing to be as wide awake and as engaged as you possibly can. For some reason, I had this feeling of 'You better not sleep it away. You better not waste it. You better not fool around because you don't have much time.'" Mortality was her pain point.

Linda Stone, a technology innovation leader who started her career as a teacher and school librarian, never set her sights on achieving the top-level positions that have marked her distinguished trajectory, from working with the CEO of Apple to working for the CEO of Microsoft and beyond. "I had no particular career plan," she told me. "I was guided by my interests and a passion for figuring out how technology might best serve the humans who use it."

Her eclectic interests shared certain common themes. "I was really curious to understand creativity, intelligence, how people learn and think, and how people solve problems. When personal computers came out, I was fascinated by the human-machine relationship. I was interested not in how humans could be more efficient, like machines are. My interest was always in how machines could support us in being the best humans we could be."

She considers her career to be driven more by curiosity than by a goal to reach the C-suite. As she followed her curiosities, opportunities came up, and she pursued them. Her deep interests in process and innovative thinking made her a standout in the corporate environment. Her passions and curiosities were not only obvious to her, they were essential—and that self-awareness was a deep source of guidance. Her pain point—wanting to work only on things she truly cares about—has been a trustworthy guide.

Sometimes it's only in retrospect that you can recognize the pain point that marked a turning point in your life. In my own experience, just as I was launching into career possibilities and had no idea what path to choose—academia or corporate enterprise—I was excited to get a job offer from a young biotech company. I'd be working alongside some of the most brilliant researchers and innovators in biomedicine. The conversation was going great until they described the job more specifically, which was that I'd lead a small team and my specific focus would be . . . and right there, at the mention of a specific focus, my alarm bells went off. To focus strictly on one project was my worst nightmare. It ran counter to everything about me, especially the way my brain works, driven by curiosity, needing to work on multiple projects simultaneously and learn new things constantly, getting into new areas all the time, figuring out what is most important in fields that I know nothing about—

basically, what I do now. That sudden realization eclipsed everything else about the job. I heeded my internal alarm system and chose not to join the startup, shifting my attention instead to opportunities that held the kind of challenge and *lit* energy I knew I needed. I had no inkling at the time that eventually I'd be heading up my own innovation lab, but I've learned to trust the process, to use the pain points to stay in touch with what motivates me, and to follow those cues.

LEARN WHAT MOVES YOUR NEEDLE

As a mentor and professor, I'm often asked for advice by someone weighing a decision about their next step, perhaps a job or study opportunity or a choice of direction in their career. They'll lay out the pros and the cons, the risks, benefits, and trade-offs, and share the advice they've gotten that leans one way or the other. Younger students often struggle with making a decision because they're not sure whose advice to follow: parents', peers', or professors'? Those with more experience may still wrestle with the strategic pros and cons of the options. What's the best path?

The question that's so often been overlooked is one I've learned to ask myself through the years: Of these choices, which one will you be most excited to go in and do? Imagine yourself waking up each day—what are you going to be most fired up to do? Answering that question helps cut through vagueness about things you can't know and makes you tune in to your feelings, your intuitive sense, which has its own kind of intelligence.

If your answer is "I don't know," that's an invitation for you to experiment more and figure out what drives you and excites you. If constraints on your time or resources mean that you can't get away for that dream trip retreat to think about it, then be where you are, as the saying goes; pay attention to what really gets your positive emotions going. Take notes. Even text message yourself—that's how I do it. As you go about your day, try to remember or record what triggers positive feelings and what brings on frustration. It takes a little concentration and a certain measure of self-awareness, but pay attention to what you find exciting and what you really want to do with your time.

Take some risks, and try lots of things. Give yourself a chance to get over the initial discomfort of doing something unfamiliar and look for signs that something resonates for you. Something will. And positive things come of the exploration itself. First, you're developing greater self-awareness, practicing taking your emotional pulse to see what you genuinely enjoy and what you don't, learning to discern between "me" and the "not-me" experiences. With that information, you can put greater attention and energy into the things that are most likely to give you a positive return on your investment. That, in turn, will boost your motivation to pursue those interests.

Getting in touch with those feelings can be difficult. Many of us were raised to believe and deeply feel the need to make choices that please other people: parents, family members, friends and coworkers, bosses. Just about anyone but ourselves. It's easy to overlook our own needs when our habit is to defer to those of others.

It helps to develop an awareness of what is going to move the needle for you personally. Identify decisions you can make today—or this week or any other time—that will maximize your excitement for the longest period. That inner drive will be what fortifies you for the harder stretches, those periods between the high points when things can be difficult or discouraging.

In science and medicine, we use biometrics to measure the presence and interactions of certain biological factors. Blood tests and other diagnostic tools reveal biomarkers for cancer and other diseases, which in turn help with diagnosis and treatment. Biometrics also include other biological or behavioral characteristics that identify something unique about you and your responses. The idea makes a useful DIY feedback tool for reading your motivational energy for a given activity. What energizes you and what doesn't, or doesn't as much as it needs to, to keep your motivation and satisfaction strong? How is your experience shaped by your environment? Do you prefer to exercise solo or with an exercise partner? Walk on a treadmill or an outdoor path? Maybe you decided a long time ago that you're "not a math person" or not athletic or artistic, because those things didn't click with you at some younger formative time. But those past impressions are always worth revisiting. A new context, fresh approach, supportive teacher or coach, and your own life experience and development can make a significant difference the next time around.

We need to become aware of the context that might define what excites us or not and use that strategically. Set yourself up for success by controlling the variables—time, place, social factors—that you can. Know thyself, and you'll discover that you can even use some of your perceived faults to your advantage. For example, there are many things I love doing, but I'll procrastinate just to build up motivational energy to be excited to finally get to them. I used to get upset at myself for procrastinating. It felt wrong, like a character flaw. But I eventually realized that for me, it was actually part of an effective process—a way for my brain to wander freely before turning to a focused task. Once I recognized that, I stopped wasting valuable energy badgering myself or feeling bad about myself and used that insight to accomplish more.

Confronted with time pressures like everyone else, I began to pay more attention to what I was spending my time on. At that point, early in my career, I was pursuing some passions but often wasn't fully present to others that mattered a lot to me. It's not that every moment must be productive, but my pattern was to find ways to get hooked on something I was working on, stay up late at night to battle my ADHD to feel productive, get tired, tune out, and be frustrated that I wasn't doing the things that deep down I felt were most important. It wasn't sustainable.

There is always more I can do: more possibilities to think about, more projects to start, more funding to apply for, more ways I can spend time meeting with students to provide guidance, more efforts I can make to be a good father and a good husband and support my family. The exhilaration and just plain positive feelings resulting from certain activities are biometrics that I've learned to read as measures of the deeper way they affect me and sustain me. I now update my internal review frequently. I inventory what I love doing, and what I'm doing or not doing that bothers me—what occupies my thoughts when my head hits the pillow. These give me an indication of whether my choices are good ones.

The more sensitive I've become to those inner cues and the more I base my day-to-day decisions on them, the more fully I can engage—and recognize when I need to rest, play, or focus more or differently on what I'm doing. Just interacting with others can be a way to take readings on your own state of mind and whether you're living your values and priorities. How others respond to you may suggest something about the vibe you're giving off. Today my *lit* response to feeling tired is: *tune in*. I focus more fully so I can be present to whatever I am doing, whomever I'm with, whether work-related meetings, family time, or turning off devices and turning in for sound sleep. I've become more vigilant about my media use, reining in some mindless habits but also using it more deliberately for good. For example, I take five-minute breaks throughout the day to play chess puzzles and found that I can use them as a test of how tired I am. The chess puzzles require being sharp and thinking several moves ahead to get them right, and when I am tired I just can't do that. So if I find myself unable to solve the puzzles, I know I need to get more sleep! I use wearable devices to experiment in other ways with my daily routines to improve my sleep. For me, that's a *lit* move: What can I experiment with in my life to improve it in ways that matter most to me?

Today, I generally push through, power up, feel energized by the "champions always do one more" mantra—within reason. Sometimes I'm less motivated to, say, track things. I'd rather just be, exist without the quantitative details. When I feel a shift like this, I'll review my habits to ask about each: Is this still serving me well? If I decide it's not, I'll shift to something different. I'm also aware that what no longer serves me today might serve me at some point in the future.

The interesting thing I find is that the activation energy needed to push beyond the tiredness is far less than it used to be. Yes, I need to get more sleep from time to time, and yes, I need more play in my life, and I'm working on that. But by filling my life with things that I'm passionate about, I find it much easier to recognize actual weariness versus lack of motivation. I'm still able to push and get lots of things done and then feel great about it, compared to the past, when I'd give in (give up) to the tiredness and then feel unproductive and lazy, which negatively affected my mood and everyone around me. Targeting my pain points leads me to feel some degree of struggle pretty much every day. Whether it's a mental struggle to figure something out or the struggle just to keep moving toward a goal, I've accepted it as part of the natural rhythm of my day.

For a quick read on the energy gain or drain tied to your daily tasks, look for contrasts. "The greater the contrast, the greater the potential," noted Carl Jung, the father of analytic psychology. "Great energy only comes from a correspondingly great tension of opposites." When do you feel confident, in the zone, exhilarated? When do you feel bored or slow to get started? When and where can you most easily sense these contrasts? The pandemic narrowed our explorations, narrowed our interactions outside of not only our personal bubbles but our immediate communities. Take stock of your patterns of exploration and take an intentional step to expand them. Start with one or two choices that target smaller things that matter to you. Maybe it's making a trip to the museum that you've continually put off because the activity wasn't high on anyone else's list. Maybe it's taking a walk through your neighborhood. Or reading a book, listening to a new podcast, or trying out a new recipe, instead of doom scrolling on social media. Start small. Pay attention to how you feel. If it lights you up, write it up!

Once you begin to respond to your own interests in this way, you build into your thought process the idea that you *can* make changes that make your life better. I would never suggest that the needs and choices of others don't matter, but the only way to find your passions in life is to think in a focused way about yourself. If that feels impossible in the moment, then let that bother you—and use any other LIT tool to provide the spark for action.

WRONG FIT? SHED THE SHOE

Although it might look to an outsider as if my path in science and biomedical innovation was reasonable, logical, and well planned, that's not how it has ever felt. I was guided by the pain point of how I felt when I was not aligning my choices with my curiosity. I needed to focus on what I was most curious about; if I ignored that inner guidance, I could feel the wrong fit like a bad shoe—or the wrong boot for a long hike. So along my journey, I learned to follow my interests, discovering a new one and then another. For me, as for Linda Stone, it was my curiosities that drove me, and working without that energy was a pain point that kept me focused, like guideposts on a trail.

I had to learn to live with, even thrive with, the element of uncertainty on that path. In other words, I couldn't let avoiding uncertainty become the pain point, choosing options because they felt safer or more secure. I had to reframe impostor syndrome as merely a sign that I was exploring new and unfamiliar territory that stoked my interest and curiosity. This is one of the cornerstones of the lab now, constantly getting into new areas of science or medicine that I am curious about but unqualified for. We push ahead and find ways to bring in people with the right skills who can help guide us. You don't have to have certainty or even confidence that something you want to try will work. But as you head into the unknown, know that you are, once again, training yourself to discern, to tell when ideas are working and when they are not. It's this process of learning what works and what doesn't that can, in and of itself, inject a sense of excitement into your life. Uncertainty is intrinsic to that process, and there is so much energy in it: having an idea, believing in it, and going for it.

James Ankrum's favorite takeaway from his sink-or-swim start: "We had a saying in the lab when I was there: 'Do something!' It can be easy to get stuck in the planning and hypothetical stages of a project and never actually pull the trigger to try something new and learn. So 'Do something!' was our way to push each other to take risks." He also remembers, laughing now, the lab meeting when I heard them saying this to each other, and I immediately reframed it as "Do something *big*! Do something *important*!"

Today Ankrum leads a lab where he creates an environment of impassioned, purpose-driven possibility for others. So many times we are bothered by feeling that we should intuitively know what to do next. Instead of thinking about what you should do next or thinking of your future as a single thing, shift your attention to figuring out what you are curious about. What excites you? What could you do next that you could enjoy for a while, long enough to gain insight into what you like or don't like, to guide your future decisions? What bothers you enough to want to do something about it?

SHARING A CALL TO ACTION

Shared pain points can create a will and a way to accomplish important things on a global scale. Until climate change and related environmental concerns and natural disasters register as a pain point for more people and that urgency carries through to government and leadership at every level, we're dooming ourselves to repeat these devastating lessons.

Something that really resonates for me is the way Lisa Sasaki at the Smithsonian referred to culture. One reason innovation typically suffers at a global level is that politics and economics are a game of dare: none of the big players wants to be the first to change course toward a more collaborative, less power-driven model—of government, of business, of social change—for fear of yielding power to others who might exploit it for themselves. But this ignores the suffering and pain points of those who bear the burden of their policies. Biologically, pain points signal quick action for survival; break a bone, and you go to the doctor. We need to find a way to amplify the pain points and turn up the dial, not wait until we personally experience the pain to act. Consider the planet your home, the natural world your neighborhood, and those struggling your neighbors. Look for the pain points. Get bothered, and find what moves you.

Find your traction for action in what baffles, bugs, or blows you away.

Notice your desire for change: *bothered awareness*. That's your pain point. To uncover your motivating sources, try these steps:

- **LOOK AROUND. CONNECT THE DOTS.** Awareness becomes recognition. Your brain is constantly engaged in pattern recognition.

In low-energy mode, our thinking routinely defaults to the familiar responses we've used before. You can change that from an unconscious response to a conscious choice to introduce a new response and a *lit* moment for your brain.

- ENGAGE WITH INTENTION. Recognize the stimuli in your life that pull you into immediate actions, and know that you have a choice. Pause to consider your choices in real time: Do you want to stick with an old habit or choose something different that supports your new intention?

- CONNECT WITH YOUR OWN POWER. Accept that you hold the key; you're in charge. Reconnect with your pain point or motivation for an extra surge of energy. It's empowering to feel that connection.

- BE TRANSPARENT. When you focus on changing something for the positive in your life, try being open and transparent about it. Your change may affect someone else's thinking or motivation. That's a spark, and with it, the possibility of change opens for others as well.

- PASS IT FORWARD. Encourage and support others on their own paths. The energy transfer in *lit* action is powerful. As you make changes, you're changing yourself for the better. That has a ripple effect on both you and those around you. They may be inspired to want a positive change for themselves and be moved to act on it. In any case, we stand to benefit when we allow our inner discomfort to bubble up and stir our intuitive sense about changes we want to see, changes we want to make.

BE AN ACTIVE OPPORTUNIST

Scout Ideas, Insights, and Inspiration Everywhere

Train your brain to seek diverse experiences and seize opportunities.

No wonder people create so-called echo chambers, surrounding themselves with news and views that reinforce what they already believe—it reduces the metabolic cost and unpleasantness of learning something new. Unfortunately, it also reduces the odds of learning something that could change a person's mind.

—LISA FELDMAN BARRETT

In the world of science and technology, there is a structure that, like us, is hardwired for vibrant, creative connection with others, that thrives on receiving and sharing information, synthesizes it to generate new energy and possibilities, and withers without the connection. This is the neuron, the connection and relay point for data in your brain, continually active, ready for growth and change. "The neuron changes constantly; it grows, and when growing it samples the environment," wrote Daniel Câmara in *Bio-inspired Networking*.

Be like a neuron! That's the essence of what it means in *lit* life to be an active opportunist. Sample your environment constantly, proactively scouting for sources of inspiration, information, and insight. Seek out people, places, and experiences that create opportunities to learn, grow, connect, and collaborate to make good things happen, whatever sphere of life you inhabit. In other words, channel your inner neuron.

Why do that? A recent study assessing the social interactions and happiness of more than fifty thousand people found that those interacting with a more diverse set of relationship types—including distant acquaintances and even strangers—were happier than those whose range of social interactions was narrower. Based on previous studies and public data from governmental and public health agencies, the group of researchers reported that "Over and above people's total amount of social interaction and the diversity of activities they engage in, the relational diversity of their social portfolio is a unique predictor of well-being, both between individuals and within individuals over time." The more conversations people had across those categories of relationship, the more satisfied they were, and the findings held true across a large sample of many countries, said Hanne Collins, a Harvard Business School doctoral student who coauthored the study. Particularly interesting was their finding that interactions with "weak ties" (i.e., distant others) could generate "surprisingly positive experiences." This was especially so in one-on-one conversations where the relational stakes are lower, they said, concluding that weak ties "play a critical role in bolstering one's network, by serving as bridges that provide access to information and resources."

I know that the word *opportunist* can have negative connotations. It is often linked to bad actors who seek wealth or power, as in "a person who exploits circumstances to gain immediate advantage rather than being guided by consistent principles or plans." I use the word in a nonsinister sense. In research, we must recognize opportunities when they arise—ideas, previously overlooked possibilities, bolts of insight out of the blue—and then pursue them to see where they might lead. We must be opportunistic, in other words, to grasp our chances and explore their potential. What's more, as hard as it is for introverted people of science to project themselves socially, we must multiply our chances to be opportunistic by continually networking, often with people who, at first glance, seemingly work in disciplines that are wholly foreign to us—in the *lit* life. Opportunism *lit* is grounded in contributions, cultivating connections and relationships for action that serves a greater good.

Active opportunism is the antidote for the brain's LEB mode, with its drift toward the familiar. When we engage with others, we alert the brain with a natural ping and a nudge to action.

Networking to build professional contacts lost its shine when it became a dull, obligatory, transactional career-builder grind. By contrast, in nature's playbook, networking is a fundamental feature, a wildly creative, energy-charged phenomenon. For neurons, it can be a matter of life or death; they flourish as networkers, and the loss of connectivity to other neurons is the death knell in disease and some cell life cycles. Cross-pollination is a necessity for some plants to reproduce, and they depend on birds, bees, and other means to help them. Ants and termites use a collective algorithm of localized pheromones to coordinate movement and tasks. Bacteria release molecules to coordinate colonization of hosts and for defense. Swarm behavior, or (at its best) swarm or group intelligence, embodies the networking advantage. Among social species, from ants and bees to birds and mammals, the contributions of each individual can boost a group's collective intelligence. Sometimes the synergy among individuals in the group "presents an intelligence that goes far beyond the intelligence of each," as Câmara explained.

Our choice in the matter and our intentional follow-through is the *lit* factor. Connection and vibrant interaction are life forces for us as humans, too, and we can energize our search-and-sample process across time, distance, and cultural differences. Reaching out can be an antidote to loneliness, a growing mental health concern. As the psychiatrist/therapist and author Phil Stutz pointed out in *Stutz*, the Netflix documentary, "Your relationships are like handholds to let yourself get pulled back into life. The key of it is you have to take the initiative."

Lateral thinking, a term coined by the psychologist, physician, and inventor Edward de Bono in 1967, popularized the concept of thinking outside the box with the metaphor of using different "thinking hats," representing different perspectives as a strategy for driving innovation in organizational settings. More recently, neuroscience research has deepened and expanded our understanding of the brain's networked systems, revealing a vast interconnectivity through which we draw intel continuously from sources within us and around us, or what the author Annie Murphy Paul calls "the extended mind" in her book *The Extended Mind: The Power of Thinking Outside the Brain*. Contrary to the long-held assumption that the mind is "brain bound"—contained and operative solely in the skull—Paul draws from neuroscience and philosophy to describe a host of extraneural resources that infuse the brain and shape the mind. "The mind extends beyond the skull, beyond the brain, into our bodies, or the sensations and movements of our bodies into physical space, the spaces in which we think and learn and work, into our relationships with other people and into our tools with which we do our thinking," she says.

What has proven golden as approaches to problem solving and innovation can illuminate every facet of our lives, including our most intimate thoughts and relationships, imagination, dreams, and daily life, *lit* with that intention. In practical terms, all of these involve active outreach: seeking out information, insights, perspectives, opinions, and experiences from those outside our immediate circle. Leveraging the high-energy brain of *lit* mode, we can cross-pollinate our thinking. Or as the artist, technologist, and philosopher James Bridle wrote in *Ways of Being: Animals, Plants, Machines: The Search for a Planetary Intelligence*, "to look beyond the horizon of our own selves and our own creations to glimpse another kind, or many different kinds, of intelligence, which have been here, right in front of us, the whole time—and in many cases have preceded us."

Not only embracing diversity of all kinds but actively seeking it out transforms everything, from the neural networks that enable you to read (or listen to) this book to the energy you pass forward as you move through your day. After all, energy exists beyond words, outside the lines, and travels in ways that science cannot yet explain.

PHILLIP SHARP:
TALK WITH PEOPLE WHO KNOW SOMETHING
DIFFERENT THAN YOU DO

When the geneticist Phillip Sharp, an institute professor at MIT's Koch Institute for Integrative Cancer Research, talks about the evolution of his work in cell biology that led to the Nobel Prize, a noteworthy thread that runs through it—besides the science itself—is his desire to be in conversation with and learning from others. "I like to talk to people who know something different than I do," he told me. He described scientific inspiration as a process "that comes out of life journeys." What struck me was how he looks at things beyond his interests to deepen his interests and maximize his impact.

When we are pursuing a passion and realize along the way that there's something else we're more interested in—a higher purpose, perhaps—an opportunity emerges to connect with a deeper intention that might lead us to a completely new path, a new environment. The more we align with our deepest interests, the more gravitational pull draws others to connect and collaborate with the energy that we are tapped into.

That's what any great organization or institution is about, and the same can be said for any community or in the space of one's own life. As Sharp described it, the diverse, stimulating science minds around him, younger and older, were more than an influence, they were an environment—a petri dish for growth. As he noted in an interview with the MIT Infinite History Project, "as you enter that community . . . you know, you look around and you say who's got the most valuable and interesting ideas. Who's getting things done? Who's moving the show?" As you engage in a fertile environment, he says, "you add information and insight, it stimulates a lot of people around you to go out and solve problems. And they bring tools and ideas back to you. So then you see from different perspectives . . . new ways of actually solving problems. And so this interface is fascinating."

Sharp's childhood years on his family's small farm in Kentucky, living close to the Earth and the animals, stoked his curiosity in science. As he pursued that path, traveling to attend conferences, he'd take along colleagues' research papers to read in transit and keep learning. "It's just terribly enjoyable being able to understand in detail how other people think and how problems unfold and adding your own little bit to it and creating something new. That's a wonderful life," he said.

At various times in the years ahead, Sharp would seek out opportunities to participate in other labs' regular meetings to discuss work under way, sharing his own as well, and expanding the scientific dialogue with an ever-growing sphere of colleagues. Eventually he stepped into the entrepreneurial role. He saw an opportunity to bring academic technologies to patients, and despite being told that he wouldn't last a year, he helped launch the biotech industry when he cofounded Biogen in 1978 and turned Boston's Kendall Square from an urban swamp and industrial wasteland into a bustling biotech capital of the world. "The thing that entrepreneurship pulls out of you," he says, "is you have to engage with a much larger sector of society to make that work . . . just meeting all these people and trying to understand what motivates them, and how they do their work. . . . It has led me to a greater appreciation of the talent, the diverse number of people in society."

"This process has reoccurred multiple times in my life," he told me. "I read outside of the specific interests that I have, then accumulate contacts with people with different interests, and then begin to connect the dots. Through this process, I have been able to make contributions that have shaped the field and shaped biotech."

Along the Licking River in Falmouth, Kentucky, Sharp's family raised cattle and grew tobacco, and he took on a share of the work to pay for his college education. He encourages more engineers and scientists to talk with rural and resource-poor students, especially, as a way of inspiring the next generation of researchers. In some of those communities, he said, students don't routinely see people who have made contributions. "Someone standing in front of them and telling them how exciting it is can have a profound impact on a young mind."

Children are the living messages we send
to a time we will not see.

—NEIL POSTMAN, *THE DISAPPEARANCE OF CHILDHOOD*

OUTWARD BOUND FOR THE BRAIN

You can practice active opportunism in many ways. Opportunities flow in two directions: outgoing (you initiate) or incoming (initiated by others, but you've got to recognize them). Either way, you want to train your brain to perk up—recognize opportunities to connect with others—and be proactive about following through. When something or someone strikes a chord that resonates with you or simply rouses your curiosity, that's a cue, an intuitive heads-up to your analytical brain: *Check this out!* Act on it. This is how one opportunity becomes an infinitude of them. It may come during a call from someone new or a chance encounter that leads you in a new direction. You never know when going on a coffee date with someone can lead to something interesting.

> *If your knowledge is very narrow or regional, then what are the odds of making the right decision?*
> —CHRIS HADFIELD, ASTRONAUT

Here's an example of *outgoing* active opportunism: Almost from day one, when I started my lab, I decided to meet with all kinds of people involved in the fields we'd need to tap to succeed. As I've mentioned, coming out of my postdoc, I was fired up to embark on a career focused on translational medicine, which, as Phillip Sharp notes, requires that you anticipate all the key steps that will be needed to bring new scientific advances from bench to bedside—from the lab to treatment settings. But I knew I didn't have the right tools to do it. By that I mean the necessary range of expertise. Generally in academia, with the exception of those with business degrees, we are not trained to bring products forward to create value in the world. I'd studied alongside Bob Langer, my mentor, and I had seen him do it and knew it was possible. But Langer makes it look as natural as breathing. It didn't come naturally to me at all.

Knowing I lacked the relevant skills and a useful strategy, I decided that I needed to meet people with the skill sets essential to translate technologies. They included patent and corporate lawyers, reimbursement and regulatory experts, manufacturing experts, entrepreneurs, people in all kinds of companies, and investors, none of whom was well represented among the regulars at the coffee kiosk by the lab. I decided that an energizing yet manageable pace would be to meet someone new every two to three weeks. Before our meetups, I prepared questions and went prepared to listen deeply and learn. I focused on quickly processing what I was learning so that I could advance the conversation with new questions. And I wanted to be respectful of people's time, especially since not all such meetings would lead to a formal collaboration. I found ways to reciprocate with insights or contacts, even if we weren't going to work together at the present time.

Networking events can feel torturous, especially when they're required of you. All that awkward, formalized small talk! I didn't always feel like meeting new people. Calling someone who didn't know me or introducing myself to someone at an event—sometimes just getting out the door was the hardest part! After all, fear triggers are built into our genetics and hesitation to engage is a feature of our species. So I tended to shy away from those events, thinking they were not only awkward but also inefficient. But sometimes all we need is a spark to override our reluctance and reignite connection.

When I shifted my attitude about the events and appreciated the potential for a genuine connection, my energy for them improved. Eventually, that intention—relational instead of transactional—helped lower the activation energy of the rest. They felt less onerous; I felt less resistant. Framing them as a self-challenge helped me flip the switch. I could stay centered in my purpose, with the goal to do it a few times a month. Eventually, it became an expedition to find people I connect with energetically. My goal crystalized: to develop genuine relationships, share ideas, get feedback, and learn and share from my experiences. That in itself is a great outcome.

As a result, I've found valued collaborators I might never have met through familiar channels. One December day in 2010, I made a decision to get over myself to attend a medical device networking event and try to genuinely value conversations with people I met. Among them was the serial entrepreneur Nancy Briefs, who was in the process of selling her current company. I had just secured a grant from the Wallace H. Coulter Foundation, which supports translational research collaborations between biomedical engineers and clinicians. Our grant was to advance autostop needle technology and included funds to hire an adviser. I took a leap of faith and introduced myself to Nancy, and something just clicked. Knowing that she had a deep and successful entrepreneurial background, I asked her to work with us, and in the months ahead, our collaboration flourished as we worked together on presentations. Her wisdom, warmth, confidence, and drive have been a catalyst in so many ways, and eventually we teamed up with Ali Tavakkoli, the bariatric surgeon, and Yuhan Lee, then a postdoc in my laboratory, now an assistant professor, to create the new surgery-in-a-pill technology to treat metabolic disorders such as type 2 diabetes. Tavakkoli had reached out to me with the idea, an example of incoming opportunity. All that from the simple decision to get over myself and step out, aim for authenticity, and genuinely value the conversations and the people I meet this way.

Incoming opportunities such as this feel like live wires, charged with energy, potential, and serendipity. The autostop needle technology I just mentioned came about that way, too. I overlapped with the anesthesiologist Omid Farokhzad when we were both postdocs in Bob Langer's lab, and one day during lunch in a conference room he described a problem with epidural anesthesia and overshoot injuries. Epidural needles are used to inject anesthetics into the narrow epidural space around the spinal cord. They are often used in childbirth to temporarily reduce the pain. Targeting specific tissues such as the epidural space using a conventional needle can be difficult, often requiring a highly trained individual, and complications can arise if the needle overshoots the targeted tissue. In the past century there had been minimal innovation to the needle itself. That could be an opportunity to develop better, more accurate devices to improve tissue targeting while keeping the design as simple as possible for ease of use.

An hour later we were the only two left in the conference room. I was immediately curious but had no experience in that space. We had ideas about how to create a needle that would prevent overshoot injuries, but we needed to bring aboard someone with expertise to build the prototypes and iterate the ideas. Eventually I found a collaborator at MIT with expertise in designing various probes. Together, we wrote grants, found funding, produced prototypes, and iterated, eventually inventing a new kind of needle—an intelligent injector—that could sense changes between layers of tissue and automatically stop before overshooting. That led to an offshoot in my lab to create a needle that could stop in between the tiny layers of the eye to deliver gene therapy to the back of the eye (imagine injecting fluid between two balloons; it goes everywhere between them). Currently, there are no widespread approaches to safely and efficiently delivering drugs to the back of the eye. We got it to work and—boom—started a company called Bullseye Therapeutics. It was acquired by a company that is now advancing it to deliver gene therapy to treat macular degeneration.

We are drowning in information while starving for wisdom.
The world henceforth will be run by synthesizers, people able
to put together the right information at the right time, think
critically about it, and make important choices wisely.
—EDWARD O. WILSON

A CHEMIST AND HIS CARTOONS

It also helps to modify your mental search engine to take advantage of unexpected opportunities. In July 2007, the same month I started my laboratory, Praveen Kumar Vemula applied for a position. His résumé was impressive, but he was a chemist and I didn't have a position available that matched his qualifications. I was scrolling through his résumé when something unusual at the very end caught my eye. It was a summary in which he'd detailed each major accomplishment—in a simplified cartoon. I was fascinated. I'd never thought to show data in cartoon format in a résumé! When I looked closer, I saw that the images were self-explanatory—you didn't have to read the text at all. He'd communicated the essential information quickly and in an irresistible visual.

Vemula was a supercommunicator. Beyond his notable work as a scientist, he had the storyteller's knack for creating images that conveyed the key points of the science; he had a science radio show on which he explained science concepts to a general audience. I scrolled further and saw that he had some interesting hobbies, including serious badminton chops. All of that shouted that he was a creative person aligned with his passions. Although I didn't have an ongoing project that was a perfect fit for his skills, I offered him a job because I knew it was important for us to have creative diversity in the lab.

Vemula displayed boundless curiosity and a desire to put his skills and efforts to good use. He was keen not only to advance knowledge in his field but to find practical applications for the knowledge. For him, chemistry was another kind of artist's workshop, and molecules were his medium. In one instance, he used specialized molecules to form a hydrogel (the consistency of butter at room temperature) that, when applied or injected, could allow the targeted release of medicine at an arthritic joint or inflammation site. The engineered molecule could be broken in half—basically disassembled—in response to inflammatory enzymes and used to release all kinds of drugs that were placed in the gel during the assembly process.

A formidable snag, however, was the complex regulatory approval and manufacturing process that would be necessary, which could easily doom efforts to bring the new material into practical use. We'd developed a new process using a new material, but the key question was: Now that we've got the process, is there a material that is on the FDA's Generally Recognized as Safe (GRAS) list that could possibly work instead? If so, we'd be able to use a readily available and cost-effective substance in a new way. We were ecstatic to find alternative agents on the GRAS list, including long-acting vitamin C and an emulsifier used to make ice cream that could self-assemble into the world's simplest inflammation response drug delivery system.

Vemula's work led to the advancement of two more nanotechnologies for ailments that afflict tens of millions of people in the United States alone. The first was for the treatment of skin contact allergies (such as nickel allergy), which affect an estimated 10 to 20 percent of the population. The second, which is being readied for clinical trials, is for the treatment of inflammatory bowel disease (IBD), which affects an estimated 23.5 million people in the United States; it can also be used to treat other inflammatory diseases.

Vermula proved to be one of those hidden-gem people who arrive unannounced in your inbox. As an active opportunist, he put himself out there, ignored the conventional boundaries and résumé style for a chemist's job hunt, and took a more creative approach to the search. Working with Vermula has been a highlight of my career. If I weren't an active opportunist myself, I'd have stopped reviewing his résumé when I saw that he was a chemist, knowing that I had no specific opening for that role. We both got lucky—but we'd stacked the odds in our favor as active opportunists with spirited search engine energy.

LINDA STONE:
MAXIMIZING THE POTENTIAL TO GET LUCKY

People often attribute their success to the good luck of being in the right place at the right time. But what does that really mean? What if you could maximize your potential to get lucky? A hole in one is an unusual achievement for anyone, but if you're a professional golfer, your chances are five times those of a nonpro. With the right practice, we can increase our chances to get lucky in any field!

Take the story of Linda Stone's rise as a pioneering leader in technology innovation, from an early career as a schoolteacher and librarian to Microsoft VP. No one would suggest that she just got lucky. She worked hard from the outset and followed her passions at every step, driven by the desire to advance the ways technology can improve our lives. She's been doing that ever since. As we spoke about her career, I was struck by the number of times she had seized a moment, sometimes an awkward or adverse one, and turned it into an opportunity by acting on it. Here's what I mean.

As a young person, she'd always been interested in technology and computers and made a move from a Chicago suburb to Washington State to attend the Evergreen State College. She chose Evergreen after she saw the unconventional public liberal arts and sciences college featured on TV's *60 Minutes*. Her reason was simple: "I thought it looked interesting and decided to go." Evergreen was a celebrated haven for creative thinkers, and she thrived in that rigorous, nonconformist milieu.

In the library basement at Evergreen, she found a fully equipped wood shop and made wooden spoons. She also found an early PLATO computer system and began fiddling with punch cards for a variety of programs.

When Stone graduated from Evergreen, she took a job as a teacher and children's librarian. She also taught in-service and preservice teachers. When she was seriously injured in a car accident and lost the use of her right leg through a long recovery period, she had to scuttle her plans for a cross-country ski trip with her boyfriend. But on his way out of town (yes, he went anyway), he dropped off a 4K Timex Sinclair computer and a book on BASIC (Beginners' All-purpose Symbolic Instruction Code). She used her recovery time to learn more about technology and eventually helped pioneer the introduction of computers into the school district where she worked. She also conducted in-service professional development programs to teach teachers the Logo computer language and about how computers could be used in education.

Stone still marvels at the serendipity of her circuitous career path. For example, in 1984, Stone paid her own way to the first Logo conference, hosted by Seymour Papert and the MIT Media Lab. She was listening to a talk on creativity and afterward began chatting with the woman sitting next to her. She mentioned that the speaker's talk reminded her of the company Synectics and a related book, as well as some experiences she'd had at Evergreen. "I work for Synectics!" the woman exclaimed, and suddenly Stone was in that orbit.

"What are the chances?" Stone asks, still astonished by that stroke of luck and what followed. When she visited the Synectics offices, she shared that she was interested in bringing its approach into her school district and asked if the company would consider sharing its training if she got grants to support the effort. The company officials countered by proposing that she help them open their first sales accounts.

Despite having no sales experience, she said yes. That school year, during her lunch breaks, she cold-called companies to sell Synectics' services. Her school district gave her release time to attend Synectics training a few times during the year, and much to her amazement, she was able to secure a few accounts for Synectics in Seattle. Even more surprising to Stone, every time she attended a Synectics workshop, she was pulled aside by corporate participants offering her job opportunities.

One day at one of the workshops, someone from Apple Computer approached her to talk about coming aboard there. She used Apple products, so it was an exciting opportunity, but what really got her attention was why the company was interested in her. "We like to hire people like you," the person said. "We don't always look for a specific skill set. Sometimes we just look for someone who thinks out of the box. You're an out-of-the box thinker."

She made the move. And each move after that, from Apple to Microsoft, was made for the same reason: she wanted to explore what was coming up around the corner, wanted to work on ways technology could enhance our lives, maximizing creativity both individually and collectively, and wanted to work with others passionate in the same way.

STEPHEN WILKES: TIME TRAVELING FOR INSPIRATION

There's an unpredictable chemistry to the idea of networking that we often can't appreciate until we look back to see how serendipity emerges over time. I was reminded of that when I spoke with Stephen Wilkes, the renowned photographer whose signature panoramas appear to be a single still shot but are actually layered images shot from the same vantage point. His fantastical landscapes basically compress time. In his epic exhibit titled *Day to Night*, each panoramic image incorporates more than a thousand single-exposure images that Wilkes took of the same location, continuously shooting through a day and night to capture the changing light. From Central Park to the Serengeti, he has developed his singular style and technique over decades of creative process. He was quick to acknowledge during our conversation the importance of the diverse creative influences that have shaped his approach to his work. In a sense, those, too, have been layered over time.

For instance, the contemporary cityscapes and people he captures in meticulous detail couldn't seem further removed from sixteenth-century Dutch peasant life, but he describes his earliest influences—Hieronymus Bosch and Pieter Bruegel the Elder—with a sense of immediacy that skips centuries. He recalled a seventh-grade field trip to the Metropolitan Museum of Art in New York City and the first time he saw a painting by Bruegel: *The Harvesters*.

He remembered standing in front of it, mesmerized. "I'd never seen anything quite like it. I remember walking up to it and looking at these little people in the fields. I could almost feel the sweat coming off their brow. Each one, busy with their different tasks, seemed to have their own story going within this epic landscape. I just found it completely spellbinding. This landscape, painted like that, and these narrative stories painted within that, just touched me in a very deep, deep, emotional way. People ask me, where is my inspiration? When I saw that painting, it imprinted me in a very strong way."

Young Wilkes soon discovered Bosch, another Dutch master, who had influenced Bruegel. He mused about the roughly four-hundred-year age difference between them and himself: "Inspiration in art transcends generations."

It's been a fascinating journey. I do find that if I keep
that energy around me, that positive energy of people
who are believers, and who want to stay the course,
that this can happen—we'll get the shot, the animals
will show up at the watering hole.
—STEPHEN WILKES

In the postpandemic world, *lit* has a surprising role to play in social reengagement. We're a social species, and the pandemic was a dramatic disruption—as though a storm went through and pulled down all the power lines. However urgent that disruption had to be as a public health measure, intentional reengagement became a necessity.

As we do when our computer crashes and we hit reset or "restore settings," anytime our social structures are disrupted, we can use the opportunity to choose our new settings with greater intention; restore the ones that we now recognize as valuable; and perhaps make some different choices regarding others, replacing the previous habituated settings with ones that do more to actively illuminate the world for us in a fresh light.

Serendipity and good luck have a mystical quality about them, but you don't have to wait for the stars to align and hope for the best. Some of us are hesitant to engage, some aren't; it's a feature of our social species. Sometimes all that's needed is a spark to reignite connection. We can also be aware of our individual fear triggers, such as fear of rejection, and realize that fear is built into our genetics but we can override it to be more actively opportunistic, to fuel the best versions of ourselves.

SYNERGIZE YOUR SUPERPOWERS

As individuals, our neurodiversity means that we've all had many different experiences, and they've rewired us all in different ways. We might even come from the same family and have grown up in the same place, but our brain-based differences mean that we may gravitate toward different things or make decisions that vary widely. My sister and I are just a few years apart in age and grew up in arguably the same environment, but we were quite different as kids, and, later, geographical distance added to sibling drift. It took us about thirty years and a shared concern for our parents to bring us together and rediscover qualities, from the practical to the spiritual, that we could appreciate in each other as adults.

In families and beyond, there is a richness to be explored as we interact with others, always open to new things we can learn and contribute. This applies in the most general way to how we can expand our social circles, community involvements, and participation in local and broader initiatives and collaborations. In our lab and other workplace settings, synergizing the strengths of a diverse team improves our problem-solving efforts.

Temple Grandin has made the point that we often get overly focused on the things that need to be fixed—buildings, bridges, and other infrastructure, for instance—but overlook the question of who will be able to do the work. She presses for greater attention to neurodivergent thinking, and specifically the hyper-focus that is a classic characteristic of it, as "critical for innovation and invention."

To stoke the *lit* factor to create more generative—and enjoyable—interactions and collaborations, keep these points in mind:

- A mix of experience and expertise helps frame a discussion broadly so that no one point of view is likely to dominate.
- Diversity in how to approach problems and generate solutions is exciting, specifically teams that include people from different countries, cultures, and educational systems who aren't bound to Western thought processes.
- An ethos in which the goal is to minimize ego and maximize exchange across disciplines encourages people to take intellectual risks and challenge one another in the spirit of accomplishing the group's goal.
- An active opportunist environment is one in which everyone comes well read and well prepared to energetically engage on the topic and advance the conversation and the team's thinking.

When the team is right, the outcomes can be spectacular.

"The power of collaborative thinking is something I recognized in the lab," Susan Hockfield told me. As a neuroscientist, before she moved into top leadership roles at Yale and MIT, she was part of lab meetings that generated ideas and new approaches for research problems. "For me, that was the magic, a bunch of smart people working on related pieces of this new problem. And someone coming up with an idea that no one would have had on her or his own is that magic of bringing things together. It's not one person; it's a group of people who can puzzle around something that's maddeningly complex and hard, and somehow that magic mix of minds produces something great."

*Our environments, our world, our communities aren't
healthy if there is only one type of thinking.*
—LISA SASAKI, SMITHSONIAN INSTITUTION

CONTAGIOUS ALTRUISM: *LIT* FOR GOOD

Shortly after Russia invaded Ukraine in early 2022 and more than 10 million people were believed to have fled their homes, many people around the world wanted to help but couldn't see how to do so. I was among them. One morning, someone I know on LinkedIn posted about opening her laboratory in the United Kingdom to student refugees from Ukraine. I thought about that for a few days, then realized that I could do the same thing. I put a post on LinkedIn, and suddenly it had 48,000 views with deep, purposeful engagement and discussion. I asked a few people in the lab if they would be interested to help, and immediately they were 100 percent on board. I asked the vice president of research at the hospital if he could help us if needed with visas and so on, and he, too, was eager to help. The process eventually led to helping in ways I had never imagined, including creating job opportunities for a dental student, a transplant surgeon, and a pediatrician. And all it took was a small spark to catalyze the contribution of many people who wanted to make a difference.

When you look at the world as one vast opportunity to connect across divides, to learn from others and learn about them, to share, and to make a positive impact, it doesn't take long to find someone two steps ahead of you on your path and borrow from their success. As we look for such opportunities, I'm inspired by the many ways people have found to use social media and community activism to connect quickly with those in need and mobilize responses to make a difference. The impulse for altruism, which some say is part of our genetic code—a so-called selfless gene or protective, compassionate impulse to extend a hand when someone is in need—moves us from inclination to action for a greater good. Like gravitational pull, this evolutionary inheritance can bring resources into alignment, overcoming obstacles of distance, apathy, and organizational inertia.

"Our mammalian and hominid evolution have crafted a species—us—with remarkable tendencies toward kindness, play, generosity, reverence and self-sacrifice, which are vital to the classic tasks of evolution—survival, gene replication and smooth functioning groups," said Dacher Keltner, the director of the Berkeley Social Interaction Laboratory, when talking about his book *Born to Be Good: The Science of a Meaningful Life*. Imagine that every time you feel touched, moved, empathetic, sympathetic, protective, caring, or compassionate, your brain lights up, ready to jump at the opportunity to act on that feeling. And when you do and someone else is touched by the thought, their brain lights up too—*lit!*

Active Opportunists Search for, Swap, and Synthesize Ideas

See infinite potential as the reality: high-energy brain without borders. Access knowledge, insights, ideas, and expertise—energy and enthusiasm, too—to inspire fresh thinking and accelerate the good. Books and magazines, podcasts, TED Talks, hobbies, and travel are easy access points. Our brains like to home in on things—shine a narrow penlight on them—but we can push back with an expansive mindset and both see and seek opportunities for connection in the widest way. The more you actively engage with the world, the more you boost your chances of lucky breaks and success. Of lateral thinking, de Bono also famously said, "You cannot dig a hole in a different place by digging the same hole deeper." Plays on the hats and holes metaphors have proliferated since, including "don't dig deeper, dig elsewhere." The active opportunist digs deeper *and* elsewhere! Some *lit* strategies for active opportunism:

- Open doors so opportunity doesn't need to knock. Chat with strangers. Meet a friend's friend. Engage with others who know something different from you. When I take an Uber, I chat with the driver and usually come away thinking later about something they've said.

- Make a point of recognizing where your personal experience is limited in ways that can create blind spots or unconscious biases that you can change through intentional efforts to see and learn more and engage more actively.
- Value neurodiversity as an asset. The term is so often used to identify someone's learning deficits or differences but not to identify their assets. We're all hardwired with strengths and capabilities; we're all on a continuum. When you meet someone who seems oriented differently from you, pay attention. The more we set out to learn from our differences, the greater the gain.
- In workplace teams, use targeted collaboration to maximize essential diversity on a small team of nimble, deep thinkers. Look for partners who bring knowledge and experience you don't already have, who bring energy and build momentum, who help think about a problem differently.
- Stay curious and open to surprises. After my daughter, Jordyn, was born in 2009, I presented to a grant committee for a small grant to secure funding for my lab but stopped during the presentation because I was so tired that I nearly fell asleep standing up! One of the committee members came up afterward and suggested that we meet for coffee. I was in a phase of submitting gazillions of grants, and my first (sleep-deprived) thought was: Do I really want to take time away and go for coffee? Then through the haze came a glimmer of a spark, and I thought: Where might that lead? I went, and our conversation led to the creation of two companies and the lab receiving four years of funding (from a different source) to continue our work.
- Develop an awareness of the skills others around you have that you lack. No shame or self-criticism is allowed—it's a straightforward self-assessment and choice to seek out those who have nailed a skill or quality and learn from them. Ask them questions about it. Study how they conduct themselves. Look for skills that can become your own skills.
- Volunteer. Follow your interests or listen for the most urgent needs and step up. It's a great way to contribute and to enrich your life with purpose.

PINCH YOUR BRAIN

Attention Is Your Superpower

Interrupt mind drift and the pull of
distractions with intentional tugs.

*The capacity to attend is ours;
we just forget how to turn it on.*
—ALEXANDRA HOROWITZ,
ON LOOKING: A WALKER'S GUIDE TO THE ART OF OBSERVATION

We moved out to the country when I was about eight years old, in third grade, and though my ADHD came with me and my dismal attention problems at school continued, I soon discovered something surprising about life in my new stomping ground. I often spent hours after school in our backyard or exploring the surrounding fields and woods, and one afternoon I was walking up our long gravel driveway past a gnarly old tree when something small hanging from a limb caught my attention. I thought it looked odd but just assumed it was part of the tree. Then I got closer and saw it was moving a bit. I focused even closer and saw the glint of tiny teeth. *Holy shit—a bat!* I was amazed to see it—and shocked! I stepped back carefully. But I couldn't stop focusing my attention on it! I finally broke away to sprint the last thousand feet (over a bridge across a creek and up the hill) to the house to tell my family.

Over the next couple years I started to realize that I was constantly amazed by all the nature around me and, despite my problems focusing in school, I could easily focus on that. Looking out to my backyard, I saw so much to explore—a forest, a farmer's field, a creek—and when I was exploring and found something that snagged my attention, I had no trouble focusing even more closely on it. Then I realized it was that way with some books, specifically fact books and joke books. I didn't need to force myself to focus on those because (a) facts were interesting, (b) jokes were funny, and (c) the material was there in just-right bite-size pieces for me.

At some point I began to wonder: Is something going on here that I can turn into a strategy to help me pay attention in school? In nature, when something interesting caught my eye, it was like a pinch—it grabbed my attention and squeezed out the other thoughts. Not only that, it *felt* different from the way distractions usually did in my ADHD brain. Instead of adding to the chaos in my mind, that kind of pinch made me feel focused and mentally calm but energized at the same time. It felt great. And in that calm and energized state of mind, I could turn to anything and the energy just flowed right into that. At the time, with my ten-year-old frame of reference informed by *Star Wars* and *Masters of the Universe*, the pinch felt like some kind of superpower.

So along with other conventional strategies I was being taught to try to tackle academics more effectively, I started to experiment with ways to use the pinch intentionally—pinch my attention to feel calm, alert, and focused on what I chose to be focused on. Making my bed in the morning, for instance: my mom always wanted me to do it, but it was always last on my priority list, so I needed to find a way to prioritize it with focused attention. Or making a meal and cleaning up after myself: it was often easier to make something than to be motivated to clean up afterward, as my mind was already on to the next thing and had little motivation to clean up. I still struggled in school, but through that process I realized that I had potential, that there was some reserve of attentional energy that I could tap; I just had to figure out how to do so reliably. I started experimenting with ways to unlock it, slowly figuring out how to apply it to everything, including school. My anxiety at school ran high, so I often hit the wall on progress there, but I tried to continue my experiments.

I had no idea why the pinch worked. It was only recently that, curious about how a physical skin pinch alters blood flow around the pinch site and whether there might be a neurological parallel, I found a possible explanation in the description of a concept in neuroscience first documented more than a century ago: *functional hyperemia*. In his work, the nineteenth-century Italian physiologist and scientist Angelo Mosso studied cerebral blood flow in patients who were brought to him with head injuries or surgical circumstances that exposed their (live) brains to direct and long-term observation. Today, neuroimaging and other research show that when neurons activate in a localized region of the brain, blood flow increases to that area, rapidly stepping up the delivery of oxygen and nutrients to the site. Presumably, it doesn't take a bat in your face to pinch your neurons and trigger the blood flow boost. When you can choose the timing and circumstances to use the pinch, all the better.

IN A SEA OF DISTRACTIONS, WHY ADD ONE MORE?

In a prescient observation in his essay in the 1971 book *Computers, Communications, and the Public Interest*, Nobel Laureate Herbert A. Simon wrote, "Hence a wealth of information creates a poverty of attention and a need to allocate that attention efficiently among the overabundance of information sources that might consume it." A half century later, we are just beginning to come to terms with the reality of that. Today, chronic distraction has become the signature quality of contemporary life.

But contemporary life isn't solely to blame. Primitive brain circuitry still drives the survival reactions that divert our attention. Our brains are "wired to wander," as the psychologist Daniel Goleman says. Think of it as the evolutionary roving gaze, this natural tendency for the brain to resort to its primal roaming mode, all senses vigilant for potential threats or opportunities. Those threats once were predators, prey, or perhaps something amiss in the vegetation or landscape that signaled potential trouble. The problem today is that devices, diversions, and the digital algorithms designed to hook and hold our attention do so by attracting the attention of that wandering primitive mind.

With the brain primed to prioritize survival cues, our attention is easily hijacked and remains on hair-trigger alert, our mental radar scanning the horizon for the next blip. But that doesn't mean we're helplessly stuck there. And it doesn't mean our distractibility is a misfit for current times. We can tap into that system, use it to our advantage.

For the human brain isn't simply wired to wander; it's also wired to *wonder*. When something or someone piques our interest, be it predator, prey, or a point of curiosity, it registers in the brain as a novelty and triggers a cascade of neurochemical responses. Some of the effects last only milliseconds, others may last several minutes, but through different mechanisms they can heighten our senses, improve our perception, increase our motivation and responsiveness, and have other positive effects on our reward processing, learning, and memory. The continual interplay of the brain's response to novelty *and* to focused attention, to wander and wonder, keeps the energy charged for the effort.

The pinch engages and holds your attention, enabling you to focus more deliberately on whatever you choose and adjust the focus as you please, like the focusing knobs on a microscope. Examining a specimen slide, you use the coarse focus knob first to bring the specimen into view, then the fine focus knob to zero in on different aspects of the specimen. Now imagine that you can direct your attention in a similar way to anything, moving from initial awareness—a general but targeted focus—to a further dimension that sharpens or widens your focus. Or think of the pinch as a penlight of attention that you focus first to illuminate something specific, then move closer for a sharper view, or move back to illuminate a greater space.

The neuroscience behind shifting from inattentiveness to focused attention involves a minuscule cluster of cells at the base of the brain where the brain connects with the spinal cord called the locus coeruleus. Whereas the frontal lobe of the brain helps us pay attention, which aids in emotional processing and inhibiting impulsive primitive urges, organizing, planning, and making decisions, this tiny cluster of cells plays a major role in our attentional focus by modulating arousal, alerting, and orienting. It's the main source of the neurotransmitter noradrenaline. This so-called blue spot governs our focus by helping us to consider relevant information. It is referred to as the blue spot because of melanin granules inside the neurons that endow it with a blue color. Interestingly, people with ADHD exhibit altered norepinephrine processing.

As the brain responds to the attentional pinch, it taps into cognitive and other brain-body processes—senses, emotions, memory—that energize more intentional thought and action. In essence, you can continue to direct and redirect or refresh your attention to maintain the heightened *lit* energy in flow. We can use our attention purposefully to enter a flow state in which we can be laser focused and experience minimal distractibility. Practicing the pinch helps develop the skill—strengthening the neural connections that create new intentional habits—and eventually trains our brain to do so at will: *lit* on demand. In practice, the continued multiple targeted pinches both precipitate and coalesce new awareness, not only of a subject we are curious or passionate about but also about ourselves. For instance, focusing first on something external—a situation or a comment someone makes—we can pinch to tune in to the emotions we're experiencing as a result and uncover something deeper within us.

As a test run, try these three steps for the pinch—and the fourth for something extra:

- Focus your attention on something that stokes your curiosity or bothers you or something that calms you: a favorite view out your window, a photo or cherished personal item, or perhaps your dog or cat. The moment you do, notice a shift in the energy of your attention.
- Use that pinch of energized attention to connect more deeply with the object of your focus: unpack the idea that's aroused your curiosity; reflect further on a source of concern; look more closely at the view out your window or the photo in hand; focus on your animal companion with extra appreciation.

- Savor this moment of heightened awareness to deepen your experience. Then repeat the pinch to focus more closely or perhaps shift perspective to a wider view.
- Go for flow. I've found that if I can resist distractions for about five minutes and focus on something of my own choosing, that combination helps me tap into a flow state.

Attention is the most powerful tool of the human spirit. We can enhance or augment our attention with practices like meditation, breathwork, and exercise, diffuse it with technologies like email, texting, and social media, or alter it with pharmaceuticals. In the end, though, we are fully responsible for how we choose to use this extraordinary resource.

—LINDA STONE, THE ATTENTION PROJECT

My experiments with attention were born of necessity, as my attention issues made it practically impossible for me to learn in school and undermined my relationships and social interactions. My mind still wanders like crazy, and not just when reading. I have a hard time listening to an audiobook or watching a movie for more than a few minutes before my mind starts to wander and I need to rewind and hear or watch it again. For years I thought that time management techniques would be the solution to my attention problems. Eventually I discovered that time management was, for me, an organizational device that missed the point. I could set aside a time to turn to something or someone, but within that space I couldn't manage my attention, either because I wasn't interested or pressured enough at the moment or I couldn't bring myself to take the first step.

Eventually, with experimentation, by the time I was thirteen, in eighth grade, I realized that with my attentional challenges in particular, (1) I need to take lots of small steps to make forward progress, and (2) no matter how many times I've taken those small steps, they are always hard to take. I need to focus my attention on tricking my brain to just land on planet Earth—and then take that step forward! Usually just a tiny amount of momentum is enough to create more and move me past that initial resistance.

The pinch proved to be perfect for that. At that time, I had no idea why it felt as though I was always up against some phantom attention-sucking force and figured it was just my weird, defective brain. My brain may be unusual in some ways, diagnosably so, but in retrospect I realize that the phantom force I sensed is a completely normal feature of the brain: yours, mine, everybody's. Scientists call it the default mode network (DMN). Neuroscience based on studies of brain wave patterns, frequencies, and other data describes the DMN as a fundamental feature of the brain, generating a steady stream of background activity. In simple terms, if you've ever blinked back from a daydream or felt caught in a reel of rumination, the DMN is likely where your brain took you. Through the *lit* lens, the DMN is like a live stream channel of information that your brain is always generating. When we're operating in LEB mode, we don't think to tune in, we just hear it as background noise. But flip the switch to *lit*—tune in with intention—and suddenly we discover it's not noise, it's our own Discovery Channel. In a study of default mode variability and ADHD, researchers found greater DMN activation patterns in patients with unmedicated ADHD compared to healthy controls. That variability was also associated with lower task performance.

BRAIN STATIC, WHITE NOISE, OR THE PINCH PLAYLIST?

In practical terms, we often experience our roaming mind as either an unhelpful distraction or a welcome diversion. The musing or spontaneous creativity or clarity that comes with the unfocused mind may be a welcome relief from the pressured pace of a day—not so much when the timing is off and we feel unfocused and scattered in ways that work against us. Is this unfettered mind friend or foe?

Until recently, scientists considered the DMN as simply neural noise, a kind of low-level static. Emerging research suggests that it may be more of a playlist, a continuous review process the brain uses to keep memory, meaning, projections, and possibilities in constant play, a kind of mashup of all the elements past, present, and predictive that make you. It may be that part of the DMN's function—what drives us nuts when we feel overwhelmed by it—is to offer up simulated scenarios in our brain of what *might* happen, what others *might* say, what the possible outcomes of three alternatives *might* be, as a way to teach ourselves without having to actually go through all the permutations; all dress rehearsals, no performance demands.

Studies suggest that when we're focused on a task, the DMN chatter becomes less intrusive; when we're unfocused, the chatter becomes more present or intrusive. Daydream, monkey mind, helpful reflection, or rumination—whatever way you experience the DMN—do you go with that flow or step in and direct it? Nature has an app for that: cognitive control, or the brain's ability to be flexible, adaptive, and goal directed. You can use this neural reactivity and adaptability as a way to interrupt and redirect your thinking. With a *lit* pinch, you might use it to sharpen your focus on the matter at hand or shift your attention to something else entirely. Either way, shifting your attention, when done with intention, taps this hardwired capacity to use as you wish.

As the novelty of a stimulus (in this case the pinch) wears off, the brain adjusts its response, typically with a less pronounced reaction, but it varies depending on other factors, such as what's going on around you and internal influences that might be physiological or perhaps other neural impulses firing at the same time.

In studies that measure brain activity, recently some scientists have adjusted the understanding of neural variability, the irregular fluctuations in the brain's impulses as it responds to stimuli. These variations were long assumed to be another example of neural noise and considered likely inconsequential. But scientists now believe that neural variability may be an adaptive balancing mechanism involved in the nervous system's responding and learning.

Evidence suggests that successful behavior may emerge because of neural variability, not in spite of it, according to researchers at the Max

Planck Institute for Human Development. Whether one is asked to process a face, remember an object, or solve a complex task, the ability to modulate moment-to-moment variability seems to be required for optimal cognitive performance. At the same time, variability declines as the process stabilizes, a good sign.

If focused attention calms neural variability and quiets noise, brainstorming is one time-honored way to stir things up. How better to keep fresh ideas—stimuli—in play than to stoke neural variability rather than calm it? I designed the lab's brainstorming process around this concept, and it's one way we can push past our comfort zones of familiar ideas and areas of expertise and out to the exciting edge of possibility. The medical problems we tackle have often come to us unsolved because they have been framed too narrowly. By bouncing between focused and unfocused states, we maximize the diversity of new ideas and frame the problem from multiple angles. Through this approach we are often able to uncover new insights that others have missed, providing novel routes toward a potential solution. Questions serve as the pinch that helps us steadily advance to new territory in our bioinspirational innovation process.

Focus like a laser, not a flashlight.
—MICHAEL JORDAN

PUSH PAST THE LIMITS OF PERCEPTION

We do this all the time in the lab. At so many junctures in our work, something takes an unexpected turn or a solution stubbornly eludes us. We try to use those moments to refocus our attention and press on with renewed energy. We continually have to "pinch past" our perceptions of what's possible. We need to constantly challenge and often disrupt groupthink, dogmas in the field, other people's assumptions, and even our own assumptions. Each of us focuses and refocuses this way, and, like a relay team, we can do it collectively. In a brainstorming environment like ours, there's often someone who's having a lightning moment that charges the atmosphere for the rest of us.

When we look at new problems, it's important to try to come up with new solutions and resist the mind's gravitational pull to consider existing technologies or solutions, which often leads to suboptimal results. We review the existing technologies in our toolbox when we start, but we're also cautious because there's a natural momentum, a gravitational pull, to just go with what you know, and you can waste precious time and resources—easily a couple years to see a research cycle through—trying to adapt existing technologies, only to encounter new complexities and eventually realize that you needed different thinking and different solutions from the beginning. We work intentionally to avoid the path of least resistance. How? We use strategic questions to pinch our attention.

What can our existing technologies do? More important, what can they *not* do? And how does this match up with the current problem definition? Because what matters most now is: What is needed? What have others tried? What has failed? What has sort of worked but not well enough? What aspects of biology, medicine, and translation (scalability, patents, clinical trials, and so on) are important to consider early in the process? What is the best result that others have achieved, and in what model system? What is the result we need to achieve if we're to electrify the field and get investors, colleagues, the industry, and the community excited about it? What will enable us to dramatically advance the field and benefit patients?

Most often this initial review process helps us define the new problem more clearly. Then we refocus solely on the new problem and place the past work, the old problem, and the old technologies we have developed to target them back on the shelf.

Here's a streamlined, slow-motion version of how we use the pinch in the lab setting to accelerate but also deepen our problem-solving process. These are some of the questions that have led to rounds of exploratory discussions and research that eventually led to multiple useful bioinspired outcomes as we looked for ways to create better medical adhesives.

QUESTION: *What problems exist in which a better medical adhesive would help?*

This forced us to do a deep dig to define the problem. We spoke with doctors, nurses, and people in medical companies and identified the need for an adhesive that would affix monitoring devices to tender newborn skin and would not tear the skin when removed, that would seal a hole inside the beating heart of a young child, and that would hold skin or tissue together like staples but not damage the skin as staples do because they must be bent in the tissue to hold fast. Staples also create an attractive place for bacteria to invade and grow in and require bulky devices for placement, which can't be easily used for minimally invasive procedures with small incisions.

QUESTION: *What adhesive mechanisms have evolved in the natural world that might provide inspiration?*

We had worked earlier on a tissue adhesive inspired by geckos, but it wasn't durable enough for challenging environments such as skin grafts or inside a beating heart. We brainstormed on how various creatures latch on to things they encounter. We considered the proboscises of mosquitoes and bees, and a colleague asked, "What about porcupine quills?"

QUESTION: *What is already known about porcupine quills?*

We did our homework. The North American porcupine (as opposed to the African porcupine) has quills with barbs that face away from the tip. The barbs are about the width of a human hair. The tip of the quill sinks into targeted tissue, but the barbs make it difficult to remove.

QUESTION: *What more do we know about how the barbs work? How do porcupine quills so easily embed themselves in—strike, stick, and stay in—their targets?*

There is almost no academic research on porcupine quills, such as how much force is needed to sink into flesh, how much to remove the quill, and so on.

QUESTION: *How can we find out?*

We poked quills into tissue and looked at the entry site. We found that most quills have several rows of barbs within a four-millimeter region at the tip. Surprisingly, it required about half the force to push a barbed quill into tissue as it does to push in a needle of the same diameter or a quill with its barbs shaved off. And unlike a standard needle or tissue staple, which makes tiny rips or tears as it enters tissue, a barbed quill makes a perfectly smooth hole, so it's easier to guard against infections that find traction in the rough edges.

QUESTION: *What if we put synthetic quills on both ends of a biodegradable staple and eliminate the need to bend the ends of the staple into the tissue?*

You get the point (so to speak). Each question helps focus our attention on the most meaningful exploration and new questions.

NUDGES AND NUANCES

My colleague Vivek Ramakrishnan suggests that as your brain gets accustomed to whatever struck it as novel previously, you might assume that you have to do or seek out something even bigger and better than before. Instead, he says, you might develop a practice, as he did, of observing the most subtle changes in things around you, or as he calls it, the impermanence of all things. We'll turn to that in more detail in the chapter "Press 'Pause,'" but in short, the idea is that by attuning ourselves to the smallest perceptible changes, the contrast from one day to the next is enough to keep the brain piqued with wonder. The pinch doesn't have to be huge; it can be something that just ignites the spark that makes the connection—gets the ball rolling—effectively lowering the activation energy for a purposeful shift rather than our having to struggle to exert control through willpower.

Successful pinch tactics for me include reading segments of text in reverse order, starting at the end of a paper and working my way forward. This helps focus my wayward attention. Admittedly, I'm an extreme example, but the idea that your attention focuses reflexively on a disruption or the novel or unfamiliar is something you can use to your advantage. To me, pinching your brain means being able to apply that process at will to anything—working on a project, talking with your partner, or planning your next career move, for example. Pinch your brain to get its attention, then focus on anything you want.

> *Let yourself be silently drawn by the stronger*
> *pull of what you truly love.*
>
> —RUMI

Your own complex lives and workplace challenges may be different from ours in the lab, but the pinch process—the *lit* process—applies universally. How we manage our attention in everyday life defines virtually every part of our lives. Anyone working to accomplish something that requires sustained attention—and that might be a project, a family, a relationship, or a life dream—knows what it feels like when the energy to do it seems to be fading. The power of the pinch injects new energy that revitalizes your attention, and simply reflecting on your options is a start.

RESIST THE PULLS; GO FOR THE PUSH

Attentional "pulls" are the things that interrupt your attention and pull it away. An attentional "push" is a shift you initiate yourself. Many of the pulls in our life are, if we're honest with ourselves, low priority and provide little value to us. They may be habits of thought: rehashing old events or feelings, ruminating, or worrying. Or they may be habits of response, for example, feeling that we must respond to everyone immediately. Sometimes there's another habit attached to it: mindless media or social media use, smoking, drinking, or eating as a diversion—or not-so-mindless but excessive media use, especially of social media.

Ironically, perhaps, "the pause" was touted even by the social media giant TikTok in congressional hearings to defend itself against accusations that it does nothing to mitigate its excessive use by young users. The platform had recently announced a new speed bump—a sixty-minute "daily screen time limit" for users under age eighteen—which young users have reported they can get past with a few taps. Research shows that pausing to decide whether to continue or log off could conceivably prompt someone to stop, TikTok's head of family safety and developmental health, Tracy Elizabeth, said. "That pause where they need to proactively think about what they're doing and make a choice if they'd like to continue using the app, that's the part that's really important."

Though this kind of speed bump is unlikely to work for everyone, it is part of an important process to recognize and reduce the low-priority pulls and try replacing them with intentional pushes—conscious choices you make to focus your attention in a meaningful way. The more you practice, the lower the activation energy—the less energy it takes—to let them pass and the easier (and more quickly rewarding) it becomes to focus your attention on what matters most to you.

"You can put frictions in place that force you to pause and think for a moment before you just mindlessly engage in a behavior," says Katy Milkman, behavioral science professor at the University of Pennsylvania's Wharton School and author of *How to Change: The Science of Getting from Where You Are to Where You Want to Be.* "And that gives you at least an opportunity for the thinking part of your mind, instead of the automatic part of your mind, to decide, Is this what I want to be doing right now?"

PILATES, PODCASTS, AND A NEW PRACTICE

When so much of what matters deeply in our life is a constant—family, friendships, even a job we love—it can easily become a backdrop we take for granted. It's said that the extraordinary is often hidden in plain sight. You may need to pinch your brain to respond to that extraordinariness.

I was slow to recognize the importance of mind-body-spirit interconnectedness, even though Jessica is a long-established Pilates instructor, a discipline that incorporates all three. So I was surprised when it was Pilates, with Jessica's gentle coaching, that ultimately opened a path for a spiritual exploration. On that path, I have found that conscious attention to our innate spiritual or intuitive capacities strengthens connections, fires up neural networks. The more I explore the inner life, the less activation energy it takes for me to try something, read something, listen to a podcast, or bring up a point for dinner table conversation with the kids.

Pilates was the pinch I needed to shift my attention, in my case inward. We all have an intuitive capacity that serves as a moral compass, an inner voice, that guides us toward what is best for us. But often we ignore those nudges. Pinching our attention to new areas of interest, including the inner life, opens exciting—and infinite—new paths.

Some pinch tactics might seem trivial, but they often work. You might take a break for a walk, especially in nature, or turn to something completely unrelated. Sometimes just shifting your attention to a different project can help. Anytime you move something from the brain's back burner to the front burner, the shift can potentially create fresh energy. In our experience, what are the most powerful, consistent, durable, and sustained attention getters for the brain? Curiosity, excitement, and purpose. These motivators turn the wander to wonder in the busy brain and ultimately to action. In everyday situations, a simple pinch can boost how you feel and think in any moment and how you engage. In meetings, especially when I find myself gravitating toward being transactional, I remind myself (a gentle pinch) that the person or people I'm meeting with are the most important people in their own lives—I am meeting with human beings! Each one is on their own journey, and that is as much a context for our conversation as any of the other aspects that may be on our agenda.

MOTIVATION PACKS A PUNCH

In studies of motivation and attention, research has shown that heightened motivational levels promote enhanced attention capabilities. Our motivation can change over time or in different circumstances, so tapping into the *what* and *why* that keep you fired up is critical to pinching your brain. When you see someone in immediate distress and you want to help them, your attention is riveted and unlikely to wander. But often our goals or objectives aren't that urgent, so if we're to reach them, we have to find a way to sustain our attention and motivation. Whether the motivation is intrinsic or an external reward—money, a promotion, a purchase, for example—reminding ourselves of our goal and why it's important to us connects us with the emotional energy, the desire that's driving us, and can provide the pinch.

FINE-TUNE YOUR ATTENTION TO MOTIVATION

Personal motivators can boost your energy for action when you direct your attention to them. Look at this list to see if one or two in particular are relevant to you at this moment. What is the present motivating factor of something in your life? Is it something you want to change or embrace more of?

Some human motivators or rewards that can focus the pinch:

Purpose	Fitness	Power
Desire	Connection	Money
Curiosity	Achievement	Novelty
Wonder	Love	Deadlines
Urgency	Survival	Fear
Healing	Expectations	Pain

PARTNERSHIP AND PARENTHOOD: POWERFUL PINCHES

When I started my faculty position in 2007, a research scientist at MIT pulled me aside and warned me about the addictive nature of being a faculty member. "You need to be careful," she said. "I've seen a lot of marriages fall apart. You get consumed by your work. You need to watch out for this." At the time I thought that could never happen. What I didn't realize was that I was already addicted to work.

When I'd met my wife, Jessica, seven years earlier, when I was working toward my Ph.D., I was already logging longer hours than most people I knew, and those were driven, hardworking people. Working harder was a way for me to avoid the shame I had experienced with my learning differences, but in a healthier way through my process—hit a snag, retool my strategies, try again—I discovered strengths that led me to discover that biomedical engineering was a perfect fit for me and my hyperactive, neuroatypical brain. Solving a problem successfully only made me want to push harder to define the more challenging problem that seemed unsolvable, a dare for an underdog.

Meanwhile, Jessica was active with her own interests in human potential, health and wellness, exercise, and spirituality, all of which seemed vaguely interesting and admirable to me but somehow far removed from my workaholic existence. We married, and as our family grew to include our two children, Josh and Jordyn, the commitments and demands of my work in the fast lane grew, too. I never wanted to be what we call the rate-limiting step—the slowest step in a chemical process or the person who holds things up. So I had a policy to get back to people the same day on everything, even if it meant pulling an all-nighter. Eventually I tripled the size of my lab, bringing aboard more brilliant, passionate researchers and, working with entrepreneurs, investors, and other translational experts, launching companies to bring the innovations into use in patient care. I loved it all—I was hooked!

Of course our family life disintegrated. Working made me feel good. Away from work I was miserable. Yet I often felt an intuitive tug signaling that something wasn't right. Jessica pressed me to spend more time with the family, but I couldn't figure out how to get out of that workaholic fast lane. I created an illusion of work-family balance to avoid feeling guilty. Still, even at school events, I would search for parents with relevant expertise to connect with to fuel my momentum on current work projects. Work-driven passion and purpose channeled my racing brain like a bullet train. When I tried to disengage to be with my family, I'd feel even more stressed because I hadn't achieved a particular work goal.

It was the same with my kids. "Just five minutes more," I would say despite my promise to do something with them. Sometimes Jessica and the kids would be waiting in the car for me while I raced to tend to a few more emails. Eventually they stopped waiting and just drove off without me. Josh, who in his earlier years had sought me out to play soccer or throw a football with him, stopped asking.

When the pandemic hit and we started working from home, my life ground to a halt right there in our living room. My lab refocused to help with Covid projects. We designed new masks, diagnostic tools, therapeutics, and a nasal spray to surround and kill viruses. I was intensely involved in the work. But now in the lockdown I could see what I'd been missing: a thoughtful, meaningful, emotionally intimate relationship with my family. I'd been an absentee, distracted father and husband, and for far too long. It became painfully clear to me: I needed to make a conscious shift to disrupt some of these old patterns.

To share time with Jordyn, I started to go along for the drive when Jessica took her to school. I wanted to wish her well and wave goodbye. Instead, we both spent the ride staring at our phones. She texted friends; I read emails, scheduled meetings, strategized. That had to change. So one morning, instead of checking my email, I passed my phone over to her and asked if she'd like to look at some old family photos. Luckily for me, she looked, then laughed and said, "You get me!" We spent the rest of the drive scrolling through the photos, enjoying the memories of fun, funny, goofy, and good times. It was a small thing, perhaps, for my daughter, but for me, it was a big deal and the start of my more conscious intention to resist the gravitational pull of my work and pinch my attention to focus more fully on my kids and our family life.

It's often said that the best strategy in any situation is to have a strategy before you walk into the room. Keep your intention front of mind, and focus on the specific steps that will keep you on track. The room can be a metaphor for anything: a person, a relationship, a project, a plan. If I'm meeting with someone and I want to stay present to the sense of appreciation for them as individuals with their own lives and priorities, it's helpful to carry that thought and intention front of mind when walking in. If I am going to be with my son in a moment when I know he really needs my support, then as I approach him, I consciously choose to channel my supportive energy. We can experiment with this deepening of intention in the ways we continue to frame and focus our attention. The energy of the pinch is endlessly renewable.

PINCH WITH PURPOSE. DIFFERENTIATE AMONG WANT TO, GOT TO, AND LOW PRIORITY. Explore and experiment to find the pinches that provide the most punch for you and use them to differentiate among what's essential to you, what's less so, and what's of little real value to you.

PINCH FOR THE POSITIVE. Focus your attention on your purpose, and aim for experiences that can create positive memories or build your energy reserves for what you consider important. As you focus your mind on your priorities, they will grow stronger and the trivial will hold less power.

WAKE UP TO WHAT'S HIDDEN IN PLAIN SIGHT. Take a quiet moment to sit with yourself and take inventory to make sure you're not neglecting important aspects of your life. No blame and no shame is necessary, just an assessment that gives you some clarity about what might need more (or less) of your attention. It might be commitments to others or to issues that are important to you, but it might also be self-care, decluttering, and vitalizing your mind through exercise, meditation, music, or art to sustain you.

UNPACK THE PINCH POINTS IN ANYTHING, ANYTIME. When was the last time you took note of the steps involved in doing something you do all the time? Walking to your mailbox or around the block with your dog? Folding the laundry? Making a meal? Bring your attention to those moments, the fact that you can do each step, the rhythm and flow of the movement, the repetition, your intention, and the outcome. Use pinch points to lower the activation energy and boost your motivation or momentum as part of a mindfulness practice. For example, you might pinch your attention to motivate yourself to cook by focusing on steps you enjoy: how nice it feels to slice through veggies with a good sharp knife or appreciate the patterns in the cross-sections.

PINCH TO RESIST THE PULLS AND CONDITION YOURSELF TO NEW CUES. Develop an awareness of your checklist lifestyle, the way we've become conditioned to reflexively respond, however superficially, to email, texts, calls, project deadlines, social media, even family time. We need to uncondition ourselves from those in order to condition ourselves toward our true intentions. Typically, I feel compelled to drop what I'm doing and respond, but now I ask, "Is this something I have invited someone to ask me right now? Is this something I planned to do at this moment? If I could choose how to be spending my work or family or me time right now, what would I be focused on?"

SNAP OUT OF IT. Shift the energy around you with a thought to how your responses or expectations may impact others. Try turning from the micro me-centered focus to the macro focus that takes others into account.

TURN TO NATURE FOR THE POP OF SOMETHING NEW AND DIFFERENT. Look around and tune in to any aspect of nature: the weed asserting itself in the sidewalk crack, the rotting stump that's teeming with insect life and the organisms of decomposition, birds collecting twigs at nesting time; the fascinating detail is endless. If you pay attention, the energy transfer will revitalize you. Nature never fails to deliver.

GET HOOKED ON MOVEMENT

It's the Key to Evolutionary Success

Take any small step—in anything—to
activate fresh energy.

*The longest journey we will ever make as human beings is
the journey from the mind to the heart.*
—CHIEF DARRELL BOB, INDIGENOUS KNOWLEDGE KEEPER
OF THE ST'AT'IMC NATION

The natural world has a lot to teach us about movement. I'm not suggesting that we should emulate the way a slug or sparrow gets about. Walking upright on two legs has worked out well for us. But look around; movement in a larger sense defines our living planet, from mass migrations of wildlife to plate tectonics, shifting seas and winding waterways, airborne seeds and spores, microbial hitchhikers, "invasive" species—and us.

"Movement of individual organisms, one of the most fundamental features of life on Earth, is a crucial component of almost any ecological and evolutionary process," wrote Ran Nathan in "An Emerging Movement Ecology Paradigm" published in the *Proceedings of the National Academy of Sciences*. As we are animals, that holds true for us in purely biological terms. However, as humans, aware as we are of the inner life and spiritual dimension that are also ours, we do well to recognize that movement encompasses that territory, too. Some species follow nature's cues to migrate across great geographical spaces, moving with the seasons and the food sources aligned with the seasonal clock. We've tailored things so we don't have to do seasonal treks to survive, but that doesn't mean we don't need the adventure that migration provides: the challenges, the shared stories, the learning to leave and come home again. Nature still speaks to us with intuitive cues to guide our movement toward physical health and to a rich and sustaining inner life.

It's the embodied conversation with nature that's relevant, the context and cues nature holds for us that we often lose sight of for ourselves but can recognize and appreciate in unlikely teachers such as birds, ants, and trees. Every living thing exists today because its species evolved in response to cues from the natural environment, a fluid dialogue. The biological conversation between organism and environment enables both of them to evolve and prosper.

In the opening lines of this chapter, the point is made that the longest journey any of us can make is "the journey from the mind to the heart." How can each of us engage our heart to move with this intention? How can we advance in this lifetime journey? "Mind creates the abyss, the heart crosses it," the Indian teacher Sri Nisargadatta Maharaj wrote. The vigilant brain often amplifies negatives, and we get stuck on problems. We can begin to create movement across the abyss by witnessing and sensing the body's reactions for insights into how we experience things. This can help to calm our body's physical reactions, quiet the mind, and create the bridge that allows us to move with heart into an undivided experience of wholeness.

Beyond the metabolic metrics of exercise and fitness, movement is intertwined with our social and emotional development, our lifelong health and well-being. If you've ever been moved by something—moved by a story, moved to tears—then you've felt the emotional energy that can move you from one state of mind to another. Or consider how meditation can transform energy from chaos to calm, having a measurable impact on the brain waves associated with those states.

For many animals, the ability to find food and shelter, migrate and adapt to follow their sources through the seasons, and mate and reproduce is the measure of evolutionary success. If we want to set our bar a little higher, not merely to survive but to thrive and live fully into our potential as contributors on this planet, we can start by embracing a more holistic appreciation of movement in all dimensions. From the most intimate landscape of the inner life to feet-on-the-ground realities and relationships to transcendent experiences, our capacity to engage and explore is infinite.

"People who are physically active are happier and more satisfied with their lives," wrote the health psychologist and educator Kelly McGonigal in *The Joy of Movement: How Exercise Helps Us Find Happiness, Hope, Connection, and Courage.* "This is true whether their preferred activity is walking, running, swimming, dancing, biking, playing sports, lifting weights, or practicing yoga." McGonigal's sweeping review of research shows that "people who are regularly active have a stronger sense of purpose, and they experience more gratitude, love, and hope. They feel more connected to their communities and are less likely to suffer from loneliness or become depressed." The benefits, which occur at every age and apply to every socioeconomic demographic, appear to be culturally universal, she says. "Importantly, the psychological and social benefits of physical activity do not depend on any particular physical ability or health status," she notes. "The joys described above—from hope and meaning to belonging—are linked first and foremost to *movement,* not to fitness."

Movement also provides a time-honored path for creative expression, calming self-regulation, and spiritual contemplation, via dance, tai chi, yoga, and other practices. The inner life flourishes with the challenge of a good "workout" no less than the body does. Action builds momentum, and momentum catalyzes energy for change, whether in our everyday life or in the world.

Me, I like the joy angle.

*The walking of which I speak has nothing in it akin
to taking exercise . . . but is itself the enterprise and
adventure of the day. If you would get exercise,
go in search of the springs of life.*

—HENRY DAVID THOREAU

Consciousness and the capacity for inspired action are signature aspects of our species, as innate as our physicality, which evolved in tandem with the demands of hunting, gathering, and the periodic need to migrate to more hospitable grounds. The holistic view of the interconnected mind-body-spirit, considered a fringe concept in Western medicine fifty years ago, is well established now, adapted from ancient Eastern practices, popularized for modern Western tastes, and more recently acknowledged as core tenets of Indigenous teachings, grounded in our origins and relationship with nature.

"We forget that the body is attached to the brain," says Caroline Williams, the author of *Move: How the New Science of Body Movement Can Set Your Mind Free*. "We can use our bodies as a tool to affect the way we think and feel, like a hotline to the mind." Gabe DeRita, the life coach who left a lucrative career in software sales without a clue as to what he'd do next, said that the one thing he had been certain of was a gut feeling that although his enviable career trajectory was moving him forward in life, the direction didn't feel right. He intuitively chose the physical challenge of a global bike trek to clear his head, engage his heart, and pursue a life of intention and oneness.

Scientific research tells us that physical activity can have many positive effects on the brain and mind by stimulating the release of neurotrophic factors, endorphins, endocannabinoids, and other neurotransmitters. To varying degrees, those benefits are associated with physical activity wherever you work out or get your steps in. However, outdoor activity does appear to provide further benefits, including exposure to natural sunlight, which, among other things, stimulates the production of natural vitamin D. The brain gets more of a workout, too, by adjusting for terrain and other factors and by being more attentive to the need to take care to avoid injury. The mechanisms of some of the benefits of outdoor activity aren't well understood, however, and scientists wonder if there's something more specific about our relationship with the environment that factors in.

What worries me, and the reason I return to the lives of ants and trees, is that the long-term survival of every species depends on its dynamic relationship with its environment, and we are losing our connection. This is more than one bioinspirational scientist's lament. "People's connectedness to nature appears to be changing and this has important implications as to how humans are now interacting with nature," wrote the authors of "The Great Outdoors: How a Green Exercise Environment Can Benefit All," a 2013 study aimed at improving access to green exercise environments. And as Dacher Keltner noted in *Awe: The New Science of Everyday Wonder and How It Can Transform Your Life*, the resonance we have with nature in outdoor settings is the result of nature's yet-to-be-defined interaction with the human nervous system. "They calm us down," he says. "There are chemical compounds in nature. You might smell a flower or tree bark, or the resin on a tree, that activate parts of the brain and the immune system. So our bodies are wired to respond in an open, empowering, strengthening way to nature."

Many reports show that humans spend nearly 90 percent of their time indoors. Only one in four US adults and one in five high school students get the recommended levels of physical activity, according to the National Center for Chronic Disease Prevention and Health Promotion. This deficit comes with high costs, contributing to heart disease, type 2 diabetes, cancer, and obesity. In addition, low levels of physical activity are responsible for $117 billion in health care costs every year. Conversely, physical activity contributes to normal growth and development, reduces the risk of developing several chronic diseases, and helps us function better throughout the day and sleep better at night. Research continues to find new evidence that even short bouts of physical activity can improve our health and wellness.

NATURE STACKS THE DECK IN OUR FAVOR

It's not that we were born to run—or exercise, to be more precise. We weren't. In fact, although we evolved to move more efficiently and effectively, we're pretty much hardwired to avoid unnecessary exertion. Humans evolved to be physically active but not to exercise, says Harvard evolutionary biologist Daniel E. Lieberman, the author of *Exercised: Why Something We Never Evolved to Do Is Healthy and Rewarding*. Our earliest survival demanded physical activity, but exercise for health and fitness, as we approach it today, runs counter to our deeper instinct to conserve energy for the hunt. "Humans have these deep-rooted instincts to avoid unnecessary physical activity, because until recently it was beneficial to avoid it," says Lieberman.

We need to nudge ourselves to get moving, especially if the modern sedentary lifestyle has replaced a physically active one in our daily life. Even though foraging and hunting have been replaced by going to grocery stores and ordering fast food, our genes are still coded for activity and our brains are meant to direct it, wrote the psychiatrist John J. Ratey in *Spark: The Revolutionary New Science of Exercise and the Brain*. "Take that activity away, and you're disrupting a delicate biological balance that has been fine-tuned over half a million years," he says. "Quite simply, we need to engage our endurance metabolism to keep our bodies and brains in optimum condition."

Nature stacks the deck in our favor if we take even the simplest steps to set ourselves in motion. The benefits for the brain and body are inextricably intertwined. During exercise your body releases several agents to protect your brain and body from stress, including brain-derived neurotrophic factor (BDNF). BDNF has known roles in promoting the survival and maturation of nerve cells and in regulating the receptors that underlie learning memory and neuroplasticity.

Think of it as a dance of the neurons. Brain-imaging studies have shown a complex pattern of moves behind our ability to dance or even tap a foot to the beat of music we hear. One study of grandmothers and granddaughters engaged in interpretive dance activities found that the shared activity encouraged exercise, promoted positive feelings, boosted mood, brought the grandmothers and granddaughters closer, and shifted the girls' perceptions of aging. Researchers see strong potential for dance as a creative intervention, especially for elders, that can improve muscle strength, balance, and endurance, prevent anxiety and depression, and help counter dementia.

"Every time you work out, you are giving your brain a neurochemical bubble bath, and these regular bubble baths can also help protect your brain in the long term from conditions like Alzheimer's and dementia," says the neuroscientist Wendy Suzuki, a professor of neuroscience and psychology at the Center for Neuroscience at New York University and the author of *Healthy Brain, Happy Life: A Personal Program to Activate Your Brain and Do Everything Better*. In a review of studies published in the journal *Brain Plasticity*, Suzuki and her team reported that even a single workout—primarily aerobic or resistance—increases the levels of neurotransmitters such as dopamine, serotonin, and noradrenaline, mood boosters that can also improve memory and focus for up to three hours afterward. The most consistent behavioral effects are improved executive function, enhanced mood, and decreased stress levels. The win-win of positive effects on cognition and mood benefits overall mental health, which is why she recommends incorporating bursts of activity into your day. Every bit helps.

INERTIA IS THE FIRST HURDLE: SMALL STEPS OVERCOME IT

Knowing what's good for us doesn't necessarily add up to the motivation to do it. If it did, you'd have to make that New Year's exercise resolution only once in your life. If information doesn't ignite the spark, inspiration can be a jump start. I often invite experts, achievers, or coaches in aspects of wellness into the lab for a lunchtime talk. One time a competitive weightlifter came in to talk with us. He didn't have us all pumping iron, but he did share his story about some of the challenges in his life and how weightlifting had helped him through, and he described how he had gotten better and better at it. We've all seen impassioned

TED Talks by athletes or others who inspired us, yet even those aren't always enough to motivate us to follow through on exercise or activity consistently.

There's no need to feel ashamed; evolution has put us between a rock and a hard place when it comes to expending energy versus conserving it. Maintaining inertia is natural, as Lieberman points out. In evolutionary terms, remember, saving energy was essential to survival.

How can we overcome the inertia or downward drag that keeps us in the low-energy brain state? Although our hard wiring defaults to eco mode to conserve energy, unlike bears in hibernation, we can override that setting with conscious attention and practical strategies to help us shift from eco mode to active mode and then stick with it.

We can borrow from the persuasive design playbook and adapt the marketing industry's hook-and-hold strategies to lower the activation energy needed to get moving—perhaps start an exercise program—minimize obstacles, maximize rewards, and consciously cultivate a habit of action over inaction to get hooked on movement. We may be hardwired for inertia to conserve energy, but we're also given the capacity to change our habits by choice, intercept that old messaging, and override it.

> *Nothing happens until something moves. When something vibrates, the electrons of the entire universe resonate with it. Everything is connected.*
> —ALBERT EINSTEIN

FIND WHAT WORKS FOR YOU: A *LIT* METHODOLOGY FOR EXPERIMENTATION

When we talk about movement as a *lit* ignition point, a tool you can use with intention, the idea is to tap into the power of movement as an energy source. How and when are going to be different for everyone and perhaps different for you at different times. Some times of day are just more conducive to doing some activities than others. Maybe you're incentivized to do a walk when you can do it with a friend, less so by yourself; you find a time that works for both of you. Our circadian rhythms and the natural fluctuations in our chemistry determine our optimal times for eating, sleeping, learning, and relaxing. To lower the activation energy for whatever you want to do, it helps to have that natural circadian lift on your side.

Experimentation is the ideal process for discovering what kind of movement works for you and when to do it. This is not a fancy process. You are the lab, the principal investigator, the singular test subject, and the author of the published article in your own journal. (No deadlines!) You might use wearable tech such as a Fitbit or a more elaborate digital watch to track some of your data or go old school and just listen to your body.

Interestingly, we know pretty quickly whether an exercise or even a meditation practice is having an effect, as we fully sense the experience. Your body, your brain and mind states, and your emotions all provide feedback; you just have to take note of them. For example, if you're running and you feel exhilarated—or even good and tired, emphasis on "good"—then you know you've done the right exercise to achieve a positive, desirable effect. You might feel great afterward, or you might feel the "good pain" of a strenuous workout. But if a particular exercise doesn't feel right or have the desired effect, you can review the factors that might be responsible and either tweak your technique or switch to something else.

Becoming attuned to these subtle inner cues can be especially helpful in starting a routine or adjusting its details to maximize benefits and minimize injuries. At one point some years ago, a reality check about a gradual weight gain I'd ignored suddenly made me highly motivated to lose the excess. Initially, I cut back on what I ate, and when that didn't work, I focused on cutting carbs, but after weeks, none of that had moved the needle. Discouraged but determined (and newly inspired by others I had seen struggle to lose weight), I decided that the only way I could lose weight was to start running. I put on my gym shoes and went for a run. At first, I quickly got out of breath and felt serious resistance to continuing the run. Sometimes I felt as though I was hyperventilating—chest tight, panicky sensation, brain screaming "Stop!" I looked online and found various suggestions for how to breathe effectively while running. I tried diaphragmatic breathing, a rhythm technique in which you inhale for the count of three foot strikes and exhale for two or three. I also experimented with other techniques. Eventually I found a breathing strategy that reduced my anxiety and enabled me to be more relaxed and run farther.

Then I hit another hurdle: soon after I started my running regimen, my ankles became so sore that I could barely walk. At one point, in a lot of pain, I hobbled into the hospital emergency department. Their advice? Just take a break. (Thankfully, the doctors there found no injury.) I researched further online and learned that it's important to stretch in the middle of a run, so I started to do that. I got a new pair of shoes, too, and the pain went away. To me, this is a page from nature's playbook: experiment and evolve. I played with the timing of my runs and with their pace and duration. What worked, what didn't? What worked six months ago but not so much now that some other factors had changed? Experimentation was key, and continued tinkering with details kept it sustainable. I was evolving an iterative system that worked for me; I was evolving myself.

> *It's weird to say this out loud, but exercising made my brain be free and "let go" and then suddenly circle back to the problem I was trying to solve but with a different perspective, a totally different approach to something.*
> —TINA KESHAVARZIAN, FORMER KARP LAB INTERN

Contemplative or meditative activity provides observable feedback, too. If a sitting mindfulness meditation heightens your sensations of anxiety, which it does for many people, try a walking meditation. Early scientific findings on the benefits of meditation often came from studies of monks and other "master meditators" who devoted themselves to the sitting practice. But today we know that many options, including walking meditation and other everyday activities done mindfully, provide measurable health benefits. The point is to experiment, listen to your body's feedback, and tinker.

One advantage of fitness-tracking technology is the detailed data it can provide that you wouldn't get any other way. Depending on the device or apps, those data may include steps, standing time, resting heart rate, heart rate average, and heart rate variability. You can use that information to tweak the timing or other aspects of your exercise, meditation, or other activity to meet your goals or follow your interests. Tracking the data in real time can be motivating, lowering the activation energy and making a meaningful difference in other ways. Daniel Gibbs, a friend and retired neurologist who has early-stage Alzheimer's disease, walks daily and hikes when he can, always aiming for the aerobic effect as a preventive health lifestyle choice that has been shown to slow cognitive decline. As he shared in his memoir, *A Tattoo on My Brain: A Neurologist's Personal Battle Against Alzheimer's Disease,* at one point he started to notice a slight decline in cognition, a bit more forgetfulness and befuddlement. He felt that he could think more clearly during and after exercise, but in science, personal observations such as that are discounted as anecdotal evidence—interesting but not acceptable as scientific data. However, the data from the tracker confirmed it. On average, his cognitive assessment score increased by 8 percent after aerobic exercise. One day, after a strenuous uphill hike, his fitness tracker reported his heart rate as 131, up from a baseline of 64 at the start of the hike. After the 1.75-mile, 57-minute hike from the start to the top of the climb, with an elevation gain of 850 feet, his cognitive assessment score had increased by 15 percent. For Gibbs, the sophisticated tracking program, the real-time feedback, and the fact that it was part of a clinical trial only added to his enjoyment of the hike. "I take pleasure in the gritty detail of the data," he said. "It's an inward-facing vista for me I can appreciate."

Heart rate variability (HRV) is the fluctuation in the amount of time between heartbeats, and I use that datum as a factor in deciding whether it's a good day to do intense exercise. I've noticed that my HRV level goes down after I do an intense workout. If my HRV is lower than usual, it means that my body is still recovering, and I might take it easier that day or excuse myself for not having enough energy instead of blaming myself for imagining that I'm tired.

Technology assisted or not, the experimental approach helps you explore the hidden factors driving your thinking and behaviors, reach some clarity about what you want to do, and free yourself from the habits that have held you back. We all have the inner pendulum that swings between affinity and aversion as if between opposite magnetic poles. Without conscious intention guiding us, it's easy to be pulled one way or the other by whatever shows up in the moment. Surprised or stressed by some unrelated event, you may suddenly feel like chucking your plan to go for that walk and then maybe "eating your feelings" with foods you wouldn't normally choose, because—well, why not, if the day's healthy goal is shot already?

Something as simple as a question you ask yourself can interrupt that impulse. A tiny case in point: One afternoon I felt like eating some chocolate, so I had some. Then I felt like eating more, so I had more. Then—the third time—I was about to do it again but stopped just long enough to wonder instead, Will I still feel like this if I don't have it for the next five minutes? I busied myself for five minutes and when the time had passed, so had the impulse. I didn't want more. We hear a lot about the power of living in the moment. But I wonder, Are we sometimes too much in the moment? If we could imagine even just five minutes ahead, we would realize that the urges and pulls that feel so compelling in the moment can be gone just that fast. This impermanence within us, the mind's changeability, can be our ally, the *lit* factor you use to revive your intention. Give yourself permission to improvise and use the power of your own impermanence to your advantage.

The more often you can get going by pausing and intercepting your thinking with *lit* intention, the more you will strengthen that pattern in your brain. As you do, the power dynamic will shift from cultural and other external factors driving your behaviors to your own locus of power. That's particularly important today, as cultural forces are amplified all the more through the always-on pull of the digital realm and social media. "Cultural evolution is now the dominant force of evolutionary change acting on the human body," notes Daniel Lieberman. "If there is any one most useful lesson to learn from our species' rich and complex evolutionary history," he cautions, "it is that culture does not allow us to transcend our biology."

Our biology says that we need to get moving.

HUMANS ARE A FORCE OF NATURE; ACT LIKE ONE

One of the greatest lessons I ever learned about endurance training came from Ed McCauley, who first taught me in ninth-grade English. I struggled a lot in his class but was determined to improve my skills, and although Ed was a tough teacher with high expectations of me, he was a wise person, one of those gems of a teacher. I would meet him often during his office hours, after school, and even sometimes on weekends. He would sit with me and help me see things from different angles. He took the time and had the patience to work with me as I improved bit by bit. I developed a passion for impressing him with my growth. Thinking back, that was a strong motivator, impressing someone I admired so much. Even if I couldn't judge my own growth with confidence, impressing Ed meant that I'd engaged the right process for improvement. And I think, a layer deeper, it was because he helped me to believe in myself. He never seemed to lose optimism, even though working with me as a student must have felt like a marathon.

I think of him now, in this context of movement and exercise and data-tracking devices, because there's something those trackers can't tell you—but Ed did back then, and you hear it sometimes as a reason to keep sports in schools and encourage kids to be on a team, regardless of their athletic ability. Ed said that the people he had seen become most successful in life were the runners—that somehow, something about running trained something deeper, an endurance for life: how to commit, push through, stay the course despite obstacles; that when you commit to running, you build stamina in many areas of life. Sometimes your body wants to stop, and it's up to you to use your brain—coach yourself—to keep going. Running isn't for everyone, but Ed's advice is: keep moving.

> *As runners, we were able to capture the rhythm of the land.*
> *We were able to feel the heartbeat of the Earth. It was what*
> *gave us the strength and endurance. The land is lifting*
> *you. And as we're running, it's through our hearts, we were*
> *able to hear the voice of our ancestors encouraging us.*
>
> —ELDER DAVE COURCHENE, RECALLING THE INDIGENOUS TEAM
> TORCHBEARER RELAY FOR THE 1967 PAN AMERICAN GAMES IN THE
> DOCUMENTARY RUN AS ONE: THE JOURNEY OF THE FRONT RUNNERS

ENDURANCE IS ITS OWN REWARD

When Joe De Sena created the Spartan endurance sports brand in 2009, it was from a bucolic Vermont farm to which he and his wife had removed from big city life and a Wall Street career to raise their family. He describes various ventures they attempted—a country store, a gas station, neither of which took off in any significant way—and he was beginning to go just a little stir crazy. His personal dive into endurance challenges had begun some years before, when they had lived in the city, and one day a broken elevator in his office building rerouted him to the stairwell, where, by chance, he met a guy who routinely trained for adventure races on those stairs. They struck up a conversation, then began a daily training routine together, and Joe was hooked. Soon he was signing on for adventure races around the globe; then he began training and coaching aspiring others.

One day a friend urged him to start an obstacle course race at his Vermont farm. "I was an entrepreneur at heart, so I'm doing these races and I'm thinking, I could do one like this—it would be fun. And boy, wouldn't it be a lot of fun to own a business where you're doing something you love?" But he had reservations about the obstacle course concept. The world of adventure races—kayaking, biking, running—felt like an Olympic sport to him, he says. "It felt legitimate." But an obstacle challenge that pitted participants against not only rugged terrain but *rigged* terrain, with mud pits and barbed wire? He recalls thinking that it was nuts. "Who would sign up for that?"

Five hundred gluttons for punishment did so, and Spartan Race was born, growing to become the world leader in obstacle course races. "Now I understand why," he says. "People are so disconnected, and they want to reconnect. So we're helping them reconnect. We're a pathway to reconnecting with Earth—and yourself. I get emails now from people saying 'You changed my life.' But we didn't. We just provided the platform. *They* changed their life. And it's funny because all they needed was some mud and some barbed wire and some sweat to realize 'Oh, my God, now, this is what I should be doing to be living healthy.'"

There's a tension we all have in ourselves about when to give up. There's always this thing about how far we will go—not just in the moment but in terms of realizing our potential. It's as if we live in a bubble of our capacity to stretch and grow but we imagine that the surface is rigid when it's actually elastic. If we are willing to push on it, we can expand our potential. But that potential can be realized only when we push out the bubble and it remains stretched.

De Sena insists that you can do it. His energy is contagious. You don't have to run a Spartan Race to be moved to action by him. He's the perfect pocket coach—the Joe in my head. When I'm ready to stop short of that little extra I *could* put into my workout or walk—or grant application or presentation or researching ideas, anything that demands sustained energy or attention—in my mind I hear: *I have the time; maybe I could do just a little more.* Joe embodies *lit* energy, and just *thinking* of Joe can push me a little further.

I like to think of people such as De Sena and others with that kind of contagious energy as available at any time to inspire us to action. My son is the quarterback of his high school varsity football team, and his coach, Chad Hunte, is a source of boundless moving energy, a true mentor who sees his players' potential and helps them unleash it, teaching leadership skills both on and off the field. I've met people like this everywhere, people who ignite a spark to shift my mindset in a moment. Who's your Joe? Who's your pocket coach?

Whether we know them personally or just read about them, it always helps to have someone whose energy and determination lights us up and helps us keep going. If you're willing to put in the work, look for people who will believe in you, support you, and encourage you to push the edge of potential out. You can do it.

> *I like movement that makes sense. That teaches me something. By practicing the movements I learn in Pilates, at my own pace and without expectations, I have created a path to guide my subconscious mind that has, for example, improved my posture. I practice moving my body fast and slow in all the ways that it was meant to move, which trains my brain and soothes my mind, and I feel wonderful.*
>
> —JESSICA SIMONETTI

CHOOSE A CONSCIOUS CADENCE

It's easy to become consumed by the need to move fast through the day. Checking things off a list quickly provides a sense of accomplishment, but it can become addictive. The faster you act, the quicker the rewards in bursts of adrenaline and endorphins arrive. But unchecked, speed swings the pendulum away from balance. So does inertia. Bring your attention to how quickly or slowly you're moving in various aspects of your life, and adjust for a conscious cadence.

For example, I discovered that during meditation my brain acts a lot like my phone, pinging me with notifications of things I need to remember to turn to: forgotten things, scheduled things, anything and everything. Life's loose ends. *I forgot I need to get back in touch with someone. How are we going to fix the problem that's holding us back in one of our projects? I haven't called my parents recently.*

When I have such thoughts during meditation practice, they create some anxiety that previously I would have translated into quick action, interrupting the meditation. But when actively meditating, although my mind may race, I've learned to disconnect the impulse to action. Instead, the physical stillness allows my mind to slow down as I come back to my mantra, the centering sound that's part of my meditation practice.

A typical week for any of us provides plenty of opportunities to notice cadence and discover ways we can adjust our pace, focus, and intensity for variety and balance. I look for periods when I can shift my mind from task to taskless to be present to deeper connections with others. It's always a work in progress, but a *lit* week includes periods of intense work, periods of getting my steps in, periods of mind wandering, periods of intentional connection with self, family, pets, and the natural world, periods of helping others through mentorship or service, and periods of struggle that often culminate in greater insights, motivation, and action.

> *With time, meditation practice makes it easier to choose what to focus on, let go of, linger with, indulge in, turn away from, enhance, or reiterate.*
>
> —JILL SATTERFIELD, "MINDFULNESS AT KNIFEPOINT"

We need to be in touch with both our slow and fast movements and aim for an awareness of this underlying cadence in all areas of life. Meditation is one of many useful strategies for experimenting to develop that awareness. For example, I've experimented (with some success) to see how I can replace common distractions from my work with meditation. I've discovered that I don't need the distractions as a break if instead I meditate for fifteen to thirty seconds—a micromeditation! I don't do this at just any time; I wait for a lull in the work or when I feel gravity pulling me toward something that is not important in the moment. I close my eyes, breathe a few breaths, and then open my eyes again, with no goal other than to just rest for a moment.

Often I'm able to return to the task at hand or at least be in a different headspace, a calmer one, and perhaps turn to some other waiting task and then return to the original one. Over the course of a day, replacing mindless distractions with even brief moments of mindful meditation—especially a calming breath or more fast-paced rhythmic breathing practice—makes a positive difference in how I think and feel.

Common distracting activities such as jumping on social media, snacking, or reacting to something in the moment can all be done quickly, but we can also do them slowly. We can pause before jumping on Instagram, chew more slowly, take a few breaths before responding to people. Get in touch with the cycles in your mind; observe how movements toward various stimuli or stillness cycle throughout your day. It's a process of discovery. You venture forth or sit with what is and read the cues from within to learn what resonates with or inspires you and lights your spirit. The journey and the process of discovery itself have purpose, and once we are able to hold that awareness, perceive the mystery and its value, that, too, lights the way. Choose a conscious cadence.

Even if we didn't evolve eager to run without reason across the savanna, neither were we genetically prepared to survive and thrive as a sedentary species feeding on junk food. We've been living a longitudinal experiment in real time, and the results aren't encouraging. Our craving for junk food is one example. The taste receptors on the human tongue evolved to help us determine which foods are safe and which are unsafe to eat. But they're no match for today's high-sugar, high-fat, high-calorie processed foods, which are engineered to exploit our vulnerability to impulsive eating.

In his book *Hooked: Food, Free Will, and How the Food Giants Exploit Our Addictions,* the Pulitzer Prize–winning investigative journalist Michael Moss described how fast foods fire up the brain's reward circuitry, hijacking our appetite and turning us into compulsive eaters. They also tap into the evolutionary drive of the brain's autopilot preference to save energy. "When we were in hunter-gatherer societies, instead of chasing down an impala for dinner, it made much more sense to grab that aardvark sitting there that can't run away—it's sort of a cheapness that's defined as 'less energy expenditure,'" Moss said in a 2021 interview with Civil Eats, a nonprofit news organization focused on critical thought about the American food system.

The easy availability of highly processed foods and the excessive salt, sugar, fat, and empty calories they contain are highly appealing but deadly over time, especially when they're coupled with less movement and less than optimal sleep, which they so often are. That late-night Oreo-Netflix fix packs a triple whammy, as Satchin Panda, a professor in the Regulatory Biology Laboratory at the Salk Institute and author of the illuminating book *The Circadian Code*, explains.

We ignore the body's inner clock at our peril, he says. "Circadian rhythms are internal timetables present in every single cell, in every organ of our body, including the brain," he clarifies, constituting "the master program that guides what time of the day or night every single gene of our twenty thousand genes turn on or off, and thereby every single cell." Well maintained, this DNA-driven program helps us to prevent disease; improve immune function; accelerate repair mechanisms; supercharge our metabolism, detoxification, and DNA repair mechanisms; and optimize brain function for improved emotional and intellectual health. Fortunately, Panda's daily circadian optimization guide is fairly simple: about eight hours of sleep on a consistent schedule; thirty minutes outside in daylight; the same for exercise; and a consistent pattern of eating that delays food for the first hour awake, focuses eating in the next eight to twelve hours, and clocks out until morning—eliminating late-night snacks. Unfortunately, contemporary life pressures us to short-change ourselves (and our kids) on the daily basics.

This laissez-faire relationship with our biological reality is unsustainable, but we've been quick to get hooked and slow to get real about the consequences: Sedentary habits make us feel sluggish. Mentally, we ease into low-energy mode. Physically, our bodies grow thicker, slower, less responsive and resilient. Absent movement, our inner lives languish as well; the inner journey is no less vital to our well-being than the outer one, and it requires attention, a special kind of energy and commitment, to reflect, reach deeper, and stay the course to explore the interior life.

Consider how prevalent alcohol use is in our society—how destructive, even deadly, it is for so many—and yet how attractive it can become as a way to cope with uncomfortable moments or thoughts that our brains generate.

I speak from past personal experience. Earlier in my career, I got to the point where I was having two shots of rum a night as a way to transition from my workday at the lab to my "night shift" of more work after I got home. I ran into predictable challenges: I felt perpetually tired and at times depressed, and less in control of my emotions. Alcohol can seem to create movement in relationships by reducing inhibitions or barriers, but meaningful movement is unlikely without considering what those obstacles are, how they got there, and how to resolve them in ways that support health rather than destroy it. Further, a side effect of alcohol is that it can take a toll on quality sleep, and reduced sleep wipes out the beneficial effects of the positive neurotransmitters we get from movement.

Our big, fancy brain can be an advantage, but only if we use it to consider the consequences of our choices and our actions (or inaction), see the pitfalls and perils on this trajectory, and make a course correction. There's no evolutionary advantage to self-destruction.

Walt Disney's Carousel of Progress has undergone periodic updates over the years, but after technical problems disabled it a few years ago, some critics suggested that it be scrapped, the concept being obsolete. Regardless of the fate of the theme park exhibit, we need to revise our storyline of progress, update it to feature humans who are active and engaged, working with nature and one another, and using technology in ways that will create a sustainable future for humankind and the planet. We can't afford to wait. We need to step off the carousel and get moving.

Step It Up!

You can step up the amount of movement in your life or try new moves in simple ways, especially if you lower the activation energy required to start, perhaps by creating a challenge or reward that boosts your motivation. Once you get moving, momentum and the positive feedback loop will help you keep going and imprint the memory of your self-starting movement. You can recall that feeling of momentum if needed in the future, perhaps after an interruption or lull in your activity, to spark it up again. Experiment with these:

- **MANUFACTURE A LITTLE FRICTION, A LITTLE TARGETED ADVERSITY.** Taking the harder path can be a positive challenge and build a mindset of toughness that will keep you moving. Adversity keeps us all moving. It raises the bar on testing our skills on a daily basis, reminding us of our strengths and points for improvement and providing direction for future growth. Joe De Sena, an endurance athlete himself, seeks out the harshest of physical tests, from Switzerland to Mongolia. You don't need to go to those lengths, of course; just create a challenge that feels like one for you.
- **DO IT FOR THE ENERGY.** Notice the inward and outward energy shifts that happen as a result of exercise. Often there's an immediate boost that you can use to sustain your progress. Notice how the energy alters your motivation and optimism, improving your mood and mental alertness, your interactions with others, and your performance on all fronts. As you get to know that pattern of heightened energy after exercise, build your challenges to take advantage of that performance boost. Work out to energize yourself.
- **START EARLY IF THAT WORKS FOR YOU.** Get a move on the day from the outset, and it's likely to energize your motivation to make healthier choices for the rest of the day, not to mention help reduce the pull toward distractions. Even if it's doing ten squats or stretches while you wait for your coffee to brew or microwave your oatmeal— just move.
- **MOVE YOUR MEETINGS AND BREAKS TO A FOOTPATH TO BOOST CREATIVE THINKING.** To be more intentional about ways to engage your divergent thinking, move brainstorming meetings out of the conference room chairs and into the world. Stanford researchers found that walking boosts creative inspiration. They examined people's creativity levels while they walked versus while they sat. The subjects' creative output increased by an average of 60 percent when walking. Walking fuels idea generation. Save your sitting

time for detail work that requires focused recall of specific, correct answers.

- **LET WHAT MATTERS TO YOU MOST MOVE YOU IN THE MOMENT.** Find the emotional charge. Do you have something or someone in your life that you love? It could be a child, your partner, an animal, even a tree or a garden. Go hug it. When I feel distracted, and especially when I'm gravitating toward technology, I go over and hug my dogs. That may sound cheesy, but that is the exact energy transfer that uplifts me, and after a short time I can return to my work with a fresh sense of energy and focused purpose.
- **GIVE YOURSELF A BREAK.** Show some self-compassion when your motivation or follow-through dips or when, for whatever reason, you need to give it a rest. Breaks can help us find a conscious cadence, giving us a moment to transition from something that we're losing interest in or momentum to do something more meaningful. Instead of shaming yourself over it, recognize that sometimes you just need a break; that to do something again, start something new, or experiment more can itself be motivating.

FALL IN LOVE WITH PRACTICE

Savor the Joys of the Brawny Brain

Enjoy the rewards of repetition and the joy
of incremental improvements.

I never practice, I always play.
—WANDA ALEKSANDRA LANDOWSKA, POLISH HARPSICHORDIST
AND PIANIST, 1879-1959

Richard Turner, perhaps the world's most celebrated "card mechanic"—or card sharp, as some might call him—is not just a proponent of practice; he is obsessed with it. Talk with him, and he has a deck of cards in one hand, flipping, fanning, and otherwise moving in ways that most people can't achieve using both hands. He manipulates cards while watching television, waiting in line, working out in the gym, eating, and in the moments that most of us would call falling asleep. With his eyes closed, his hands riffle and cut the cards and simply pause in suspended motion, cards and all, when his brain clocks out for a nap or the night, resuming the move the instant he awakens, he tells me.

"People say that practice makes perfect," says Turner, who has twice been named Close-up Magician of the Year by the Academy of Magical Arts. "I don't believe that. I think perfect practice makes perfect."

What is "perfect" in Turner's world? "I figure out what the end goal is," he told me. "Let's say the goal is to produce the seventeenth card in the deck, one-handed. So I backtrack to figure out how I can squeeze that deck in such a way that I can pivot out the seventeenth card, then crick it with my index finger and my middle finger, and then thumb turn it over one-handed, hitting it from the middle." And then he does.

I don't suggest that Richard Turner is in any way what we'd call a normal person; no ordinary person can do what he has done with a deck of cards. But he's more than simply a card-manipulating machine. He's a fitness fanatic who holds a sixth-degree black belt in Wado Kai karate. He's an inspirational speaker. And, although he doesn't like to make much of it, he is blind.

Turner developed a retina degeneration disease when he was nine, following a bout of scarlet fever, and his vision quickly diminished such that by the age of thirteen, it had deteriorated to 20/400. That's just backstory, he says if pressed. He prefers to focus the conversation on the cards, the cards, the cards, and his passion—some would say obsessive compulsion—about practice. He considers his capacity for card manipulation to be a natural gift. But it's what you do with what you've got that makes for mastery.

Practice is a process that is, for any of us, both deceptively simple and layered with subtlety, surprises, and astonishing reveals. There is more to it than meets the eye. Practice helps us learn or master a skill, but beyond that, it has an effervescent effect. In the brain, as the repetition and challenge stimulates neuroplasticity, it creates new and deepening neural pathways that intertwine and energize networked connections that affect our mood, cognition, memory, motivation, and attentional focus. Energy demands on the brain shift, too, as actions that were once new and challenging become more routine and eventually more automatic or even unconscious, freeing up resources to replenish energy stores or devote to fresh activity. The findings converge: practice creates a paradigm for growth and fulfillment in every realm—work, study, athletics, relationships, meditation, spirituality. Even household tasks can cease to be "chores" when you see them as a practice and appreciate their process and payoff.

The satisfaction and confidence that come of hard-earned progress can also transfer to other parts of our lives, creating the energy to step up our efforts. That might mean adding three more repetitions to a workout, sustaining a musical practice, or practicing a new response to an old issue—perhaps to improve communication with someone or handle certain situations differently.

It's gratifying to overcome the brain's natural resistance to exertion, both physical and mental, and achieve something that is important to us. But even if we don't believe that something is vitally important— maybe we're not competitive runners or we see no glory in folding laundry—we can still experience the rewards of practice as repetition with a purpose. Once practice begins to have an impact, the positive experience and brain-based reward make it more pleasurable and stoke the confidence that comes with becoming better at the activity. *I can do this; maybe I can also do that.*

I think of it as falling in love with practice. It's more than self-discipline and different from an obligation. The more you can appreciate its nuances and incremental gains, the more rewarding practice becomes, and the more it opens fresh possibilities for you. You may even begin to experience practice as being satisfying in and of itself—with no goal beyond being fully present in the moment. My new awareness of practice as a LIT tool has helped me (finally) develop an appreciation for the path itself, and, as Justin von Bujdoss, an American Buddhist teacher has described it, "how it twists and turns; the work we must put into it along the way."

Discipline breeds discipline. The more you do something, the more you can do of it, and also the better you'll do it.
—RICHARD TURNER

NELSON DELLIS: CLARITY IN A CRISIS

Growing up, Nelson Dellis, memory champion, did not excel at memorization. He wasn't great with math or numbers. He was, in his own words, just your average kid. But after his grandmother was diagnosed with Alzheimer's disease, Dellis became obsessed with memory, particularly with techniques that USA Memory Champions use to remember large amounts of information. He started with a deck of cards. Not a preternatural card whisperer like Turner, he struggled at first to remember the cards in the right order. Eventually, by using memory-building techniques and practice, he got it down to twenty minutes, then fifteen. He got faster and faster, and eventually it took him just forty seconds.

Dellis was not a born memory champ; there were no precocious feats of memory that stamped him for future brilliance. Practice did it. The habits that he developed around practice proved to be the transferable skill—the keen focus that ultimately saved his life on an ill-fated climb up Mount Everest in 2021, his fourth attempt at the summit.

That season on Everest was a tough one, with unusually rough weather, two cyclones back to back, and Covid concerns adding to the tension among climbing teams. The team pushed for the summit through a tight weather window, and Dellis got above 27,230 feet (8,300 meters) in altitude, into what climbers call the death zone, where the oxygen pressure is insufficient to sustain human life. At that point exhaustion set in and he decided he should turn around. "I didn't want to cause problems higher up," he said. "Tough decision, but the right one."

Breathing is challenging enough at that altitude, but oxygen deprivation also affects the brain, causing confusion and clouding judgment, which has cost climbers their lives. Just having the mental clarity to make the decision to turn around is impressive, especially considering all he had invested in training and preparation, travel, costs, and his emotional investment in succeeding that time.

As the others went ahead, Dellis waited at the camp to rejoin them for the descent. I asked him if he had experimented with any memorizing or memory recollection at high altitude.

"As a memory guy, I always bring cards with me, especially for trips where I know there will be a lot of downtime. Surprisingly, with memory techniques I've still been able to memorize a deck of cards under a minute in the death zone," he said. "Crazy, right?"

With such impressive presence of mind, from memory feats to mountain climbing, does he think he's simply hardwired for high-performance thinking?

"I've always been inclined to take on new things, both physical and mental—that's been with me since a young age. Once I won the USA Memory Championship, the idea that I could perform at a high level if I trained hard and pushed myself started to pour into other aspects of my life. So a lot of the things I would do, whether it was memory related or climbing related or fitness related or whatever, I would approach at the same high level, always purpose driven."

Eventually, perhaps not surprisingly, the same purpose-driven motivation for commitment in that period of his life led him to shift his priorities a decade later when, now a family man and business owner, those responsibilities grew. "Before, I believed you could just throw yourself completely into something, be obsessed, work hard, and see results," he said. "Now it's not so blind and carefree anymore. With my limited time and resources, I have to be very selective and decisive on what I want to spend my time on in order to see results."

As for Everest, that challenge continues to make the cut. Having made four attempts in ten years, and having gotten within 165 vertical feet of the summit the first time, the challenge remains a powerful motivator. Although each ascent stopped short for different reasons, each time the decision required having his wits about him to make a wise choice in the worst conditions. His memory practice and skills "saved me up there," he said. Specifically, the *lit* factor of memory practice kept his mind actively engaged, helping him make the decision with clarity in the face of extreme danger.

CHRIS HADFIELD: PRACTICE FOR THE UNPREDICTABLE

Practice not only sharpens our cognitive processes but also shapes our intuitive sense—a valuable asset, as Chris Hadfield found when he needed to adapt his skills to navigate in space.

Before he became an astronaut and commander of the International Space Station, he was a downhill ski racer. On the day of a race, to fine-tune his mental visualization of the course, he would walk the entire course in reverse direction, starting at the finish gate and walking up the slope. "I wanted to get the fine nuance of the course and compare it to my mental visualization—do everything I could to get a clear picture in my mind," he says. He practiced visualization the same way to prepare to walk in space and live and work on the spacecraft for five months.

Human instinct didn't evolve to serve a space explorer or a fighter jet pilot, he says. "To develop that skill set, you have to deliberately change your instincts so that you have a chance at succeeding when there isn't time to do a full analysis. And the only way to develop that entire instinctive skill set is to have clearly identified your objective, to have studied and worked to understand all the variables," and, just as he did for the ski slopes, "then practice relentlessly, over and over and over again in ever more realistic circumstances."

More down-to-earth applications of practice can strengthen interpersonal skills. As one who has struggled to bring fresh energy to practice myself, I've been inspired to hear how others have used practice creatively—and deliberately—to tackle their unique challenges. And it's not always in service of a competitive edge. In the case of one colleague, it was a laughing matter.

The infectious disease epidemiologist Steffanie Strathdee goes by the moniker "Superbug Slayer" on Twitter. It's a hint of humor that wasn't always natural for the professor and associate dean of Global Health Sciences at the University of California San Diego School of Medicine. When she was a teenager, Strathdee realized she didn't understand the nuances of humor. She took everything literally, from billboards to banter. She remembered seeing an advertisement for a lottery that said, "Retire a Millionaire!," prompting her to muse, *Why would anyone want to put a millionaire out of a job?* Eventually it dawned on her that she had misunderstood the message.

Years later, well along in an accomplished career, she recognized that her brain sees things differently from most people's, which was a strength as a scientist. But she still couldn't pick up on the cues for humor, and she got tired of missing out on an aspect of social life that she saw everyone else enjoying. She came to realize that that frustrating gap might be neurological—perhaps attributable to a neuroatypical brain that she recognized in herself and in descriptions of high-functioning autism. Her analytical acumen was one of her great strengths, however, and knowing that the analytical approach is how she learns best, she decided to apply that skill to develop this distinct facet of social intelligence: a sense of humor. She studied Gary Larson's *The Far Side* comics to deconstruct the elements of humor, analyze them, and decode them. She began to incorporate comics into her lectures and to develop her own style the same way anyone learns anything new: with study, good coaching (by her wry-humored husband), and practice. It worked, she explains with a laugh, but it took a *lot* of practice over time. "I had to learn to stop trying to explain my own jokes to people. If a joke needed explaining, it probably wasn't funny."

With deliberate practice, she was able to consciously attune herself to humor around her, and her decoding process got faster. Today her sense of humor is, as her husband puts it, "nerdy but endearing." She's still fine-tuning. A friend pointed out to her that she has two distinct laughs in response to jokes: one is a belly laugh when she "gets it"; the other is a hollow laugh, usually a few seconds after everyone else, when she realizes she didn't get it but everyone else did. She recognizes the misses now and makes a mental note, she says. "I store it in a box in my brain until I can analyze it, then adjust the algorithm."

Practice puts brains in your muscles.
—SAM SNEAD, PROFESSIONAL GOLF LEGEND, RECORD HOLDER FOR
WINNING THE MOST PGA TOUR EVENTS

JOANN DEAK:
PRACTICE BUILDS THE BRAWNY BRAIN

Whatever fitness or lifestyle goals you may achieve with practice, you can also appreciate that practicing in effect takes your brain to the gym for a workout. "I like the metaphor of muscularity," says JoAnn Deak, a

preventive psychologist, author, and lecturer who helps parents, teachers, and children understand how the brain works so they can engage
it more effectively—and happily. In the brain, the repetition of neurological "sets," spending time repeating a particular task, changes the
chemistry of all the neurons used. As a strength-building technique,
repetition helps muscularize the brain by stimulating dendrites—the
branching ends of the neuron—to grow, making new connections and
strengthening the existing ones.

Steady practice lowers the activation energy required to start and
then perform a task, because the brain is no longer required to start
from scratch and forge new connections. It can more readily do what it
already is primed to do with each successive round of neurochemicals
used for the task, and do it faster.

With practice, and the combination of leaving a chemical trace that's
easily followed, growing dendrites, and lowering the wattage required,
Deak says, "you get to the point where playing a complicated Mozart
piece on your violin still takes a lot of energy, but nothing like it did ten
years before."

If this aspect of practice to create energy-saving brain circuitry
sounds suspiciously similar to LEB—the low-energy brain state we aim
to shake awake using LIT tools—that's because it uses the same circuitry that enables the brain to skip past rote detail. How you use that
fast-forward feature is your choice: Will you allow autopilot to dull your
thinking or use practice to free up brainpower and energize your brain
for more creative or challenging effort?

Sometimes practice leads us to the limits of our capacity or motivation for something at a particular time. I love to run, but no amount of
practice would turn me into an Olympic runner. And although I was
curious about developing a meditation practice for years, it was more
stop-and-go tourism than a dedicated drive. I never gained any traction
until a strong motivation—wanting to be more mindful and present to
my family—kicked in.

Motivation matters. What is important to us, how we think about a
goal or intention, literally moves us. Motivation is energizing, a fundamental element of our interaction with the world and with one another.

As a *lit* booster for practice, motivation also lowers the activation energy, jump-starts our effort, and continually refreshes our commitment to practice.

BREAK IT UP! TRY MORE AND SHORTER PRACTICE SESSIONS

The role of practice in creating new synaptic connections was partially what interested Molly Gebrian, a music professor and neuroscientist at the University of Arizona, when she considered how students are taught to play the viola, her instrument. For reasons both historic and amusing, for centuries the viola played second fiddle to the smaller, higher-toned violin in music compositions. But in the twentieth century, as the viola rose in esteem through its role in string quartets and more modern music forms, materials to teach viola students—etudes, scales, and atonal techniques—lagged behind the need.

"It is possible, unfortunately, as a violinist to get through one's entire musical education never having performed a solo piece written after 1900," Gebrian wrote in her doctoral dissertation at Rice University. Now imagine, she said, a music student who, since early childhood, has practiced traditional scales, rhythms, and tones who suddenly must play music in which few or none of those conventions is present. "Because of the strength of muscle memory, scalar passages that don't fit into a major/minor framework can become even more challenging because the player must simultaneously override the automatic muscle memory for tonal scales and also play accurately the pattern the composer has written." Posttonal modern music, she said, is an entirely different musical language for instrumentalists to learn.

This problem has been a central point of Gebrian's neuroscientific interests. Musicians tend to practice techniques and musical compositions for four or five hours a day. But like most people, few understand how to practice most effectively, she says. "The ways in which the brain learns most efficiently are often quite counterintuitive," she told us. "Musicians tend to think they need to practice for a big block of time, working really, really hard. If you have an hour, you spend that whole hour on just one thing. This is not the most efficient way to learn."

In terms of practice duration, Gebrian says, it is better to practice for many short periods, such as fifteen minutes in the morning, fifteen minutes at midday, and another fifteen in the evening. That's because practice stimulates the brain to establish new or stronger synaptic links, but not during practice itself. "The learning takes place in the breaks between practice," she says. "The brain has to actually undergo physical changes to learn, which is retaining information. For the brain to do that kind of reconstruction, you can't be using it at the same time."

Studies suggest that the brain can establish links that begin the process of retention in as little as an hour. Reinforcing a lesson—fingering, bowing, memorization of a piece—with subsequent practice helps seal the learning in place. Over time, certain actions that once were difficult become automatic as more neurons establish more connections.

Recent studies demonstrate that practicing a skill also helps build myelin, a substance that acts as an insulator in the electrical pathways of the brain. As the myelin sheaths thicken, they help create a kind of electrical superhighway, which again adds to skill retention.

Then there's a stage of practice called "overlearning," training that continues beyond the point of mastering a skill. You may no longer improve your performance, but continuing to practice the skill at a high level of difficulty can seal your ability to perform it. However, studies also show that overlearning can be so powerful that it temporarily prevents new learning. The new skill simply doesn't take until the old one is fully absorbed. A parallel drawback can result from excessive specialization and practice, particularly in brain development during the formative years of childhood and adolescence, Deak points out. "Be careful with inordinate amount of time on task, because of the areas that you're *not* spending time on," she says. "Once you do a lot of practice, once you have created more dendrites, lower capacitance, and chemical traces, then the brain wants to do that. It wants to do the easier stuff—it doesn't want to be frustrated and feel the load of work" that other things, such as social and emotional development, require.

Breaks from practice, especially when learning a new skill, also create a startle effect in the brain, which amounts to a slight disruption in the way the brain retains new input, Gebrian says. "When you come back to practice it again later, the brain is at a higher level of readiness to learn. But it has also had a chance to forget a little. New practice reminds it and helps solidify the lesson," Gebrian says.

A break can be the catalyst for connection in the brain between points past and present. We have this trail of experience for everything in our lives, meaning that we've already lowered the activation energy for most things. We just need to remember the dots and then connect them! Often all we need is a quick ping about possibilities to help us pick up the thread.

I like to think of practice as a tool to cultivate confidence, precision, and intuition with the current skill we have under development. The neural feedback loops we engage along the way build confidence for an expanding skill set. So practice not only expands a specific capability, it opens up a universe of possibilities, and it doesn't matter where you start. From sports to music to hobbies and even to social interactions or reconnecting with the Earth, focused practice cultivates evolution in everything.

THE JOY OF PERSISTENCE

Nelson Dellis describes three motivations that keep him passionate about practicing feats of memory. "I practice because I have this desperate appetite for achieving some goal," he says. It might be a target number or a record held by someone else. "So the feeling I get when I chip away at that progression toward the number, the better I feel. That feeling is why I return to practice each day." Data are another motivating factor. He tracks the data after each practice to see his progress and analyze factors he might tweak to improve. He keeps a record of his scores, the time of day he practiced, and any outside factors that could have contributed to his performance, for better or for worse. "Having that data in front of my eyes every day helps remind me of the progress I've made from the start," he says. Finally, there is what he calls self-accountability. "Seeing my data from every day is like seeing a calendar filled with Xs that shows the days I practiced without missing a day. I get addicted to keeping the streak alive. Missing a day of practice becomes more of the thing I want to avoid rather than the motivation making me *do* the practice."

Whatever energizes you can become the joy of practice, at least the way it registers as such in your brain. As Deak explains, there's some evidence that as you perform, or advance in your practice of anything, the brain produces dopamine and serotonin, which affect your emotional system and give you a good feeling. The so-called runner's high is an elusive reward that many people—even athletes at the peak of their performance—never experience. But understanding what you are doing for your brain when you practice can be a more interesting, reliable, and lasting reward. The more positive feeling you can weave into practice—appreciating the incremental progress and what's happening in your brain, for instance—the more your practice will trigger those feel-good rewards and increase your motivation to continue. Studies suggest that being in love produces a similar swell in those neurochemicals, so why not fall in love with practice and enjoy it more?

After years of pushing myself to practice, practice, practice all skills, that was a tricky thing for me to fully appreciate. I thought that aiming for the runner's high was the incentive I was looking for. Deak set me straight—and then I smashed my finger and found out she was right. I shattered the little finger on my left hand while throwing a football with my son and had to wear a splint. But what a lucky break! Fortunately, I didn't need surgery, and being me, I was fascinated by the wound healing and rehabilitation process. Bone regeneration and the cascade of other healing processes are biologically painstaking, complex, and slow. Under a microscope, the action would be spectacular, yet all of it remains invisible to the naked eye. Our only window into the healing process is surprisingly old-fashioned: what we see and feel.

For my pinky finger, physical and occupational therapy involved daily exercises to slowly restore its strength, flexibility, and range of motion, millimeter by millimeter. My physical therapist showed me the exact movements to make, over and over again.

That was the part of recovery I came to appreciate, even enjoy. It was exciting to work on something, practice dutifully, and see and feel progress. I knew that if I didn't work hard at regaining movement, I would be limited in what I could do in the future, and that motivated me even more. It was rewarding to see the progress of my finger moving just an extra millimeter!

If anyone had ever told me that one day I'd be excited about such a small, incremental piece of progress, with that small finger at the center of attention, I'd have laughed. Yet that was what happened. I improved, and that was my reward; no great high, just progress: a lithe little finger and a brawnier brain.

Sometimes it is practicing patience that pays off—patience with ourselves and patience with process. Think back on your own life, and you'll likely find your own great reminder, but for me, it was a high school experience as a "least likely" member of the school's track-and-field team. I was never a sporty kid; in fact, I was typically the last to be chosen for teams during recess or after school. But in high school I signed up to do discus, javelin, and shot put. I wasn't a particularly promising competitor, but I liked throwing the discus: the spin, staying in the circle, throwing, the angle of the discus, how it released off my fingers. The art teacher, Mr. Wade, ran the discus event because he had thrown as a child, and when I asked for help, he agreed to show me some mechanics of throwing.

I'm the type of person who never gets things the first time, or even the tenth time. I need to see things over and over for them to lock in. But he was patient with me, and I realize now, years later, that he was in effect teaching me to be patient with myself and focus on the process. It amazed me at the time that I could make small adjustments and see myself improve, and when the day came for the big competition, I placed second in my school, which qualified me to compete in the all-city track-and-field meet, where I placed third with a personal-best throw. I was elated, but the most important thing I learned—a lasting life lesson—was to trust the process. For example, I learned recently that the positive stimuli I was getting from learning a particular way—reinforcement learning—was what made practice feel good. I also learned that habit formation is more responsive to context than to goals. The more positive cues (including dopamine rewards) you get to practice a behavior, the more likely you are to do it and the more likely that the practiced behavior will become a habit. For instance, early survival in humans involved locating environments where food is found, which leads to dopamine production. I was able to create new habits to be productive, delivering dopamine in the context of work.

There's a place in our lives for both the comfort of the routine and pleasures that practice can bring and the excitement of the new, as Rudolph Tanzi points out, having found both in the worlds of science and music. We can actively practice both, especially if we see practice as part of a continuum—not static drudge work or necessarily heavily goal directed, but a pathway to something satisfying in and of itself.

Pablo Casals, perhaps the greatest cellist of all time, who started playing music on three instruments when he was four years old, was asked at age eighty why he kept practicing for hours each day. "Because," he said, "I think I am making progress."

To change an old habit or develop a new one is a creative act in that we can choose what works best for us, choose our individual path to practice, and choose to persist. Consider the ant, celebrated for its seemingly robotic persistence but, in its own way, fickle about choice. In his 1907 dissertation, "The Homing of Ants: An Experimental Study of Ant Behavior," the scientist and educator Charles Henry Turner, known for his pioneering studies on insect behavior, described an experiment in which he introduced a small obstacle—an incline called a section-lifter—in the path of ants engaged in a routine housekeeping task. Contrary to the scientific assumptions of the day, which would have predicted uniformity in the ants' response, he found otherwise. "Thus I had two individuals of the same colony, at the same time and under identical external conditions, responding to the same stimulus in quite different ways. To the one the incline had no psychic value, to the other it was a stimulus to pass to and from the stage. To one the section-lifter was a repellent stimulus, to the other an attractive stimulus. Each had acquired a different way of accomplishing the same purpose and each had retained and utilized what it had gained by experience." The ants were hardly robotic! Furthermore, they appeared to invest "psychic value" in one choice over the other.

Turner then reflected on the power of habit—and persistence—in the ants, and that of our species as well: "Not only do ants retain, for at least a few hours, what they have learned; but a habit once formed is hard to break. From time to time I have performed experiments for the purpose of breaking up habits. Often I have failed, my patience not being a match for the persistence of the ant; in other cases, by patient persistence, I have succeeded."

Celebrate All Your Goals and Gains Along the Way

To reap energy from practicing, it helps to uncover insights about single steps we might experiment with to improve or grow in what we are trying to achieve. Several years ago, inspired by Jessica's physical flexibility, I wondered if I had a similar potential. So with curiosity as my lead, every few days I would try to touch my toes. I would stretch as far as I could go and count quickly to thirty. Then I started counting to thirty and then back to one. When I started, I could barely reach past my knees. But I kept practicing that simple movement, eventually doing it once a day easily while I waited for something to heat in the microwave. My reach got better and better, and the practice became easier. A couple months in, I could touch my toes—it felt great! I craved doing the stretch all the time. What impressed me most wasn't my newfound flexibility, though I felt good about achieving my goal; it was that something so simple and perhaps inconsequential could have captured my imagination and commitment. That felt great, too. (And at my next yearly physical, my doctor announced that I'd grown half an inch!)

Research points to the power of motivation to boost the brain's response to anything. Motivation lowers activation energy and boosts overall energy, enhancing the rewards of your effort. The brawny brain becomes a happier brain, too. Try these *lit* boosters:

SOCIALIZE IT. If practicing alone seems daunting, engage your "social brain" to boost your motivation and rewards. We are a social species. Practice with a friend or a group—just get the first session onto your calendar and lower the activation energy for the rest to fall into place. The presence of others whose energy and attitude are a good fit for you will register as positive, supportive, and encouraging. If you relish competitive energy or a drill sergeant approach, then seek out a group or a person who will energize you that way. If you feel you're slipping into a rut with practice, revive by connecting with someone who has more skill or by changing your work environment. There are now all kinds of in-person coworking spaces and online coworking rooms where you can get together with strangers, quickly share your goals for the next hour or two, work, and then meet back at the end to discuss what you've achieved.

USE INSPIRATION TO IGNITE MOTIVATION. Turn to media to draw inspiration and insights from others. Documentaries about musicians, artists, and athletes often reveal their practice process, and witnessing that level of passion and commitment can energize your own. The documentary *Running the Sahara,* chronicling three men who ran more than 4,300 miles across the desert to raise consciousness (and money) for a clean water initiative in Africa, put the challenges I face on a daily basis into a completely different light. Surprisingly, it gave me a sense of empowerment to see what was possible for human potential—and how much further I could go, how much more potential I could extract in myself. Inspiration is a great example of *lit* energy transfer.

TUNE IN TO FORWARD-LOOKING CONFIDENCE TO ENERGIZE CONNECTION AND IMPACT. Limitless potential, joy, liberation, and fulfillment await us, but they often feel out of reach until we take the first step. Other rewards of progressing toward long-term goals include connection with others and confidence that we can do something more beneficial for ourselves and/or our community. As we develop skills, we discover our ability to mentor others and harness the *lit* principle of energy transfer to bolster their efforts and our own. This synergism builds more confidence that we can practice when developing a new or different skill.

BREAK FREE FROM RIGID EXPECTATIONS, AND ENGAGE THE PLEASURES OF PRACTICE. We typically think of practicing to achieve mastery, but sometimes we unnecessarily prize performance over pleasure. When my family moved near a public golf course, I decided I had to improve my game—no more excuses! I practiced dutifully, but soon it became frustrating and futile. To revive my interest, I watched instructional videos online, focused on specific parts of a swing, then practiced it on the driving range. I felt the change immediately—in my swing and my mood—as I reframed my focus each week. It was fun again. And now I am practicing *not* golfing, so that I can focus on shared time with my family and develop other skills. It's up to us to reframe our expectations of ourselves around practice to reflect changing priorities and interests, and own the challenge and the liberation that come with it.

USE GROUP MOMENTUM TO BOOST YOUR OWN. A group practice can push your limits and have you feel part of something beyond yourself. Jessica and I take Djembe drumming classes together, in a drum circle with others. Our instructor, Alan Tauber, says that all you need to do is show up, relax, and play. Amazingly, he has us play complex pieces we couldn't imagine we'd be able to play when we walked in. But we start together, and, however imperfect, it quickly sounds great as people make adjustments. Even if you can't play all the notes, you can play many of them, and you can hear the sound of your drum and that of others and the harmony. We always leave surprised—and all we need to do is show up!

SAVOR PEACE *FROM* MIND IN THE PRACTICE MOMENT. Practicing for a period of time helps reduce the distracted or transactional nature of the mind—the worries, anxieties, desire to accomplish something, or other intrusive thoughts that dog us throughout the day. Practice can be meditative, such as folding laundry or doing dishes. Focus your attention on this aspect of repetition to leave the rest behind.

DO NEW, DO DIFFERENT

Invite Surprise and Serendipity

Play with nuance and novelty to generate
new possibilities.

*You need change, or you lose the energy
to do something new.*
—RUDOLPH TANZI, NEUROSCIENTIST AT HARVARD MEDICAL SCHOOL
AND LEADING ALZHEIMER'S RESEARCHER

Even Thoreau left Walden Pond. After two years of sauntering around the countryside discovering new dimensions of creativity and spirituality along the fabled road less traveled, he realized that eventually a fresh path becomes a rut in thinking. "I left the woods for as good a reason as I went there," he wrote in the conclusion to *Walden*. To do new. Writing of the inevitable dulling effect of routine, even when it's one you chose, he concluded, "It is remarkable how easily and insensibly we fall into a particular route, and make a beaten track for ourselves."

Today, the most advanced neuroimaging studies show not only the rut effect that Thoreau lamented but something more encouraging: the power of new, different, or surprising stimuli to energize the brain. In response, the brain forges new neural pathways that promote not only skill building, as we might associate with athletics or technical mastery, but also creativity. A 2022 study involving "exceptionally creative" (or "Big C") visual artists and scientists and a "smart comparison group" suggested that in the brain, "Big C creativity is associated with more 'random' rather than more 'efficient' global network functional architecture," wrote Ariana Anderson and her collaborators. "This more random connectivity may be less efficient much of the time, but the architecture enables brain activity to 'take a road less traveled' and make novel connections," they wrote.

Practice expands and deepens that growth, as we saw earlier, but in the beginning, the *lit* factor is learning something new. When we learn something a certain way, we establish a path or "pave the road" in the brain. Continuing the metaphor, if we learn to drive on hard pavement, it is tricky to drive on, say, a gravel road because we apply the strategies we originally learned on the hard surface. We need to develop new synaptic connections and practice them to adapt our driving style to the different surface. The novelty and motivation involved light up the brain and help lower the activation energy.

Conversely, familiarity breeds not necessarily contempt but complacency and blind spots, or at least attentional ones in the brain's visual awareness. Known as the Troxler effect, the perceptual phenomenon was named for the Swiss physician and polymath Ignaz Paul Vital Troxler, who used optical illusions to demonstrate the brain's fading attention to certain objects and colors in our peripheral vision and its preference for novelty. The more habituated we become, the more static images fade from view. A function of the brain's wiring for efficiency, that habituation was what made it possible for me to ignore the TV and pinball machine in my study room in college but not the novel email notifications that began in the mid-nineties. Years later, I realized the power of novelty as being a LIT tool that we can use intentionally.

In a world of complexity and sophistication where expertise is considered essential to success, often the most extraordinary developments owe a debt to chance encounters and bringing a beginner's mind to new situations. Whether at work or at home, when everyone is counting on you to keep doing what you do best, take a deliberate step to do something new. Surprise yourself. Not only will the rush of neurochemicals that respond to the unexpected invigorate your neural networks, but the ripple effect of your action will shake open other possibilities.

The many interests of Grace (Teo) Katzschmann epitomize a life lived on the edge of the new: new things to learn, new ways to explore her interests, and new jobs that exemplify her eagerness to jump full throttle into fresh opportunities.

Katzschmann, who joined the lab in 2009, had interned here the year before, then returned to Boston fresh from earning a bachelor's degree in chemical and biomedical engineering from Singapore's Nanyang Technological University. She came our way to earn a Ph.D. in those same areas and during her five years with us became an expert in the biology and engineering of stem cells in the context of stem cell therapy.

But eventually what caught her attention was a comment by a patient with muscular dystrophy (MD) whom she met one day, which had nothing to do with her work in the lab—except a course requirement that she get out of the lab and into the real world.

"As part of my program, we were given the opportunity to spend up to three months in a clinical setting, speaking with clinicians and patients to understand real-world problems," says Katzschmann. "One of my favorite questions for patients was 'What do you miss most about being healthy?'" When she posed that question to the patient with MD, the woman told her that it had taken her an hour to get dressed that morning. "She missed her independence in small but daily activities like dressing," Katzschmann says.

That struck a personal chord with her for two reasons. First, as she was growing up, her older sister had gone through more than ten corrective surgeries to repair a cleft palate and upper lip. The last surgery, when she was eighteen, was to be cosmetic, with the aim of fixing her nose symmetry. "She declined the surgery, saying it was her nose and she accepted it," Katzschmann says. "That sort of confidence in her appearance was very inspiring for me. Also, when she was younger, someone told her that she would have to work harder in life because of 'how she looks.' That made me quite aware that looks can have great impact on how one gets through life." Further, she says, "my dream when I was younger was to be the wardrobe designer on film and TV sets—I liked the idea of being able to transform people and create narratives through clothing."

Sparked by the patient's reply, Katzschmann had an idea, something entirely new on her career path. "I wanted to start designing clothing that would be attractive and easy for people with disabilities to put on," she said. The challenge? "I had a very standard science-oriented education and zero background in design."

So Katzschmann turned her problem-solving skills to learning about design; specifically, how to design attractive garments for people with a limited range of motion or who were differently abled. Together with a friend, she devised an educational program involving designers, engineers, occupational therapists, and people with disabilities, who together create dressing solutions. The nonprofit organization, called Open Style Lab, was launched in 2014 and has held annual research, design, and development events ever since. It is now integrated into the curriculum at the Parsons School of Design and has been replicated at other academic institutions.

"The biggest thing Open Style Lab gave me was confidence to dive into completely new fields and figure things out step by step," says Katzschmann, who has gone on to work as a lecturer at MIT, venture capitalist, biotech analyst, and research director and is now a biotech consultant in Switzerland. "I'm inclined to like to try out new things."

Not all of us are prepared to launch new ventures in unfamiliar terrain, but we do have one thing in common: new experiences, people, ideas, and physical challenges excite our brains and launch networks of possibility, synapse by synapse. New experiences make us feel *lit*. And we can start where we are.

I was struck by the Nobel Prize–winning geneticist Phillip Sharp's purposeful commitment to meeting new people and hearing fresh perspectives not only in science but more generally. Because so many people want his attention, he came up with a way to protect time for both. He divides meeting requests into two categories he considers of equal importance. The first attends to long-term commitments, the second to opportunities that allow him "to jump over the routine" and make time to meet or experience somebody new or experience something new. "Avoid the routine, but use time to sample a new space and new ideas," he advises. "It's terribly important, and you need to keep it on your calendar."

Rudy Tanzi points to the value of variety in our everyday habits. When you are performing familiar routines, your brain fires the same networks over and over because you know them. Those neural networks contain your habits, patterns, likes, and dislikes, all established over time—but also, potentially, an obstacle to achieving *lit* states of mind. To learn and practice new things draws on mental energy but generates it, too.

"It's important to understand conditioning, repetition, and patterns that create order are like a structure, like a house," Tanzi says. "Anytime you break out and do something new, you introduce chaos and disruption. The change keeps you fresh and gives you energy."

Pattern is the enemy, he says. "Pattern creates order, but the same pattern repeated over and over becomes stagnant and decays. You need change, or you lose the energy to do something new."

Tanzi talks about fear and desire as the two primal motivations that drive all we do. We avoid what we fear and are drawn to what we desire. His own history of working through fear to do something out of his comfort zone, coupled with the resulting positive experiences, has helped him focus past the fear, he says. Our amygdala may still trigger an alarm, but we don't have to respond to it fearfully. We can choose to redirect that energy and connect with positive anticipation instead of dread.

> *You must do the thing you think you cannot do.*
> —ELEANOR ROOSEVELT

Katzschmann, for instance, says she is relatively unfazed by the fear factor when she's motivated to try something new. She attributes this to selective memory, enthusiasm, and a willingness to ask for help when she needs it. "I have a really bad memory for low moments in my life," she explains. "It's difficult for me to remember specific moments I felt stumped, but I think I generally circumvented those moments by looking for people who knew what they were doing in the areas where I felt lost and inviting them to help out." We can do the same with intention— mimic the upside of a bad memory—by developing the skill of letting things go, not grabbing onto negative thoughts or fear in our brain, just acknowledging the thoughts and then letting them pass through as one might do on a road trip, stopping in many places but none as the final destination. That practice of detachment can lower the activation energy of doing something new and perhaps intimidating.

Tanzi notes that even with his preference for shaking things up, it isn't always easy. But when he feels a pang of anxiety, he uses a simple meditation in the moment, closing his eyes to focus on his breath, which enables him to focus on his purpose. That positive reward disarms the resistance. Do that, and your brain will be your ally, with the neuroplasticity that enables it to adapt to new demands by altering its structure and networks—growing and linking neurons in response to new demands while pruning lightly or unused patterns from the past.

Experiment with different strategies to identify tools that help you step past fear to try new things. One that often works for me is not to overthink the situation; give the analytical brain a time out and lead with an intuitive leap instead. I try not to let past experiences get in the way or bias me against engaging in new experiences. Other tools:

- Try to identify the source of the fear and determine if the fear is truly useful.
- Practice becoming more comfortable with having less control over situations, so that the element of uncertainty doesn't itself become a trigger for fear. Patterns in our thinking often validate uncomfortable thoughts, giving them veto power, in essence allowing discomfort to drive our decisions. For example, in a situation where we have less control, we might be inclined to dwell on all that could go wrong and then decide to quit or not engage. Instead, we might try letting those thoughts exist but not basing our decisions on them.
- Question thoughts or beliefs that don't serve you well rather than leave them unchallenged. Ask yourself if the thought is an absolute. Is this really bad for me? Is this going to harm me? What is the worst that could happen? Could I learn from this? Could I gain insights? Might something arise that is helpful?

Challenging the thoughts that hold us back opens the space and frees the energy for an internal dialogue. Tanzi suggests a simple visualization exercise to shift the brain-based skills you bring to the task. To disrupt or dispute the negative thought pattern, "bat away the words"—in effect, reduce the energy and attention you give them. With no words for traction, you can begin to train your brain to disengage from the message. In other words, we can train our brains to be less analytical and more in touch with the fuller experience of the moment. When I notice that unhelpful thoughts have hijacked me, I try to check myself during or afterward to ask why I'm dwelling in my own head and confining and limiting myself instead of connecting with the outside world. I've spent a lifetime honing skills to focus my attention and my analytical brain, but sometimes we need to disrupt with intention when that's what serves us best.

> *Neuroplasticity is better than mind over matter.*
> *It's mind turning into matter as your thoughts*
> *create new neural growth.*
> —DEEPAK CHOPRA AND RUDOLPH E. TANZI,
> *SUPER BRAIN: UNLEASHING THE EXPLOSIVE POWER OF YOUR MIND TO*
> *MAXIMIZE HEALTH, HAPPINESS, AND SPIRITUAL WELL-BEING*

GO AGAINST THE COGNITIVE GRAIN

Not everybody has passion projects to dive into, as Katzschmann does, or, like Rudy Tanzi, an exciting array of options that can take him from analyzing spreadsheets of deep data to testifying at congressional hearings to playing keyboard center stage with a headliner rock band. That's okay. What matters is the act of doing something different in the moment. Almost anything you do—the smallest departure from a familiar routine—rouses your brain, overrides for an instant the brain's natural resistance to change, and creates an opening for neurons to network with fresh creativity. The smallest changes can ignite the brain and rev the engine of possibility. Something as simple as writing with your nondominant hand, walking or driving a different route to a familiar destination, or speaking with a stranger or someone you usually pass by activates learning circuits in your brain. Even if your sole purpose is that alone, nothing lofty or dramatic but the simple intention to give your brain a healthy boost, mission accomplished. Asking your brain to go against the grain creates cognitive irritation, which can stimulate creativity, and attempting something new or risky triggers the release of dopamine, rewarding the effort. Remember Joe De Sena's workout advice to manufacture some targeted adversity. Turns out that the brain loves a good workout, too.

We tend to think in terms of cultivating cognitive development in children, and we look to schools and educational toys and activities to do it. However, even as we age, the brain is wired to make the most of doing new. As we progress through adult developmental stages, we engage differently with experiences that hold new potential for us precisely because in the mature brain, at middle age, the two hemispheres of the brain begin to work more closely together. "Any activity that uses both sides of the brain optimally is, in effect, savored by the brain," says Gene D. Cohen, a pioneer in the field of geriatric psychiatry. "It's like chocolate to the brain. It's like you have a new capacity or skill."

At one hundred, I have a mind that is superior—thanks to experience—than when I was twenty.
—RITA LEVI-MONTALCINI, ITALIAN NEUROLOGIST
AND NOBEL PRIZE WINNER

In the 2014 study The Synapse Project, which looked at the impact of sustained engagement on cognitive function in older adults, researchers found that learning new skills that are cognitively demanding—in this case quilting and digital photography—and sticking with them (for at least three months in the study) enhanced memory function in older adults.

The ripple effect of novelty or the cognitive stretch in the brain is also impressive. "No single part of the brain ever works by itself," the psychologist and author JoAnn Deak told us. "So for instance, when I go to push a button, I'm not just using my motor sector. I'm using the area that receives information from proprioceptors. I'm using my visual cortex and my processing cortex. At any point, even the simplest task is using ten to thirty to forty different sectors of the brain."

The Olympic medalist Adam Rippon said he had been drawn to participating in *Dancing with the Stars* specifically because it was a stretch for him—the kind of experience he seeks out. "As a competitor, I found that when I pushed myself out of my comfort zone, that's really when I felt like I was the most alive, or getting the most out of myself," he told me. "*Dancing with the Stars* was completely out of my element, but that was totally the draw. It was something that was different, something I hadn't done before.

"When you step out of your comfort zone, you learn more about yourself," he said. "You learn more about how you deal with different situations and how you deal with different pressures. So I'm so glad that I took the time to do it, even though it was a crazy time—more than I imagined. But at the same time, it was so fun and so rewarding."

"DEFAMILIARIZE" YOURSELF TO TRANSFORM YOUR PERSPECTIVE

Choosing to see something through fresh eyes can make for a surprising new experience. The poet and theologian Pádraig Ó Tuama reflected on his favorite word in Russian, остранение (ostraneniye), which translates into English as "defamiliarization." In art and literature, the word has been used to describe works that take the familiar and portray it in strikingly unfamiliar ways that jar our senses and stimulate fresh perspective. Think of Andy Warhol's giant Campbell's soup can paintings, which transformed the ubiquitous brand into celebrated art, or novels such as George Orwell's *Animal Farm*, which cast barnyard animals as the complex humanlike characters in a dark political drama. But Ó Tuama appreciates the way defamiliarization can help us see something with fresh eyes in everyday ways, such as during an unhurried conversation you might have with a new acquaintance or even a stranger in a coffee shop or on a flight.

"Defamiliarization is one of the functions I hope for in good conversation," Ó Tuama wrote in an email introduction to the weekly *On Being* podcast. "I hear something and it makes me look at their world in a new way, and change my actions correspondingly. I hope for moments to see old ideas in a new light, where the familiar feels less familiar."

Astronauts (and more lately celebrity travelers who've orbited the Earth) have described a similar effect—the so-called overview effect—as they've rocketed into space and observed the Earth from that vast distance. For the rest of us, a handy experience of defamiliarization is as close as your thumb. The ancient Greek concept of *holon* describes the awareness that something can be a whole in and of itself and at the same time an integral part of something larger. You can look at your thumb, for instance, and see it as a thumb, but if you widen your field of vision, you see it as part of your hand and then your hand as part of your arm, your arm as part of your body, and so on. Eventually you can widen your field of vision to see yourself (or anyone) as part of humanity or a species among others sharing the planet.

"The concept of *holon* is so important because as soon as you think you see the whole picture, the wholeness of something, you realize you're really only seeing a part of a larger whole. And as soon as that clicks in your head, it actually changes your perspective on everything in the world—everything," says Deak, who uses the thumb exercise in teaching kids about the brain. "You can't look at a car the same way, or a bug or anything else, because everything all of a sudden is holonic."

The point is not only to be open to surprise and welcome it but, if need be, to create the element of surprise for yourself by consciously changing your perspective to see something in a different context. Or simply look more closely. Novelty may snag your attention, but nuance can hold it indefinitely because there is no end to our capacity to see anew. Seeing the next layer, the next personal discovery of how things are connected and interconnected, makes the same thing new again.

Substituting nuance for novelty is what experts do, and that is why they are never bored.
—ANGELA DUCKWORTH

In the lab, that's an essential, and exciting, part of our process, perhaps nowhere more evident than in our weekly Wednesday presentations.

Each Wednesday, someone from the lab presents a summary of their project. People who are new to the lab often start their presentations the way most young scientists do, by showing slide after slide of experimental methods, data, and results. I'll interrupt, asking them questions that people unfamiliar with the work might ask, such as "Why are your experiments the right ones to do?," "What is the most critical thing we could learn?," and "Why are your results important?" One of my favorites, in the spirit of engagement: "What is the best published result anyone has ever achieved, and how much better do we need to do?" It's the "So what?" question—the simplest trigger question to challenge your own conclusions.

Often the response starts off with a superficial answer, such as "We're doing this experiment to help patients" or "We're doing this experiment to test X or Y." But after some probing, people start digging past the surface level for their answers. The real point of the discussion is to ensure that we don't lose touch with the deeper and higher-level goals: What are we trying to learn, and how is that going to help us move the needle for patients and society? In the lab, the do-new ethos generates exciting innovation, sometimes by flipping conventional approaches or coming at a problem from a completely different angle. Here are two recent examples:

A NASAL SPRAY TO FORM A BARRIER COATING IN THE NOSE THAT CAN CAPTURE AND KILL VIRUSES AND BACTERIA. When Covid hit, we repurposed the lab to help in any way we could. One published paper that caught our attention described how the virus thrived in nasal epithelial cells—the lining of the nose. We had already been working on some pilot experiments to create a nasal spray to deliver drugs through the epithelial lining, but in that new context we saw an opportunity to flip the script. Instead of using the nasal lining as a conduit, we reimagined it as a protective barrier and set out to create a long-acting barrier film in the nose to limit exposure to pathogens and to rapidly kill them.

AN INJECTABLE GEL THAT TARGETS THE DELIVERY AND TIMED RELEASE OF ANTIPAIN MEDICATIONS. One problem with existing injections and devices for the management of back and knee pain is that many of them don't work well enough or their effects are short lived. We decided to collaborate with an expert in the area on an approach that starts with a drug that is designed to work for a short time but then protects the drug in the body, releasing it slowly and exactly where it is needed, potentially providing relief for months from only one injection.

TAKE A CHANCE ON CHANCE ENCOUNTERS

Our genetics incline us, as a species, to be supersocial and quick adapters by our propensity to generate dynamic connections with others. We're biologically and psychologically equipped to adapt to the randomness of life and then to connect with others and remain in sync amid our neuro-variability and the random environment. Yet our social interactions tend to become narrow in content because we often gravitate toward familiar social circles, which narrows the aperture of our exposure to new stimuli and limits that source of creativity. In 2015, an opportunity arose for me to move the laboratory from near MIT in Cambridge to a new building in the Longwood Medical and Academic Area in Boston. There was no obvious immediate reason to move—the lab had been there for eight years and everything was great—and initially I was against the idea.

I feared the move because it would be a lot of effort. We would have to shut the lab down during the move, and it presented some challenges—moving lots of chemicals. But the more I thought about it, the more I realized that change can shake things up, especially when it puts you into the flow of activity that provides greater opportunity for random encounters with people and projects of interest. So in 2017, we made the move to the new building, which is part of the Brigham and Women's Hospital (my home institution), and this has in fact led to all kinds of new chance encounters with doctors and colleagues, from hallway encounters to presentations and discussion groups. This ease of exchange has led to many new projects in collaboration with infectious disease doctors, pulmonologists, and anesthesiologists I'd never have bumped into in our previous location. The building also houses a robust clinical operation (patient care), where I landed for treatment myself in the orthopedic department a couple summers ago when I injured my wrist when I accidentally hit a rock while golfing. More important, we're now in close proximity to a setting and the people—patients and clinicians—who inspire our work in the first place.

It might seem counterintuitive to think that you can bring intention to randomness. But it's your *relationship* with randomness that you can change and, in doing so, boost your brain's capacity for creativity. Here's one way to think about it, from nature's playbook, drawing from different theories, synthesized and greatly simplified: We are hardwired for adaptability, born into an environment that is awash in spontaneous, random events, from unpredictable molecules to anomalies in the weather and the social behavior of people around us. One of the functions that scientists have theorized about the brain's default mode network (DMN), that always-on roam mode, is that it picks up on the random bits and is constantly processing them as part of the loose narrative the mind weaves and reweaves about past, hypothetical, and future events. Human creativity is highly adaptive; below our level of awareness our brain is constantly sampling the environment and devising ways to respond to it. Our minds often gravitate toward the comforts of structure, which can be helpful in comparing and contrasting everything we experience as a way to learn. However, we can also develop an awareness that cues us when we are gravitating toward structure, and structure is not necessarily beneficial (e.g., bureaucracy, harmful cultural norms). Randomness is a useful ping in that creative system.

Serendipity, random events, and encounters that put you in the path of fortuitous social "collisions" with new people and new experiences will happen with some effort on your part.

> *It's really important to take yourself completely out of your comfort zone. In the morning, take a cold shower—do something so bad it makes the rest of the day easy.*
>
> —JOE DE SENA

Step Out of Your Comfort Zone and into the *Lit* Zone

Here are some simple steps that can get your mind ready for larger changes. The bigger the leaps of faith (the more risks you take), the bigger the leaps you'll make next time (the more risks you'll be willing to take). Feeling some resistance? Remember that it's natural but also that anxiety, fear, and other uncomfortable sensations can be rocket fuel for growth.

Lower the activation energy by focusing on the positive aspects and recuing discomfort as a positive sign. Work on developing a new skill that takes you out of your comfort zone. Say "yes" to tasks outside your area of expertise, with the understanding that you'll find others with more experience as you need them. You'll also be building resilience against future (inevitable and expected) failure.

Some strategies I've found that help make new easier to do:

- Prioritize with a calendar assist. Put it on your calendar. Make a practice of meeting new contacts in other fields—try for at least once a month—to learn more about them and their work and see what you might share that could be of interest to them.
- Say "yes" to tasks or invitations outside the zone of your expertise. Deliberately placing yourself in unfamiliar settings or roles for which you may feel poorly qualified can stimulate your creative energy to meet a challenge. In the process, your brain will develop new connections that will give you greater resources, resilience, and confidence going forward.
- Change up some simple habits, such as the hand you use to brush your teeth, hold your fork, or soap yourself in the shower. Try throwing a ball or Frisbee with your nondominant hand. When you sit down to eat, try closing your eyes for a few bites and feel how your awareness wakes up to the flavor and texture of your food.
- Make a notes file on your computer and brainstorm some things that you might like to try. Include a mix of quick dips—visiting a new

park, trying an unfamiliar cuisine, learning beginner dance moves on YouTube. Strive for variety, including easy short-term goals and more challenging long-term goals. Look at the list often to add ideas and get inspiration.

- Attend a talk (in person or via Zoom) by an expert in something you're curious about.
- Add a song or two to your playlist from outside your usual musical preferences.
- Send a personal note of appreciation to someone you routinely see.
- Try ending your shower with a brisk and bracing switch to icy cold water. Then try starting your shower with cold water. Saunas are said to lead to the release of dopamine and beta-endorphins (pain suppressors) that create a sense of euphoria, calm, and pain tolerance, and cold creates hormetic stress, which increases the brains sensitivity to endorphins and norepinephrine, boosting stress tolerance.
- Turn to household tasks with a conscious appreciation for the things you can do to make your habitat more habitable.
- Put yourself where fortuitous social collisions with new people and new experiences can happen with little effort on your part. Start a conversation with someone in a checkout line, or volunteer at a local food bank or animal shelter and chat with others.
- Try timing the start of your day to see the sunrise, take a walk at sunset, or pick any moment outdoors to pay attention to the nuances in light, colors, sounds, temperature, and other sensory experiences.
- Pivot your perspective. If you're consumed with detail, shift to the wider view. Observe a situation from a different point of view. Shift from heavy thinking to hands-on doing—something physical to get yourself moving.

FOCUS BEYOND FAILURE

Tee Up Energy for Renewed Action

Use the emotional charge of failure to
fine-tune where you channel your
purposeful efforts.

I've missed more than nine thousand shots in my career.
I've lost almost three hundred games. Twenty-six times,
I've been trusted to take the game-winning shot and
missed. I've failed over and over and over again in my life.
And that is why I succeed.

—MICHAEL JORDAN

Diana Nyad, the famed endurance swimmer, first gained fame in 1975 when she completed a twenty-eight-mile swim around Manhattan in record time. Four years later, on her thirtieth birthday, she swam 102 miles, from North Bimini Island in the Bahamas to Juno Beach, Florida. At that time it was the longest recorded ocean swim, and she completed it in twenty-seven hours, twenty-eight minutes, an amazing feat.

Less well known are Nyad's failures. I mention them here because, in the pantheon of failures—minor to significant, insignificant to ruinous—they were "good" ones. But the value of each failure wasn't obvious at the time.

In her twenties, Nyad set as one of her goals a nonstop swim from Cuba to Florida, a distance of 110 miles—the equivalent of almost four marathons—through often stormy waters swarming with sharks and especially poisonous stinging jellyfish. Her first try came in 1978. For safety, she swam inside a shark cage. She swam for forty-two hours, traveling 76 miles, but contrary winds and eight-foot swells pushed her away from Florida toward Texas. The rough water slammed her into the cage, and she was forced to abandon the attempt. The following year, after the Bimini–to–Juno Beach exploit, she retired from long-distance swimming and began a long career in journalism and broadcasting.

But she never lost the desire to swim from Cuba to Florida. And so, more than thirty years after the first failure, she organized a support team and began training for another attempt. She failed twice in 2011, once because of an asthma attack and once when a massive swarm of jellyfish wrapped their tentacles around her neck, around her right biceps, down her right arm, and across her back.

A lightning storm ended attempt number four after fifty-one hours in the water, and you might think that that would have been the quest's end. But in 2013, on her fifth try and at the age of sixty-four, she completed a crossing in fifty-two hours, fifty-four minutes.

Staggering onto shore, surrounded by a cheering crowd, she urged others to persevere in pursuit of their dreams and to take three points to heart: First, "never, ever give up." Second, "you never are too old to chase your dreams." And third, work with others when that's what it takes, as she did. "It looks like a solitary sport, but it's a team," she said.

What changed between her first failed attempt, her three subsequent failures, and her final success? She *learned* from each swim. She got rid of the shark cage, relying instead on teammates skilled in repelling sharks. She learned how to protect herself from jellyfish stings. She worked on navigation management. She never stopped training.

"Life isn't the way we want it to be," she told me. "The best thing we can do is engage. I don't have a fear of failing; I have a fear of not trying."

As we talked, I realized that I was hearing an epic story of personal evolution—one *aha*, one modification at a time—which, put all together and with some luck with variables such as weather, came to this successful conclusion: Nyad, battered and exhausted, yet succeeding, making it onto the beach. It reminded me of the work we do in the lab and how it trains us to focus forward and treat failure as an intrinsic—valuable and essential—part of success.

BOB LANGER: DON'T GET LOST IN FAILURES

We live in a culture that frowns on failure. And of course, no one likes to fail. Yet failure happens; horrendous failures, such as the space shuttle *Columbia* and *Challenger* disasters, as well as more commonplace failures, such as the demise of a business venture or a poor grade on a test. Though it's important to learn from failures, what's more important is the process you engage in responding to them and how you change that process over time.

This is drilled into anyone who works in scientific research. In my lab, nine of every ten experiments fail. We get no result, or the result we got isn't at all what we had expected. Doing good science requires the determination to keep trying, keep reflecting, keep asking deeper questions, and keep thinking about new ways to approach a problem. Some may say that we haven't failed until we give up trying. Iteration—the continual massaging of ideas until the most effective approach emerges—is a powerful tool for gaining a deep understanding of a problem and ways to approach and solve it. That includes complications, setbacks, and unexpected results, including failure.

Of course, sometimes failures are crushing to our intellect, spirit, and bank account, especially if we've invested too much personal capital in a particular solution that flops. The *lit* response embraces the opportunity that emerges from failure. Reflect deeply on it. Sleep on it. Collect insights and cultivate a new iteration of the plan. Take the idea of a "growth mindset" and set it on fire. Referring to the concepts developed and popularized by the psychologist and Stanford professor Carol Dweck in her book *Mindset: The New Psychology of Success*, executive coaching CEO Peter Bregman writes in *Harvard Business Review:* "If you have a growth mindset, then you use your failures to improve. If you have a fixed mindset, you may never fail, but neither do you learn or grow." Every time I've failed I feel as though I've been punched in the face! But try to remember that examples of success are often correlated with similar examples of failure through which someone persevered.

In 2007, when I first became a junior faculty member at Brigham and Women's Hospital after about three years of learning in my mentor Bob Langer's lab at MIT, I was excited to pursue a whole range of projects. But to do that, I needed research grants to support myself, my small team, and the lab. Grants don't fall from trees. They are graded by review committees that look at every request skeptically. At the National Institutes for Health, for example, fewer than 20 percent of research requests are successful, and the number can drop to less than 10 percent for certain institutes and types of grants.

During my first two and a half years on the faculty, my personal grant success rate was abysmal. I submitted more than a hundred proposals for funding, and almost all of them were rejected. Every time I was rejected, I felt like I was letting everyone down. Often I only made matters worse when I let my ego jump in. When I received a grant or paper rejection, I would tell myself that the reviewers had been crazy to reject it, that the process was unfair, that my hard work entitled me to the rewards.

At the time, I was caught up in the indignity of failure and desperate to succeed. I thought about grants every day and every night as I tried to fall asleep. It was brutal, so much so that more than once Jessica asked me whether I had made the right career choice. The pressure was immense.

But Bob Langer taught me not to get lost in my failures. He said, "It's the grants you *get* that count!" So I worked to learn why my grant proposals weren't working. I attended seminars and lectures on proposal writing. I began to listen more carefully to peers and mentors, who said that my submissions needed more preliminary data as a first proof of concept. I paid close attention to feedback I received that the methods we were proposing were not going deep enough, that we hadn't detailed our backup plan, that the project was too risky, or that I lacked the expertise necessary to be successful.

I learned that each grant submission has to be "derisked" by including data to show promise, a lab team that includes necessary expertise, extremely detailed work and experiment plans, reviews of work that others have done in the area, and proof that we're asking the right questions to make a difference. In *lit* terms, I needed to shift the focus of my grant proposals from potential energy to action and impact. The feedback I was getting was iterative gold for learning how to successfully prepare grant applications. I eventually realized that I was not failing at writing grant proposals; I was engaged in a process of being schooled in grantsmanship. With each miss, I internalized the feedback and looked for opportunities to incorporate it into my next proposal. I slowly started to think of my "product" as my evolving approach as much as a finished grant. Finally, in year three of my lab, I won three large NIH grants, and my lab's financial foundation was secure.

I still worry about funding; that never goes away entirely. But I worry from an entirely different base, because my purpose-driven colleagues and I have shown that we have a deep sense of *why*—that we know how to tackle problems, shape answers, and translate new knowledge into medical advances that can improve the lives of millions of people.

It became more and more apparent that the real obstacle to innovation is that people are afraid of failing.
—SAMUEL WEST, CREATOR OF THE MUSEUM OF FAILURE

A BIAS AGAINST FAILING KEEPS US FROM MANAGING FAILURE BETTER

Why are we so reluctant to talk about our failures? It robs us of the opportunity to make the most of them. This silence costs us, says Allison S. Catalano, who researched learning from failure for her doctoral degree at Imperial College, London. Catalano and her colleagues have studied why, and how, instances of failure are rarely mentioned in the academic literature despite its ubiquity in practice. "Despite the central role failure plays in every human endeavor, the words we use to describe our deviation from an ideal outcome carry emotional baggage and social stigma," she wrote. "We instinctively understand that experiencing setbacks offers powerful opportunities for learning and growth but also internalize messages from an early age that failure is something to be avoided, and therefore deny ourselves the chance to learn from such failures."

Catalano's research focused on teams and organizations working in environmental conservation, the field of protecting and maintaining ecosystems. She suggests that practitioners in her discipline—and others—begin "with an acceptance of the inevitable nature of failure." She finds it unhelpful that academic journals, websites, and newsletters traditionally discourage authors from writing about their failures. "Ultimately, success breeds complacency and overconfidence, reinforces the status quo, generates a cultural milieu less tolerant of experimentation and change, and increases risk aversion," she wrote. None of which makes good science.

Catalano and her colleagues identified a series of cognitive biases that often discourage managers from acknowledging failure and using it wisely. (The same applies to all of us in the way cognitive biases limit our ability to confront failure and learn from it.) In addition to some familiar biases, such as confirmation bias and blind spots, the study suggests that other biases may be in play if you tend to:

- Assume that your own worldview is the "real" one and that others who do not agree must be ignorant, unreasonable, irrational, or wrong (known as "naive realism")
- Strongly prefer avoiding losses to acquiring gains (referred to as "loss aversion")
- Blame bad outcomes on another person's personal shortcomings rather than situational factors that may have been beyond the person's control (known as the "fundamental attribution error")
- Link an unrelated series of events together into a seemingly logical story by imposing a pattern of causality on what you observe (called the "narrative fallacy")
- Systematically overlook critical, easily accessible, and relevant information (referred to as "bounded awareness")

Overcoming these biases opens a more accurate, expansive, and nuanced view of both success and failure. With that clarity, you may discover greater value in some of your failures and fresh insights that could add to the value of any success.

SUCCESSFULLY PROVING THAT SOMETHING DOESN'T WORK

Wilhelm Conrad Röntgen, the German mechanical engineer and physicist who won the first Nobel Prize in Physics, discovered X-rays quite unexpectedly as he studied cathode radiation, which is produced when an electrical charge is applied to two metal plates inside a vacuum tube. Röntgen noticed that a light-sensitive screen nearby gave off a faint light. He spent weeks searching for the source of that surprising glow, leading to the discovery of X-rays. Röntgen's tale of discovery, like that of so many others in the Nobel Prize pantheon, celebrates the circuitous routes that eventually lead to (sometimes surprising) success.

Closer to our own time, the 2011 physics Nobel was awarded to Saul Perlmutter of the Lawrence Berkeley National Laboratory and the team of Brian P. Schmidt of the Australian National University and Adam G. Riess of Johns Hopkins University and the Space Telescope Science Institute. The Perlmutter and Schmidt/Riess teams thought their work would show that expansion of the universe is slowing. Instead, in 1997, they found that the universe's expansion was actually speeding up because of "dark energy," a cosmological constant that pervades all space. "When we started the project, I thought we were just going out and doing a simple measurement of the brightness of exploding stars, and finding out whether the universe was going to end," Perlmutter said in an interview years later. "It turned out that what we discovered was a huge surprise. We have been comparing it to throwing an apple up in the air, and finding that it doesn't fall back to Earth but instead blasts off into outer space, mysteriously moving faster and faster."

Perlmutter emphasizes that "science isn't a matter of trying to prove something—it is a matter of trying to figure out how you are wrong and trying to find your mistakes."

It's important to remember that Perlmutter had begun his work eighteen years earlier. Nothing about his research was direct, as in "If we find A, that will lead us to B." Rather, it was a dogged pursuit for information about supernovae, using land-based and space telescopes, self-made computer software that analyzed great swaths of starry space, resets of plans based on the discovery of a new subclass of supernovae, construction of a new wide-field camera type, and much, much more—iterations of iterations, based on work at home, abroad, and in space.

Very few people in the world are engaged in such intensive scientific inquiry, but the following principles of how to respond productively to surprises, disappointments, and failures are the same for all of us:

- Regard bumps in the road as opportunities to iterate your process. Failure hurts, but it sets the stage for the next advance. Make the most of it. A good night's sleep can help the hurt fade quickly, and the reflection and even the emotions it brings out almost always lead to new ideas.

- Cultivate a culture at work and at home in which unsuccessful attempts (or successful attempts at proving something doesn't work) are a source of beneficial discussion and action. When failure is understood as being part of a process—an expectation of it— both kinds of outcomes become opportunities to spur creativity, maximize learning, and nourish collaboration and teamwork. Everyone gets to improve their problem-solving process.

- Look for cognitive bias that might be interfering with your analysis of a situation. I often find if I am sure I'm right about something that has gone wrong, chances are I need to rethink my assumptions.

AIM FOR CONSTRUCTIVE FAILURE

Even great ideas fail when there is insufficient appreciation of how they must interact with the real world. It happens to people in all walks of life;

they discover belatedly that their great idea doesn't have buy-in from the rest of the team or organization (or family!) or that they didn't take into account some practical considerations that present new problems. In my line of work, I hear about researchers who start a company to bring their inventions to others, yet don't understand that the market for their product or service is extremely small. Or who don't appreciate that a new approach to a problem must fit into an established distribution system or use industry-standard nomenclature and not scientific terms that we might use in the lab. The thinking is narrow—"My idea will revolutionize this process"—and there is no understanding of whether the idea fits with established practice. Some version of that was in play years ago when I failed to secure funding for the stem cell–targeting project because it was too complex. The prospective investor saw that right away. I hadn't. But that lesson transformed the lab's process going forward.

When we feel burned by such things, it's often because there's the heat of emotional attachment. But when that cools, it's possible to emerge with valuable insights and often more of a laser focus to use on the next venture. If you can take humbling first tries in stride, distill their lessons, and move on to the next thing, your chance of success becomes much greater.

Four points to keep in mind with this live-and-learn process:

- Failure plus forward motion is a winning strategy—provided that you have an evolving process for how you become aware of and absorb the insights gained. Without a process for moving forward more wisely, boring plateaus can bring you down if you're stuck there for too long. And your process needs to be personalized to work for *you*.
- Learning from others is critical, but what it lacks is figuring out what works best for you at any given moment. Observing others' processes, even trying them out, is important. At the same time, recognize that you have your own wiring that is going to connect well with certain things and not with others and that your wiring and those connections can change and evolve.
- The best-laid plans and steps to execute are great when things are working, but when they are not, switching to creative mode can

be exciting. The key is to identify insights that will enable you to experience some progress. However incremental, progress injects new energy.

- Focus on constructive failure: fail first, to learn and gain key insights that then open up a targeted process of iteration. As Michael Jordan said, "To learn to succeed, you must first learn to fail."

So many of the people we admire have come this route, learned hard lessons, and used them to guide their way forward. In the lab, it's what motivates us to find ways around an obstacle or setback. We move quickly from creative mode to execution, and if things don't work out, we switch back to creative mode, always a fun place to be. Doing so refuels our energy for another go at the problem, and this time we're often more energized than when we started and have a greater chance for success. Those we know as winners often offer the most cogent perspective on losing. NBA star Giannis Antetokounmpo did just that after his team, the Milwaukee Bucks, got knocked out of the 2023 NBA playoffs by the Miami Heat. "It's not a failure, there are steps to success," he said in a postgame press conference. "Michael Jordan played fifteen years and won six championships. The other nine years were a failure? That's what you're telling me? Exactly, so why ask me that question? It's the wrong question. There's no failure in sports. There are good days and bad days, some days you're able to be successful, and some days you're not."

NOWHERE TO HIDE

My most memorable failure (because the emotional sting makes memories stick) was in the middle of a TED Talk, my first. I forgot my lines.

It was the high-profile talk I mentioned earlier—the one I'd been so nervous about when I had been invited to do it that initially I'd said no. I hadn't memorized anything substantial since grade school when I had made short speeches, and worse still, I'd transferred out of my biology program at McGill University because I didn't want to have to memorize. I didn't know if I had it in me. But I signed on anyway.

I knew I'd need help preparing the talk, and I found it, but memorization is an inside job, and my brain makes it a nightmare. I struggled and experimented and finally found that I could memorize twenty-second bites if I practiced them over and over and over again; then I strung them together. But I also found it hard to figure out which twenty-second pieces went together. Even though I'd memorize them in the right order, nothing felt cohesive in my brain and I'd mix them up. Then I had to practice the transitions to make sure I could get them right. Once I got the fifteen-minute talk memorized, I had to practice the delivery. I practiced in front of group after group; I even rented an auditorium at MIT to feel what it would be like. The groups' feedback was useful, but any change threw off my memorization and I had to start again.

I was crazy nervous going into the speech. The technical crew told us beforehand that the slide changer goes only forward, not backward, so if we needed to go backward, we would need to yell out to people behind the curtain. That was not how I'd practiced. They tried to be encouraging to those of us readying to take the stage, telling us, "If you stop, just smile and try to regroup."

The night beforehand, I barely slept. Right before stepping up, I ate a pack of cough drops to give me a sugar boost. Onstage at last at the John F. Kennedy Center for the Performing Arts in Washington, D.C., five high-definition cameras were trained on me to live stream my speech around the world—intimidating! The president of my hospital was there, too, in the audience, also slated to give a talk.

Everything started well. In fact, I knew the talk so well that I started thinking of other things while giving it—it's just the way I'm wired. And then suddenly, I realized I'd missed a line. *Oh, shit!* Then I got so focused on my error that I stumbled, completely forgot where I was in the talk that I knew so well it was almost robotic. And then I stopped. *Shit shit shit—they told me to smile—just do that!* So then I was smiling but thinking *Oh, shit,* and I smiled for what felt like forever. In that highest-pressure moment of my life, with everyone watching, all I could think was *I have failed publicly and spectacularly. What can I do? What can I do? Advance the slides.* I did—and the next one was blank. Then I remembered that I'd put the blank slide there myself as a cue, and I moved ahead.

I recovered, and as I was leaving, the cheerful organizer assured me that the talk had gone well and the production team could easily cut out the pause in production. Afterward, people came up and said they'd seen me pause, "but what a recovery!"

From then on, I knew that if it happened again, I could recover. That alone lowered the activation energy to do more. Better yet, I learned what I needed to do to improve my process, to prepare myself and my materials more effectively for that kind of venue—including being prepared for the unexpected.

Chris Hadfield is often asked about setbacks and surprises he has experienced over his long career as a fighter pilot, space station commander, and speaker. "Sure, that can happen regularly," he told me. "But hopefully, before you've gotten into a situation where the consequences are really high or where the ripple effect is irreversible, you've gained enough of a skill set that even if it may not go the way you want, you won't go down in flames. You hardly ever do anything perfectly, but to expect failure is a big part of succeeding and high performance. In fact, *eagerly* seek out failure; you want it to happen as early as possible, when the consequences are still low."

Stuart Firestein, a Columbia University biology professor, in his book *Failure: Why Science Is So Successful*, described failure as "a challenge, almost a sport in the way it gets your adrenaline going." He suggested that we square off with failure and tap the fight in our fight-or-flight response. Channel Rocky Balboa. "Figuring out why this or that experiment failed becomes a mission. It's you against the forces of failure," he wrote. "Can you see how an important discovery is more likely to happen in this state than when you are simply tabulating the results of a 'successful' experimental run? Indeed, failure truly favors the prepared mind, and it prepares that mind."

Great expectations can be inspiring and motivating, but a rigid all-or-nothing mindset sets you up for a fall that can make it hard to pick yourself up, learn from the failure, and improve in the next round. Seeing any failure as part of the process helps.

Maria Pereira, the cofounder and chief innovation officer of Tissium, which engineers biodegradable materials for tissue reconstruction, worked on research in the Karp Lab that led to the creation of an adhesive that can seal holes in large blood vessels and inside a beating heart. Repeated failures were inevitable, given the mix of factors that had to align perfectly for the new technology to succeed, and managing everyone's expectations and disappointment was essential to keep the energy high. "It's not just about keeping your motivation," she says, "but also to help others to understand that it's part of the process and keep them engaged."

> *There's nothing wrong with having a goal. It's being attached to the goal, expecting an outcome, and being resistant to change that creates unhappiness.*
> —JAMES DOTY

YOU'VE COME A LONG WAY—GIVE YOURSELF CREDIT FOR DOING SO

Every creature or plant that is alive today has overcome all kinds of challenges and solved insurmountable problems. Do you see dinosaurs as a failure? They ruled the Earth for 150 million years! *Homo sapiens* have been around for only a few hundred thousand years. If dinosaurs had "succeeded," we might not be around to have this conversation. Obviously, there's no way to know what evolution has in store for us. Perhaps nature itself doesn't even "know" what's in store for us—evolution is a process. But part of our distinct repertoire of adaptive survival skills is that we can choose to use our intelligence in the most, well, intelligent way. We can step up from whatever version of primordial swamp thinking has us mired and uninspired, and choose a response that truly serves us. In my own case, one of my failure responses is to shame myself, versus just considering what I may do differently next time should a similar situation arise, and how much better that will go—flip the switch from negative to positive. I'm working on it.

When we're accustomed to being in a dependably safe environment, our genetics understandably program us to avoid all failure in order to survive. We are also programmed to learn from failure to avoid future failures. But we can tweak this to our advantage by embracing the value of failure for the potential insights gained, harvesting whatever is useful from every experience. Don't let fear keep you from taking actions that have minimal risk and a huge potential upside.

Flip Failure to Jump-Start Creativity

Nobody wants to review their disappointments when they're still in the struggle, but eventually we find our way forward. Sometimes that's to a successful outcome on a project or in a situation. Sometimes it's to changes or shifts that eventually lead to better times. When you can, take a moment to reflect and perhaps jot down hurdles or memorable setbacks that felt like failures and appreciate the role they played in the eventual positive outcome. Refer to the list the next time you need to remember what you've overcome before. My own list has a couple dozen entries at least. I now see every one of my grant proposal rejections (more than a hundred) in a very different light from when they were fresh disappointments.

Consider these ways to reframe and reflect on failure for success:

- Embrace failure as a problem-solving tool. Every innovation is the product of continuous iteration, adjustments to our thinking or the process as we uncover new or overlooked insights. In science, the goal isn't to succeed in the beginning; it's to develop a process for learning through experimentation. In the lab, we never have all the information we need when we start. We use failure to continually discover new pieces of information, new solutions, and new insights.
- Aim for quicker rebounds. Refocus your attention, and ask high-yield questions using "back to brainstorm" mode.
- Resist being impatient with incremental improvements. It takes time to test, find weak spots in the system, and talk about them with a team of diverse thinkers and begin again, if necessary.

- Ask people in your circle who have had successes to talk about their failures and how they overcame them.
- Create a "fail fast" culture—a safe zone for failures and the process of learning from them—at home and at work to spur creativity, maximize learning, end perfection paralysis, and nourish collaboration and teamwork.
- Build a team of advisers to identify blind spots, to push you beyond your perceived capabilities and provide the *lit* spark needed to rekindle energy if it flags after a failure.
- Reflect on a past failure that eventually led to evolution or progress and how you made it through. Consider how time helped you deal with your charged emotions, find support from others, benefit from sleep, and have the opportunity to reflect and update your mindset to generate new ideas and renewed enthusiasm.
- When you're in a good place to appreciate the ups and downs that have led to a success, create a list of failures past. Mine is long! The backward glance can help you keep your failures in perspective for yourself, and your story may help others do so as well.
- Embrace trial and error, and recognize failure as part of nature's process. Evolution is a continuum on the grand scale but also in our personal evolution. We are fully empowered to sustain that continuum by utilizing our extraordinary abilities to engage in complex reasoning, introspection, and decision-making to infinitely evolve and flourish.

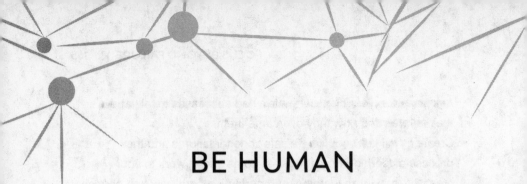

BE HUMAN

Be Humble

Let awe be your access point for inspiration
and your capacity for greater good.

Have the humility to learn from those around you.
—JOHN C. MAXWELL, LEADERSHIP CONSULTANT,
AUTHOR, AND PASTOR

In many cultures, tradition holds that when you enter someone's home, you take off your shoes and leave them by the door. It's a simple show of respect, a way of acknowledging that you're stepping into someone else's space with humility. Symbolically you've checked your ego at the door.

If somewhere along life's journey you've absorbed the idea that being humble means being meek or weak, science says otherwise. A growing body of research suggests that humble people handle stress better, are healthier both physically and mentally, and are more tolerant of ambiguity and differences than are people who are less humble. Appreciating and thinking of other people's best interests activates various neural networks, some related to cognitive learning, others to emotional intelligence, all of which foster feelings of connection to others and, more broadly, a sense of humanity—humility's expression facing outward. When you are grounded this way, your potential expands for problem solving that can do the greatest good and have the greatest impact. Love, kindness, and social intelligence, into which humility is hardwired, bring

our awareness to the fact that every single person and situation has something to teach us. Everyone on a team (or in a room or car or relationship
or society) feeling heard, appreciated, encouraged, and included builds
trust, a fundamental piece of the relationship. The dynamic benefits everyone. When you leave your ego at the door, you free up valuable space
for more important things. More specifically, humility helps us overcome
three common obstacles of our own making. Humility enables us to:

- Overcome self-absorption and me-centered thinking that obscures
  what's important to others
- Engage a larger, more complex reality that includes our
  relationship with the natural world
- Develop a sense of perspective about ourselves and the world that
  serves as an inner compass for meaning and action

MAY-BRITT MOSER: A WIN-WIN SITUATION

It might seem that humility would have nothing to do with the discovery
of brain cells essential for navigation, the science for which the Norwegian psychologist May-Britt Moser was awarded a Nobel Prize in science
in 2014. Moser passionately argues otherwise.

Moser; her then husband, Edvard; and their colleague John O'Keefe
of University College London shared the 2014 Nobel Prize in Physiology
or Medicine for their discoveries of cells that constitute a positioning
system in the brain. In 1971, O'Keefe had discovered that type of cell
close to the hippocampus, an area located in the center of the brain. In
2005, the Mosers found that when a rat passed certain points arranged
in a hexagonal grid in space, nerve cells that form a kind of coordinate
system for navigation were activated. They then went on to demonstrate
how these different cell types cooperate.

The cells, which the Mosers called grid cells, provide an internal
coordinate system essential for navigation, for knowing where you are
and how you will move to another place. In a sense, that's a fitting metaphor for the way May-Britt Moser talks about humility and a deep

collaborative sensibility as the soulful coordinates that drive the science, the people, and the environment at her lab. Without those internal values as coordinates, she insists, it's unlikely that the passion and purpose that brought them to the Nobel podium would have existed to propel their work as it has.

Moser, a psychologist as well as neuroscientist, cites culture as a significant contributor—in this case, the merger of two cultures: the traditional Norwegian culture and the diverse multicultural research lab community. Traditional Norwegian culture, which has a strong emphasis on hard work, "no-upmanship," egalitarianism, respect for others, and shared social responsibility, places a high value on humility as well as excellence, she says. The globally diverse lab community, reflecting many similar values in different ways, brings a vibrant chemistry to the social and work dynamic. Research has found that humble leadership also brings out that quality in others, creating more cohesive teams that excel. Moser agrees that it's a potent prescription.

The Kavli Institute employs individuals from more than thirty nations, "because we want people who are different so that we can have very, very interesting discussions, both about science and other things," Moser says. "We all need challenges to our thinking, and these challenges make us grow to understand things we did not understand before."

Humble people see value in errors and the information that they provide for their own learning.
—CHRISTOPH SECKLER, CHAIR OF ENTREPRENEURIAL STRATEGY,
ESCP BUSINESS SCHOOL, BERLIN

Some of the greatest CEOs I've worked with are those who recognize that inevitably there will be holes in their thinking and are constantly looking for people to pressure-test and critique what they're doing. They know what they don't know and realize that someone else may illuminate something different that may be useful or lead to something that is. That outside perspective may come from someone they already consider a valuable source or from someone totally unexpected.

In the lab, a certain amount of hubris is required for any of us to take on the challenges we routinely do. When the point of your work is to find solutions to problems that no one else has managed to do, it means spending the bulk of your time confronting the limits of what is known, up close and personal with your own ignorance. That's humbling, and worse, there's no promise of immediate relief. Can jellyfish tentacles really serve as a model for ways to snag certain cells in the bloodstream? Is it possible to stimulate minute parts of the immune system so that we will have an enhanced ability to fight cancer? The answer to both is yes, we've done it—but I can vouch for the value of the humbling moments when we met the limits of what we knew and redoubled our efforts by turning elsewhere for new leads.

If you want to fully understand and solve intractable problems, you've got to get over yourself and ask for help; seek out people who know more than you or think differently, and see what you turn up when you put your heads together. We often have to hear things multiple times, in multiple different ways, in order to internalize them, make connections, and adjust our path. Sometimes the lesson in humility comes from hearing things we may not want to hear that make us confront insecurities, fears, or biases we don't want to admit we have. To use humbling experiences to shift our thinking and approach is *lit*—and that's exciting. It can also be ego bruising. To that I say: Maximize opportunities for a bruised ego!

On my own journey, it helped me—freed me up—to realize that I'm happier, more excited, and more passionate about my work when I'm constantly surrounded by opportunities to learn—be humbled—to keep me in check and stay aware of how much I don't know. It's exciting to be able to do things I would never be able to do myself and see people in the lab stretch that way, too, to advance toward our highest-value goals. This requires that I never get too comfortable and always keep open lines of communication with my lab members. I can't possibly know everything, but if I create a free-range environment with minimal hierarchy (only when it's helpful) and focus on doing important work, I try to recruit people who know a lot about things I don't, and together we can advance the conversation in new ways. At the same time, for me—with

ADHD—an ordinary day can be constantly humbling. My mind races with all kinds of thoughts and I need to make so many choices, continuously, about what to say, what not to say, what to engage with (or disengage from), and what to let go, never knowing what will pass or what will stick in my unpredictable brain.

Humility doesn't require that you habitually defer to others; if it did, it wouldn't be a LIT tool. Though you may seek out others' expertise, also be prepared to question it. Sometimes when we work with people who have expertise in areas we don't, we may have a tendency to trust or accept their judgment. But in an environment in which every assumption is tested and turned over to see what's underneath, both parties in the exchange benefit from the mutual regard and openness to what others have to offer. The American economist and Yale professor Robert J. Shiller put it this way: "Errors of human judgment can infect even the smartest people, thanks to overconfidence, lack of attention to details, and excessive trust in the judgments of others, stemming from a failure to understand that others are not making independent judgments but are themselves following still others."

It's important to be open to the discomfort of realizing what we don't know and how narrowly we think about everything, even when we believe that that's not the case. I find this stimulating; it creates energy that can be harnessed in service of innovative solutions.

I believe that there is a subtle magnetism in Nature, which, if we unconsciously yield to it, will direct us aright.
—HENRY DAVID THOREAU, "WALKING," *THE ATLANTIC*

Dacher Keltner, a founding director of the Greater Good Science Center and professor of psychology at the University of California, Berkeley, writes about awe and the power of humbling experiences to change us. In his most recent book, he described the neurophysiology of it, how experiences—even just the memory of them—change the brain. The science is cutting edge, a dramatic step forward for modern science, which has long sidestepped the subject. But Keltner notes that research findings support the traditional Indigenous teachings that have forever held that "we are part of an ecosystem, our bodies are part of them." The ideas of the "separate self" as being different from other people and different from nature are true in one sense, he says, but the larger truth is that we sync up both with other people and with the natural world.

ELDER DAVE COURCHENE: SCIENCE MEETS SPIRIT

I find deep resonance in the way that Indigenous teachings emphasize humility as a core competency and tie it directly to the quality of our relationship with nature and spirituality. Considered sacred laws, these principles are rooted in the understanding that Earth and Spirit are living forces that we can fully integrate into our lives and embrace for a good life.

"It's a very simple, basic truth, that Mother Earth is a living entity. She is alive, just as much as you and I," the late Dr. Dave Courchene, a prominent elder of the Anishinaabe Nation in Manitoba, Canada, told me when we spoke on a Zoom call during the pandemic. "We're sitting here, and we're only one part of the web of life that we call human beings. There are many other beings within the web of life. People talk about interconnectedness, that we're all related and we're all connected, and that's an absolute truth. Whatever happens to one part of that living entity within the web of life will affect the whole web of life itself."

Nature's lessons are always present to us, but to access them we first have to recognize that whatever our individual knowledge and expertise may be, we are missing essential pieces and perspectives that only others among us with different experience can provide.

Different types of knowing, types of intelligence, include scientific, intuitive, and spiritual, among others, and no one culture or way of knowing makes the others irrelevant. Elder Courchene described decades of discussions with scientists and others whose framework for addressing global problems and solutions was through shared assumptions based on classical evidence-based science. That overlooks or ignores the deep knowledge held by others based on different ways of knowing that supported humankind's survival for thousands of years previously.

Climate change has brought the deficit in discourse into sharp relief. "They're all trying to figure out what is the answer to dealing with climate change, so they come in from the point of view, from their own comfort, of what they have learned as scientists or intellectuals. Where is the conversation in terms of allowing Indigenous people to speak from their place of comfort and their own intelligence, which is in defining that relationship with the land, and the simple understanding that our people have always said, 'What you do to the land, you do to yourself; you are the land.' We see it more than ever today, that what we have done to the land, we have really done to ourselves."

Search for the Sacred in the ordinary with gratitude in your heart and you will surely find it.
—SARAH BAN BREATHNACH

We spoke the summer before Courchene passed in December 2021, having devoted his life to the creation of Turtle Lodge International Centre for Indigenous Education and Wellness in Manitoba, Canada, on the southern tip of Lake Winnipeg.

Turtle Lodge is now a thriving cultural hub not only for Indigenous communities globally but for the growing numbers of others awakening to the awareness that the knowledge and wisdom carried down through thousands of years of Indigenous experience are critically important to us all. Similar resources exist in cultures around the globe, where their deep experience with environmental factors, including the human factor, is a well of knowledge and expertise that supports life. We have everything we need to replace hubris with humility, and *lit* thinking will find new paths forward.

Some would say that spirituality creates that path, enabling us to walk the temporal realm with the touchstone of the transcendent present to us, especially through nature, a humbling influence if we allow it to be. But that can be a challenge in today's cultural landscape, Courchene said. "That's not easy to convey to people who are very highly intellectual; usually the person is quite used to scientific proof, that there must be evidence to show me that there is spirit. And that's something we cannot do. When we talk about spirit, that's a totally different realm of understanding. But within the way of life of Indigenous people, that is the reality of our world, the existence of the spiritual influence that many of us consider the higher power of influence.

"As Indigenous people, you know, when the Europeans first arrived, they did not recognize or respect that we were very advanced spiritually and how that spirituality was reflected in the way that we took care of the land and in the way that the children were centered in our communities," he told me. Despite systematic efforts by colonizers to eliminate Indigenous people—taking their land and their lives and forcing their assimilation by taking their children and forbidding the use of their native languages and traditional customs and rituals—the core values still taught today in the sacred laws and tribal education remain those that have been passed down through the millennia. The fact that humility remains an essential teaching has drawn new interest as science has begun to catch up with long-standing Indigenous intelligence, and more people are becoming interested in tapping that knowledge base and perspective to try to bring about an equilibrium in our natural world as we confront catastrophic environmental change.

> *In Indigenous ways of knowing, it is understood that each living being has a particular role to play. Every being is endowed with certain gifts, its own intelligence, its own spirit, its own story.*
>
> —ROBIN WALL KIMMERER, *GATHERING MOSS: A NATURAL AND CULTURAL HISTORY OF MOSSES*

LYNNE TWIST:
TRANSFORMING PREMISE AND POTENTIAL

The world of philanthropy was due for an overhaul when Lynne Twist, at the time a global activist working to end world hunger, was inspired to make a dramatic shift in her fundraising approach from the traditional charity model, in which moneyed donors define a problem to be solved and determine a plan to fix it, often without meaningful input from those receiving the funds. Working alongside members of Indigenous cultures around the world, she said, had exposed her to the problem with that power dynamic. The implicit bias was made explicit: the haves helped the have-nots, who were expected only to be grateful, however much the infusion of money or poorly prepared volunteers might disrupt the community. Projects often failed due to a fundamental lack of understanding about the roots of a problem. Humbled by that awareness and guided by an intuitive sense, she reconceptualized her mission as "fundraising from the heart" and pioneered a new paradigm for philanthropy grounded in problem-solving partnerships in which everyone's resources become valued contributions and a rigorous problem-solving process generates strategic action that channels money, time, specialty expertise, and deep knowledge of the problem in order to have the greatest impact. Twist went on to cofound the Pachamama Alliance, which partners with Indigenous people of the Amazon rain forest to preserve their lands and culture. She describes the coequal partnership as both essential and humbling, especially for those from outside that culture who want to support effective and sustainable change. Twist explained that she learned those lessons early on in her work with communities in sub-Saharan Africa and Asia, where the key to addressing hunger and poverty was to empower women as strong community and business leaders.

When the Pachamama Alliance began partnering with Indigenous peoples in the Amazon rain forest, Twist came prepared for a similar dynamic but discovered something very different. The communities were neither impoverished nor going hungry. And the women had a different view of their power and strategies as changemakers than the Western version of empowerment and voice. In fact, early direct actions to change particular customs in the community were rebuffed by the women themselves. So for more than a decade, the partnership focused on other solutions to challenges the communities faced, as deforestation threatened their survival.

Eventually the women sought out the help they determined they needed: access to a midwifery program to dramatically improve women's education and practices supporting safer pregnancy and childbirth, which they then created with their Pachamama partners. To accomplish their goal to share this knowledge among the tribes in their region, the women launched literacy and leadership initiatives for girls and women and began traveling from community to community to teach the techniques. The result of the childbirth education program has been significantly fewer deaths of women and their babies in the vulnerable pre- and postnatal period, Twist says.

Leaving her preconceived ideas and assumptions at the door, developing relationships based on respect, and listening to learn was and continues to be essential, she says. "I really learned that whatever *I* think about what they could or should be doing, it's not even helpful. It's what *they* see the opening is for them. And once they see that opening, then we can offer a coequal partnership. It's not giving to 'have-nots.' It's women who know the territory, know the local language, know what the needs are, know what they can and can't accommodate. Those are the assets that they have, and we bring the financial resources that can be helpful in making that program work."

Those closest to the problem are often closest to the solution.
It is as important to know when to step back as it is to
know when to step up.
—REGINALD "REGGIE" SHUFORD, EXECUTIVE DIRECTOR,
NORTH CAROLINA JUSTICE CENTER

AWESOME, HUMBLING—AND *LIT*

Almost any day in the lab, we are at some point in a project that has us tracking leads on ways that nature has solved a problem. In the patterns, processes, and ingenious designs evolved across geological time, a spider's web is no less spectacular than the Grand Canyon. What we encounter in that search is truly awe inspiring, and it's humbling to see nature's intrinsic creativity and precision as a problem solver—and mentor. One example gives me brain goose bumps just remembering it: jellyfish tentacles.

In the treatment of metastatic cancer, even after a patient's primary tumor is surgically removed, the challenge remains to identify the drug that can kill the residual cancer. A promising approach involves taking a sample of blood from the patient and passing it through a device to isolate the circulating tumor cells that are coming from the metastatic sites. The problem is that the device involves the capture of cells on a surface, and cells that are streaming by—just a human hair away—are not captured. Those that are captured are so tightly bound to the surface (by antibodies) that it's nearly impossible to remove them intact to identify the drug needed to kill them.

So we asked: What creature in nature can capture things at a distance? Jellyfish! They have long tentacles that extend far from the main body to capture food and prey. So we developed synthetic tentacles made of DNA that could specifically attach to the surface of cancer cells, wrap around them, and immobilize them on our device. We were able to match the high efficiency rate of previous methods but also do it at ten times the flow rate, meaning we could flow ten times as much blood through our device in the same amount of time. And because the artificial tentacles are made of DNA, we could simply add enzymes to release the cells in pristine, viable condition to study to find the drug match that would kill the residual tumor cells. After a year or so of research and development, the moment with the microscope when we were able to witness the effect of the DNA tentacles capturing the cancer cells was simply breathtaking. I can still see it in my mind's eye and feel the awe that swept through us all. We were thrilled—and humbled—that a solution nature had designed for jellyfish survival had worked through the human imagination to evolve a new tool for cancer patients' survival.

Bioinspirational work is routinely humbling this way. But that's only the half of it. There's also the human factor. People can be so awesome when you take the time to hear their stories or witness their everyday acts of what Dacher Keltner calls "moral beauty": kindness, courage, overcoming obstacles, saving lives. Based on the 2,600 narratives he collected globally and analyzed for purposes of his book, he identified and ranked the most common sources of awe people reported. "Time and time again the most common source of awe is other people," he said. "And you wouldn't think that given what we look at on Twitter and Instagram, but it's a deep, deep tendency to choke up and get tears thinking about what people can do."

You don't have to look far to find awe that way. In the lab, as in so many workplaces, over time we hear one another's stories woven through casual conversation. Some are about family members or individual hopes and dreams, challenges and setbacks, and the perseverance that brought them through. Another way we share our stories is intentional. Two or three times a year, our regular Wednesday meeting for project discussion takes an irregular turn. We set aside that time for individuals to present a three-minute talk on a topic they are curious or passionate about. It could be anything. Recent headliners included someone who was curious about stand-up comedy and did a routine for us; another person talked about a bakery their family had run for years and years that had had to shut down during Covid and their resilience as they determined that they would build it back up as a life mission. Someone spoke about competitive synchronized swimming and passing out underwater during a routine because they needed to hold their breath for so long. Someone spoke about being in their high school band and had us close our eyes as they played music by it. An all-time hit was a musical review of the best hamburgers in Boston, set to a rap beat, by burger lover (and cell biologist) Dustin Ammendolia.

For me, there is something awesome in hearing the stories, a kind of flow state. Part of it is the shared experience, and for me, there is something highly energetic about passion and curiosity, whether the focus is on biology or burgers. When you tap into that energy and recognize it in the people right next to you, it is captivating.

Awe tells us to go out and expand your view on things.

—DACHER KELTNER, SCIENTIST, AUTHOR

BOB LANGER:
A FATHER'S LEGACY AS A TOUCHSTONE

Bob Langer is roundly admired as a kind of force of nature, the ultimate innovator and medical science translator. Over the course of a long and distinguished career, he has made several breakthroughs that have challenged conventional wisdom in the field, revolutionizing the way drugs are delivered. These inventions have positively impacted an estimated 25 percent of the world's population, including 3.9 billion people globally who received the Moderna vaccine based on decades of drug delivery research in his lab.

Langer is celebrated for his brilliance, but among those who know him, his humble nature is as legendary. He sees the potential in everyone and shows it. He makes everyone feel important, respecting their time, efforts, and interests. He is quick to give credit to others and express appreciation for their individual work and contributions. On projects, he points people in a positive direction and aligns them with the mission. He talks about his greatest source of pride not as his accomplishments but as the people who have trained in his labs.

This especially stands out in the academic world, where competition and ego can crowd out better angels such as kindness.

Langer considers himself to be a happy person, with just cause, thanks to a loving family, the passion and purpose he finds in (and brings to) his life's work, and his belief in the basic goodness of others, he says.

"I've been lucky," he says. His mother, a lifelong homemaker, still issues caring edicts when she calls to be sure he has dressed adequately for inclement weather. His father, who died at age sixty-one, when Bob was twenty-eight, left him with two stories that have always stayed close to his heart, touchstones for trying times and a formative inspiration for his worldview.

One was personal. "My dad grew up in the Great Depression, a really tough time, and he saw a lot of successful people kill themselves because they went from being zillionaires to having no money. Then he fought in World War II and had friends die, saw a lot of people who didn't make it back. Those were tough things to live through, humbling times." Whatever else happened, he says, "my dad always said that he felt that every day he got after World War II was a gift. That was useful to me."

The other belongs to baseball history but transcends it and is never far from Langer's mind as he works to advance innovations in medicine. New York Yankees legend Lou Gehrig died of amyotrophic lateral sclerosis (ALS), also called Lou Gehrig's disease, in 1941, when he was just thirty-seven years old. The debilitating disease forced him to leave baseball, but the stirring farewell speech he gave at a recognition day for him two years before he died was a source of inspiration that Langer's dad shared with him through the years. "He gave this amazing speech, thanked his mother and his father, thanked many people, and he said, basically, 'I know a lot of people think I've been given a bad break, but today I consider myself the luckiest man on the face of the Earth. I've been given so much.' And I thought, what a great way to look at life. Here's a guy, he ended up dying in the prime of his life from a terrible disease, and he told the world he was the luckiest man on the face of the Earth. Every time I think of that story and all the people who got ALS after him, all the people who have had bad breaks, I think, *But what a way to look at life.*"

> *The humble are those who are concerned not simply with the past but also with the future, since they know how to look ahead, to spread their branches, remembering the past with gratitude. . . . The proud, on the other hand, simply repeat, grow rigid, and enclose themselves in that repetition, feeling certain about what they know and fearful of anything new because they cannot control it.*
>
> —POPE FRANCIS

BRINGING IT HOME

Some of the most humbling lessons I learn are as a parent. Kids don't sign on to be our teachers, but if we're lucky, they find a way to outlast our worst inclinations and eventually enlighten us. As problem solving goes, sometimes it's a circuitous path, and the "expertise" I think I have, having once been a kid myself, has been an obstacle. Best-case scenario: you remember what it was like to be your child's age, and you empathize. Worst-case scenario, or at least a problematic one: you flick right past empathy or even interest and set about directing, assuming that what worked for you at their age can work for them—not only *can* but *must*. If it doesn't, the failure is on them, not you, because the evidence from your own experience says it should work.

Problem definition and problem solving are what I do for a living, and it would be only natural to assume that I can seamlessly transfer those skills to the home front. The thing is, in the lab and in every other work relationship, an essential part of problem solving is the iterative process—the back-and-forth where we define the problem together and brainstorm about solutions and the way forward. Lots of listening and learning are built into that process. In our families, the evolution of our definition of what is important to us often gets lost. As parents, we may consider only what is important to us today, in the moment, with the emphasis on *us*. We forget to check in on what our children deem important. The biggest disconnects I have experienced at home or at work have come from not pausing to consider someone else's definition of what is important to them. Sometimes support is all that is important, all they need.

So it came as a surprise to me when Josh's seventh-grade tutor pulled me aside and suggested that I reconsider my parental version of a "campaign for excellence" to develop one's full potential. Why? I asked. The tutor told me that it was getting in the way of my son's own efforts to do just that.

I had a long think. I had drawn from my own challenging years in school and my hard-won lessons and winning strategies for achieving excellence. I thought of them as road tested. Eager to save my kids from the painful parts of my childhood, I found myself forcing my methods on both of them. I failed to take into account that using my playbook for my version of commitment and my version of success wasn't working, because my children are not me—they are their own people. Once

I accepted that obvious (to everyone but me) fact, I was able to toss my playbook and learn some new strategies.

That took practice. I needed to learn how to listen without being reactive, share a conversation instead of issuing edicts packaged as encouragement, appreciate the person each of them is, and enjoy them as they grow.

My kids continue to reinforce these lessons in humility for me. I've come to realize that the best *lit* thinking sometimes means being present just to listen, to be available, to be nearby, to give someone—especially our kids—our attention without distractions, without judgment. One thing I already envy: both my kids are hard workers, yet they have a far better work-life-play balance than anything I've ever been able to achieve. I'm taking notes.

I could have saved everyone (myself included) a lot of angst if I'd taken my own advice and left my shoes—and my ego—at the door several years ago. But I'm educable. I'm humbled. I'm learning.

The beauty of embracing your humanity—and humility as part of that—as a LIT tool is that you can start where you are right now, no prerequisites, and the activation energy is low. In the next conversation you have with someone or the next thought you have about a situation or a person, try framing it through a lens of intentional appreciation and interest, even if just for a few moments. If someone is trying to connect with you in a conversation but is managing only to push your buttons, consider that they may be unsure in the moment or running some internal algorithm built upon bad habits. Look for a way to neutralize your own reactive impulse, give them an out, or reframe the conversation to allow for a truer connection.

Opportunities abound. Often when I feel a knot of resistance or a need to be right rising from within, if I pause to consider why, I realize that something about the situation has triggered an impulse to defend or protect that little fortress sense of self. I ask myself why, and almost always I realize that the reaction is likely some primitive survival instinct that has misfired. Shifting from a me-centric to a you-centric frame of mind helps me appreciate more keenly what others are bringing to the situation.

For other practical ways to access awe and put humility into practice, consider experimenting with these:

- Tune in to nature any way you can. We are a tiny, tiny speck in the vastness of the universe yet a critical spoke in the wheel of humanity and, more broadly, nature. Sit with that. Appreciating our part in an ecosystem is a spiritually humbling experience.
- Look for the moral beauty—kindness, courage, overcoming obstacles—in everyday people and hold that thought. Hold the feeling.
- Praise others not for their end result but for the courage they had to try, their persistence to practice, the attitude they chose to keep moving forward, the risks they took despite the adversity, the effort they put in.
- Be quick to share the credit when you're singled out for praise.
- Hear criticism as an opportunity to learn how you're affecting others, regardless of your good intentions. When someone tells you that you've misstepped, strive to acknowledge it and reflect on how you might channel that insight into self-evolution.
- Take time to think through and express a meaningful apology when you've made a mistake.
- If you have skills that others don't, share your process for acquiring those skills and offer to help them learn.
- Cultivate a habit of finding the good in others, and acknowledge it, especially with children.
- Try switching from *me* thinking to *you* thinking. Listen for what's important to others. Care to ask.
- Listen when those you trust "call it as they see it" about something you're saying or doing with the intention to help you see what you're not seeing.
- Try to appreciate life's humbling moments. The more you care enough to keep trying, the more humbling—and illuminating—it may be.

PRESS "PAUSE"

Protect Time to Be and Behold

Prioritize time for unhurried play, solitude,
and silence to recharge your spirit.

*We all need to be reminded to stay connected to the essence
of who we are, to take care of ourselves along the way,
to reach out to others, to pause to wonder, and to connect to
that place from which everything is possible.*

—ARIANNA HUFFINGTON

I'd met Vivek Ramakrishnan ten years earlier in a single conversation via a chance introduction by a mutual friend, and we hadn't spoken since, when a Zoom call during Covid brought the three of us together, again somewhat by chance. Ramakrishnan is the director of venture development at the University of Connecticut, and by the time we signed off on our call, I had invited him to speak at the lab. But it was not about his work in venture capital and medical innovation; it was about his unusual meditation practice.

In our call, we had each been reflecting on our careers but also about how Covid had affected all of us. Ramakrishnan mentioned that he'd begun to study meditation and the intersection with the default mode network (DMN) more closely, brainstorming regularly with one noted neuroscientist and attending meditation retreats to focus on developing his own practice. I had recently begun experimenting with meditation techniques myself, so I was more than casually interested; I was in-trigued.

Always looking for ways to bring fresh insights and ideas to the lab, I asked if he would be open to joining us in a video call, and it was a convergence of energies. Since his first lab talk, he has returned by pop-ular demand and now speaks with us every few months. He shares new insights into the nature of impermanence, a long-standing philosophical inquiry and photo project on his blog, and a related interest, strategies for managing the brain's mind-wandering DMN rather than feeling cut helplessly adrift or distracted by it. The impermanence project is one of those strategies, a simple hands-on activity that requires only you, your camera (phone camera is fine), and a moment of your attention.

We'll turn to that shortly, but whatever way you choose to shift the energy in your day, whether by changing the pace or redirecting your attention, giving yourself a meaningful break gives your brain, mind, body, and spirit a chance to resync. It's a skill, learning how to slow down. But it's necessary to give the brain time to fully process not only the information pouring in from the world around (via sight, sound, taste, smell, touch) but also from within. The brain is constantly re-ceiving chemical and electrical signals from our organ systems, as well as from emotional and other more subtle intuitive sources. (The "gut feeling" we think of as an intuitive sense about something has biologi-cal underpinnings in the communication between gut and brain.) And finally, the brain must integrate that information to coordinate a real-time response. All of this—billions of neurons sorting and sending sig-nals and coordinating responses—happens faster than we can observe it. But we *can* intercept it. We can choose to pause to allow the rhythms of the brain to reconnect with the most fundamental rhythms of na-ture in all its surprising dimensions. We can also treat intuitive cues as invitations to pause and be receptive to different energies that emerge when we do so.

Sometimes we just need a break to clarify our thoughts and inten-tions for a course correction. Or to get unstuck. Reactive behavior can get us stuck or overswinging, distancing ourselves from people when simple connection is all we desire. But we lead with the emotional response because it has a lower activation energy; it's easier to explode than calm that impulse.

BORROW FROM WINTER'S WISDOM

The rhythms of nature show us that downtime, far from being empty or wasted time, is rich in life-sustaining activity that's different from what we typically think of as activity. In nature, the downtime of winter might look spent and barren, but it is a critical period in which the Earth and most plants and animals replenish themselves and prepare for the creative, energy-intensive activity of spring and summer. That timeless cycle carries evolution's seed of survival intelligence for us in this unnatural time of digital speed, stress, and constant activity.

All life depends on the rejuvenating power of the pause. The biological cues for it are hardwired into our circadian rhythms. We know intuitively and science confirms that the pause we get from sleep is essential for life. Ordinarily our bodies cue us to sleep at night or when we're tired, and ideally we rely on a predictable time for that pause. Sleep science tells us that sleep frees the brain to divert energy to, among other things, systemwide maintenance and regenerative processes, including routine maintenance of neurons, flushing out cellular waste, and prepping the system for a fresh restart. When we wake up feeling refreshed, there's a reason for that: the brain has been busy—actively sleeping! Chronic sleep deprivation or poor sleep, the norm for many people in the workplace and for parents of infants and young children, leads to adverse health effects. Ultimately, if we don't sleep, we die.

We need not only the pause of sleep but pauses during the day to maximize functioning and our mental health. Yet, too often we've pushed the snooze alarm on those alerts or failed to hear them, especially in the din of the digital age. The cues are still coming, but as we've moved farther and farther from attunement with nature, we've become inured to them.

We need a strategy in our lives to pause intentionally. Just like the rest of our planet in winter, we need to take time to conserve our energy, rest, restore, and prepare to resume with renewed energy. To take it a *lit* step further, we don't need to wait for signs that our energy is waning and we need a break. We can be proactive and pause and restore ourselves before our energy is spent. Through circadian rhythms, nature tells us to prioritize, to interrupt the artificial schedule that culture-driven demands impose on us and use our agency as humans to push back. It's not selfish or self-indulgent any more than other basic human needs are. Downtime is an essential phase in the brain's energy cycle. It is a necessity, not an option.

Researchers Sooyeol Kim, of the National University of Singapore; Seonghee Cho, of North Carolina State University; and YoungAh Park, of the University of Illinois, found that even microbreaks—very short periods of relaxation during the working day—boost work engagement and reduce end-of-work fatigue. Microbreaks are "an effective energy management strategy while at work," they wrote, encouraging organizations to employ microbreaks to "take an active role in promoting a health-friendly culture and high autonomy."

Music practice provides a useful analogy, as Molly Gebrian's observation about optimal practice sessions for musicians shows. Practice stimulates the brain to establish new or stronger synaptic links, but not during practice itself, she said. "The learning takes place in the breaks between practice. . . . The brain has to actually undergo physical changes to learn, which is retaining information. For the brain to do that kind of reconstruction, you can't be using it at the same time." The open, "empty" spaces, the rests between the notes in our busy lives, are vital to creativity and all of our mental processes. It is in the pauses that the brain consolidates and restores its energy reserves for new rounds of active duty.

Pair a pause with music, and all the better. Music resonates for any of us with measurable effects. Depending on the tempo and how closely our breathing matches the beat, music affects our cardiovascular and respiratory systems, and it arouses or focuses our attention, according to a study that compared the effects of music on musicians and non-musicians. Both groups enjoyed beneficial effects by listening to music, and interestingly, a pause in the music brought about an added measure of relaxation. It appears that both our learning and our relaxation groove on the pauses.

*Mindfulness is a pause—the space between stimulus
and response: that's where choice lies.*

—TARA BRACH

AN EXCITING EXPERIMENT IN IMPERMANENCE

The brain's "constant chatter, inner monologue, and random stream of thoughts make it difficult for most people to sit alone with their thoughts for extended periods of time," says Ramakrishnan. Rather than feel besieged by those things, we can befriend them. Using intention to cue a pause helps retrain the brain for it and develop the skill. "The very act of observation alters how the brain processes information and how it assigns values to our highs and lows," Ramakrishnan says. "It changes the threshold of your awareness. You don't need a big high to get pleasure, and the brain does not assign an arbitrarily low value if things don't go your way. You can train your brain to notice small changes in your everyday life, and there is a subtle joy that comes from noticing how beautiful change can be."

The wandering mind is, after all, still working in its own way. Consider it a random walk, like the one that early humans would have taken across the savanna, alert and aware of their surroundings, vigilant for threats or things of interest. Emerging research suggests that the adaptive value of this random stream of thoughts is that there is a great potential for gaining insight due to random connections. That can be annoying if you're in a circumstance that calls for focus and sustained attention. But when the pressure is off, your DMN can become an asset, one that is accessible only if you give yourself the time and permission to "go there"—and with enthusiasm. As a purely practical tool to observe a live stream of what's truly on your mind, the DMN is always on. In LEB mode, we're inclined to hear the stream as simply static, just as scientists once considered it to be. Now we know it as a creative current we can tap into at will.

As our lab members experimented with impermanence project

activities, some focused on snapping a picture of something and, while doing so, paused to connect with the subject and their feelings while taking the picture. Whatever way you choose to engage in observing nature's nuances, with or without a camera, appreciation is the important thing. It rewires the brain for greater engagement.

I decided to take images of the same flower over several days and notice subtle changes that I tend to miss. I might see a tree full of leaves but notice that it's losing leaves only when they're half gone. By taking daily pictures of the flower, I began to notice many interesting changes, such as changes in the flower's color and the direction it was facing. Those were fairly dramatic changes, but I wouldn't have noticed them otherwise, even though I see it every day. I still may not always notice the individual changes, but I've become more attuned to the dynamic vibrance of it all, and with that I feel a flash of awe. More recently I became aware that I notice treetops as they sway in the wind, something I didn't used to see unless I intentionally looked for it. Now each morning I try to eat my breakfast with an eye out the window to notice any movement in nature and capture a little wonder to start my day.

The pressured pace of our days, to which we have become habituated, means that our brain has to exert extra effort to slow down and pause. We need to learn that skill and practice it to make it stick, especially when the human-made environment of manufactured things, commercial media, and messaging exerts such a strong pull. A lot about life is also teaching yourself what you are capable of and how to advance along your chosen path. It helps to pause periodically to check where the incremental changes in your own life are unfolding and, following nature's cue, focus with intention on your direction.

A life well lived is also very much about no goals at all.
The friends I'm most drawn to simply live in the pleasures
of the moment. I constantly have to remind myself
to look out at the horizon, up at the sky, into my
dog's eyes, and simply feel.

—DIANA NYAD

BURNED OUT:
THE NEW NORM?

Long before neuroscience existed to explain the reasons, folk wisdom already cautioned that "All work and no play makes Jack a dull boy"— bored and boring. Today we know why, and that's the reason you find Ping-Pong tables, billiard tables, foosball tables, and nap areas in so many high-tech companies and other workplaces that put a premium on creativity and fresh, innovative thinking. It's the same reason an early human forty thousand years ago took a mammoth tusk and carved it into a flute. Play lights up the brain, specifically the cerebellum. Even idle musing taps into the stream of random thoughts and images and turns the DMN into a source of fresh ideas and insights. Children develop their executive functions—monitoring behavior, attention, planning, decision making, task switching—through play, and adults can do the same. Even in the thick of work, complex considerations, or intense pressure, a short break can calm the brain or energize it, allow it to consolidate new information, and more or less catch up with itself and resume more refreshed.

All work and no play practically pushes the brain into LEB, overextended and actively searching for cognitive paths of least resistance to save energy. Boredom, depression and anxiety, mental exhaustion, and inadequate sleep are unsurprising consequences but alarming nonetheless.

David F. Dinges, professor and chief of the Division of Sleep and Chronobiology, Department of Psychiatry, at the University of Pennsylvania Perelman School of Medicine, laments that we have internalized the unhealthy expectation of round-the-clock work demands. "People have come to value time so much that sleep is often regarded as an annoying interference, a wasteful state that you enter into when you do not have enough willpower to work harder and longer." He points out that "sleep is critical for waking cognition—that is, for the ability to think clearly, to be vigilant and alert, and sustain attention." In other words, sleep is necessary for self-regulation that enables us to manage stress and function well.

Jenny Odell, the multidisciplinary artist, educator, and author of *How to Do Nothing: Resisting the Attention Economy,* wrote that many of the ideas for her book evolved over years of teaching studio art and advocating for the importance of rest to design and engineering majors at Stanford University, "some of whom didn't see the point." She described the field trip of her design class as a simple hike during which, at some point, the group stops to "do nothing" for fifteen minutes. It is confusing or excruciating for some. "Among my students and in many of the people I know, I see so much energy, so much intensity, and so much anxiety. I see people caught up . . . in a mythology of productivity and progress, unable not only to rest but simply to see where they are."

We wouldn't have to fight so hard with ourselves to exert willpower if we recognized that it is actually self-regulation—how the brain and body manage stress physiologically—that determines our energy and thus our attention to any given task. Restorative breaks are essential to effective self-regulation. Even as the brain craves stimulation to function well, it also needs relief from overstimulation. But as we know from binge behaviors with digital games and TV, the conscious mind doesn't always know when it needs an override to change the settings. Self-awareness is an essential aspect of self-regulation because we need to be able to notice the signs that we need a break. Otherwise, we rush right past them and eventually suffer avoidable consequences. It's about the quality of your life and the contribution you make when you're awake.

The good news is that once you recognize the value of downtime, you lower the activation energy for making it a priority, and a world of options opens up.

We say peace of mind, but what we really want
is peace from mind.
—NAVAL RAVIKANT

Find everyday things that slow your pace or quiet your space.

Eavesdrop on the reactions to the change by your mind, your body, and your spiritual and other senses.

Give it a chance—savor the shift.

Press "pause" more often to connect with your core and nurture your whole being.

IF YOUR MIND WANTS TO WANDER, OPEN THE GATES!

The paradox of the brain's mind-wandering mode is that although it can be a distracting nuisance, the wandering mind can also be a rich resource that you can tap with intention when you give yourself the time to do so. "Whether or not mind-wandering is a negative depends on a lot of factors—like whether it's purposeful or spontaneous, the content of your musings, and what kind of mood you are in," noted the psychologist Jill Suttie, who writes extensively about the science of positive psychology. "In some cases, a wandering mind can lead to creativity, better moods, greater productivity, and more concrete goals."

I like Thoreau's concept of "sauntering," which he described as going forth on even the shortest walk "in the spirit of undying adventure." Close observation of nature deserves fresh attention in light of what neuroscience suggests about the collateral benefits for the brain and body. I think of it as a kind of mind meld, a way to engage a state of mind wandering in which nature not only is observed but is directing the wandering. That merged state of mind, wandering with nature in the lead, has an especially positive effect in the brain, as brain plasticity shapes around experience.

My daughter, Jordyn, and I went for a walk in the woods by our house one weekend with the dogs, and although at first she resisted going—she said she hates going into the woods—during the walk we ended up seeing all kinds of other dogs, and she clearly loved that. What had begun as one thing in her mind turned into another. I also tried to notice whether the walk affected me the rest of the day and was surprised to discover that it did. That evening when I went to bed, although the usual worries and unresolved issues entered my mind, aspects of the walk did, too. My anecdotal finding: what we expose ourselves to during the day can imprint itself on our thoughts during reflective and mind-wandering moments, potentially making the downtime mind an even richer resource.

> *I love to go for a walk and open my senses to nature. I especially like walking a beach and visually meditating as I look at stones along the sand. Anything that calms my mind I find rejuvenating. I like a short nap, and some of my best ideas come to me while I shower. You need to give yourself the space, whether it's a quiet room or a walk, to allow yourself to let go of the tension.*
>
> —STEPHEN WILKES

SECRETS OF THE SLEEPING BRAIN

Sleep has long been understood as a unique kind of downtime that's essential to physical and mental health. There's a good reason people are encouraged to "sleep on it" when confronted with an important or confusing decision, says Robert Stickgold, M.D., a professor of psychiatry at Harvard Medical School. Sleep contributes to brain plasticity, permitting the brain to consolidate memories and form new neuronal connections. "It is now clear that sleep mediates learning and memory processing," Stickgold and his colleague Matthew Walker concluded in their paper "Sleep, Memory and Plasticity" in the *Annual Review of Psychology*. Gene Cohen, the psychiatrist and creativity and aging researcher, once described how the answer to a vexing equation came to him overnight in a dream, spelled out in the letters of alphabet soup.

Perhaps most fascinating, however, when seen through the *lit* lens, is emerging research that challenges the classical notion of the brain in sleep "as an all-or-nothing phenomenon," according to the authors of a recent study published in the journal *Nature Communications*. The researchers found localized "slow waves," a pattern of brain activity that is characteristic of the transition toward sleep but is also thought to be associated with dreaming and sleepwalking and important for memory consolidation.

That means that different parts of the brain can be in different stages of sleep—so-called local sleep. All the world's religious traditions have pointed to dreams as vital spiritual events in the transformation of the self and communication with the spirit world. Some aspects of slow-wave brain activity may also help explain what's going on in the brain during waking states when we experience lapses of attention, such as when we daydream, when our mind wanders, or when our mind suddenly goes blank. This slow-wave local sleep phenomenon might also play a role in sluggish or impulsive responses, they said, and not simply when someone is overtired but also in well-rested individuals, showing up as occasional mental lapses.

All of this underscores the brain's potential to engage in different ways in a single moment—a local *lit* effect intersecting local cortical circuits in whatever their current wave state may be. It's especially exciting to consider how pressing "pause," depending on the way you do it, can play out so differently in that variable creative landscape of the brain.

You can experiment with your sleep for clues about connections between that special downtime and how you feel and function when awake. For instance, notice how close to bedtime you eat (thus, the length of your fast until the next meal) or engage in screen time or if you take melatonin or find ways to reduce your heart rate before bed by experimenting with relaxing bedtime rituals, and see how you feel the next day. Or use a wearable device to check your resting heart rate, breathing rate, and time in deep/REM sleep and HRV.

*Each person deserves a day away in which no problems
are confronted, no solutions searched for. Each of us needs
to withdraw from cares which will not withdraw from us.*

—MAYA ANGELOU

A MEDITATION EXPERIMENT

I never thought much about meditation until after graduate school, when I landed in Boston and the Langer Lab. Exhilarated, I wanted to maximize my potential, do more, follow my interest in others' approaches and my own curiosities—and do it more efficiently. I eventually discovered (and continue to learn the lesson) that when I was overcommitted and spread thin, it could feel overwhelming. I ignored that and pushed on, but over time I became aware that my mental health was beginning to suffer.

Looking for a new approach, I listened to meditation apps and podcasts on meditation, and the repetition eventually lowered the activation energy for me to experiment with it, as did the crash landing during Covid. I thought it might work for me. I remembered a high school experience with hypnotism when, as part of a leadership conference program, I volunteered to be hypnotized. I still remember how it felt in my brain. While I was hypnotized, my conscious mind slowed down and my usual inhibitions and filters felt gone. Presumably my subconscious mind felt more alert, open, and available. For those few minutes I felt removed from my usual distracted mind. That experience stayed with me, and now, years later, I was open to spirituality, meditation, and mindfulness practices. Then I realized that Jessica had been reading books about spirituality for years. I'd heard her talk about it, but it had never clicked as relevant to me.

I eventually landed on Transcendental Meditation (TM) after hearing Jerry Seinfeld talk about it on a podcast. I found a teacher of TM in Boston. I downloaded the app, did the exercises, and watched the videos. I started practicing TM for twenty minutes twice a day. I learned how to avoid holding on to distracting thoughts. Just being able to let go of them was liberating. I use TM now when I feel my mind drift to a distraction or I want to shift my energy. I simply close my eyes and repeat my mantra for fifteen to twenty seconds. The effect is quite powerful as the pull of the distraction dissipates. It creates the pause that I desperately need to be less caught up in thoughts about things that are, in the big picture, inconsequential.

Don't overthink mindfulness meditation. The tools to interrupt the primitive circuitry and take control through a simple meditative exercise are yours already, as close as your next breath. Just be quiet and pay attention. Fretting over technique can spoil a perfectly good relaxation break using meditation basics.

James Doty, the Stanford University neurosurgeon and compassion researcher, advises simply sitting quietly in a room. Sit up straight and relax with your hands on your knees. "Just simply breathing and doing nothing more than that. Don't even think about meditation, and you are in that meditative state. The nature of breathing in through your nose and exhaling through your mouth slowly puts you into that state." (You could try this right now.)

Many meditation traditions and practices, such as walking meditation, don't even call for the seated position. Vivek Ramakrishnan considers his impermanence photography practice a meditation.

Whatever your posture, a meditative experience brings about a shift from your sympathetic nervous system (the vigilant, reactive one) to your parasympathetic nervous system and the so-called rest-and-digest mode. Good things happen: your heart rate variability increases, your blood pressure declines, your cortisol levels drop, and your immune system is boosted. The propagation of inflammatory proteins is markedly diminished. You have access to your executive control function areas in the brain so that you make much more thoughtful, discerning decisions.

Almost everything will work again if you unplug it for
a few minutes . . . including you.
—ANNE LAMOTT

SILENCE VERSUS STIMULATION

After getting into the car one day with Jessica, I turned the radio on, which I always do without any particular thought. Jessica noted what a common habit that is—innocuous, really—but she wondered what impels us to do it. I turned the radio off, but what snagged my attention was looking at my decision-making process, such as it was. There's a gravitational pull toward stimulation without a thought to its purpose, just stimulation for the sake of stimulation. Not that just enjoying music or wanting to listen to a radio show or audiobook isn't reason enough; it is. But not every empty space needs to be filled. You can make a conscious choice to opt for less stimulation, even if it's just for short periods. Silence is sometimes what our overstimulated selves need more than anything.

In the car that day, I was surprised to find that engaging silence could feel so personal and liberating. Nobody else's agenda was coming through, no messaging was wafting in from marketers, no background sound was setting the tone of my day, there were no distractions, even well-meaning ones, and there was no chance of my attention being hijacked for some alternative purpose—no click bait. Basically all of my senses were in their ground state, at rest, and recharging for fresh takes on the day.

Silence is rich in so many ways. In one sense it allows us to eavesdrop on our mind, getting into touch with thoughts that exist in a quieter register, perhaps unheard until given the uncrowded space to emerge.

When choosing silence, we can get in touch with our thoughts. However random or insubstantial they may seem, our thoughts are like biomarkers in the conscious and unconscious, bits of inventory, information that tells us something about our state of mind. It's what physicians look for: biomarkers that reveal a disease or condition. We can learn to search for the biomarkers of *lit* in a similar way, by quieting and listening to our thoughts. We can detect patterns we might want to change or whole subjects that we don't need to be engaged with.

Sitting with silence outdoors can be especially rewarding, as silence there typically begins to fill with the sounds of nature, and if we listen, those resonate within us in unique ways. It's not strictly silence, then, but a respite from the sounds of the manufactured environment that usually surrounds us.

> *When I say listen, I am saying listen beyond the human voice, something beyond the human realm. Nowhere on the planet is actually silent, because there's always something living outside of humans, doing something. You're going to hear something—you'll start to hear the sounds beyond the human voice.*
> —PANDORA THOMAS, PERMACULTURE SCIENCE EXPERT,
> SOCIAL TRANSFORMATION ACTIVIST

You can actively dial down the volume on everyday human sensory stimuli in simple ways. This is, after all, the fundamental premise of *lit*—that you can intersect with your own thinking and direct it. We routinely let external influences—social media, an article, a podcast, a documentary, even advertising—affect how we feel and think. Our inner self deserves some airtime. Solitude sustains us. Choose to take the break, power down the digital devices and other interruptions or distractions.

"It takes a concerted effort to reclaim our opportunities for solitude today," Surgeon General Vivek Murthy writes in *Together: The Healing Power of Human Connection in a Sometimes Lonely World*. "What's required is the white space that allows us to deliberately suspend our mental clutter and fully experience our feelings and our thoughts. Today such freedom does not come easily, but this makes it all the more important to intentionally reserve time for solitude on a regular basis."

> *Continuity of mindfulness allows us to course-correct throughout our day. We become familiar with the places where we get caught, and over time, we start to pause more naturally. It's a little reset—a breath here, a breath there.*
> —KATHY CHERRY, "A REMINDER TO PAUSE"

UNINTENDED—AND POTENT—PAUSES

I've been intrigued to see how the pause plays out in many other ways, as people we meet, experiences we have, or things we learn that might seem random fade from our minds over time—an indefinite "break." Then, in what seems a coincidence or bit of serendipity, our paths cross again in a new context, a fresh experience, as if we've rediscovered a breadcrumb trail, and suddenly the path forward isn't random at all, but one paved with fresh energy, intention, and purpose. Sometimes in life someone will say something, then time will pass, and then it will become relevant. A friend who started a not-for-profit recently told me that someone she'd met years before had said that once they were closer to retirement they'd be interested in helping out developing countries. Ten years passed. Recently, that conversation came to her mind and she reached out to that person. They are now working on a team to improve health care in a remote village in Africa.

Another friend, Michael Gale, who struggled with alcohol use for twenty years, was driven to pause by a type 1 diabetes diagnosis when he turned forty. Around the same time, he had begun therapy, attended his first yoga festival, and found his grandfather's journal (while staying at his parents' house during the Covid pandemic). These experiences prompted him to start his own journal for his future grandchildren and also to learn about himself. In that crucible of circumstances, he had the excuse he needed to defeat the social pressure to drink and the perspective to press pause and deeply reflect. The sudden urgency of his health situation and his developing awareness led him to recognize other opportunities, and he felt strongly motivated to take active steps that began the life transformation that continues today. He sought to understand himself better and surrounded himself with intentional friends to support this adventure.

"This whole new world and mindset for me developed when I learned to say 'no' and to be more connected to my inner life, my family, and nature," he says. "My former life of saying 'yes' to every party, every trip, every drink, and new friend is fading away, and my mind is now clear to realize my full potential on this Earth. Love has new meaning for me.

And that has to do with my desire for a deep connection with myself and those around me."

Gale says he now keeps three journals: one for day-to-day personal notes, one for brainstorming, and one as more of a to-do tracker for work. Taken together, they offer something like a 3D view of where his attention and intention align, and where a gap may suggest an opportunity to reflect more consciously and let fresh insight guide him. In going through the journal that his grandfather, a physician, had kept, Gale found an unexpected nudge that affirmed his shifting life focus. His grandfather had begun the journal when he was nineteen, writing through his first two years of college. Then the entries stopped and only resumed (in the same journal!) when he was sixty-five, continuing for ten years until the end of his life. Gale noticed how his grandfather's reflections had changed from the everyday observations and worries he wrote about in college to those that consumed his thoughts in his last decade. With advancing age, he wrote almost exclusively about his children and grandchildren, occasionally about what he had found on the beach that day, and his patients' ailments. For Michael, the message that shook him awake was the power of family and the love to be shared there, something that he focuses on now with intention in his own journaling.

"Journaling and self-reflection have brought me closer to my family," he adds. "The realization that I love them very much, combined with therapy and a morning routine of breathing and meditation practice, has allowed me to realize that I can also love myself and the incredible importance of that."

So many times in life, our circumstances suddenly change—an accident, an illness, an injury, a loss—and the pause is not only unintended but unwelcome, even devastating. The pat suggestion that "everything happens for a reason" requires a whole elaborate belief system of its own, but the blunt force of the pause itself is unambiguous. The empty canvas that it creates becomes whatever we choose to make of it. This holds true from the most personal, intimate experience to the pandemic pause that became a pivot point for so many people for so many reasons. Whether we choose to pause or it is forced upon us by circumstance, in the instant that space opens up, it is primed for possibility. That's all the brain knows. And whether the pause is simply an inevitable passage of time, as it was for health clinic collaborators, or a profound turning point, we can recognize that pattern of possibility in life and watch for (and create) opportunities to re-engage with new intention and purpose.

DO WHAT MAKES YOU HAPPY

Bob Langer's standing as one of the world's leading bioscience innovators rides on a piece of his day that he says is essential for his best work: workout time. He rides an exercise bicycle, uses an elliptical machine, and walks a treadmill (low speed, high incline) several hours a day, and more often than not any call to him includes the soft whir of the workout equipment in the background.

Because everyone who knows Langer knows this about him, I asked him about the role it plays in his thinking process. He shrugged. "I don't know the answer to that. I think it just makes me happy."

Langer's creative thinking revs up when he takes a break to work out, and that does make him happy. An example: A bunch of years ago, he'd flown to Florida to give a dinner speech to the American Heart Association, and with ninety minutes free before the talk, he went to the hotel gym and got onto the exercise bike. He picked up a *Life* magazine that was handy and started reading it just for fun. "One of the things they talked about in the future is that you could have a car and if the car was in an accident and got a dent, you'd heat it up and it would heal, so to speak. And I thought to myself, *Wow, maybe what I could do is invent materials, polymers, that could help what's called shape memory.* In other words, that they could heal—change shape. And then that led me to thinking, *Well, if you could do that, you could make sutures that would tie themselves, and all kinds of things like that.* That all happened on the exercise bike, but I wasn't trying."

(P.S.: And then he invented it: biodegradable, elastic shape-memory polymers for potential biomedical applications.)

Langer's idea of downtime includes a lot of stimuli, so it might not seem to fit the idea most of us have about taking a break. But for him, it means that he pushes "pause" on all the meetings that he typically does in a day and all the work at his computer. Whether we'd want to do the same thing or not, the reward is something to aim for: Do something that makes you happy! Your workhorse of a brain will be happier, too.

Cultivate and Practice the Skill of Pressing "Pause"

For a truly restorative break, even a short one, put the to-do list fully off limits. Resist the pull to fill your break with productive catch-up tasks. When your mind wants to skip ahead to a waiting task, have a mental cue ready that helps you disengage. *It can wait. Be here now.* Pause to feel grounded in the moment, open to inner cues and those from your environment. Try these in different settings:

- Reconsider the need for speed. Notice when rushing to get things done has become habitual. Avoid bulldozing the time you need for breaks or for change to occur.
- Step outside with your camera for microbreaks to photograph trees or flowers—or take pics of house or office plants. Pause before clicking to more deeply connect with the life in front of you.
- Savor. Tune in to the sensory experience of routine moments. And make more of them. Substitute a walk for online scrolling time or close your eyes as you listen to music. Trade a fast-food meal for a slow-food option and savor the meal prep as well as the meal.
- Plan or improvise your own silent retreat. Aim for a stimulus cleanse: try travel or drive times without the audio backdrop of news, commentary, podcasts, or music.
- Use familiar downtime cues to signal your brain and body to shift gears. Experiment to find what works best for you. Sensory cues might be opening the window to let in fresh air or sounds or lighting a scented candle. Relaxing mental images or memories, stretching or meditation can help shift your energy.

- Consider underlying reasons you may gravitate to one kind of break over another and whether you might consciously pick something different for a *lit* booster. When I'm about to jump onto social media, for example, it's often because I'm bored or uncomfortable or my environment needs a change. Better options to address that include doing a twenty-second meditation, listening with your eyes closed for a moment, drinking a glass of water, stretching, walking around the house, and sitting back down in a different location.

- Put your expectations onto a sliding scale so you can thoroughly enjoy a short break for what it offers and a longer one for a different experience.

- Cultivate "third places" outside home and work where you can enjoy casual, spontaneous interaction with others, productivity-free conversation, or just relaxed hanging out. Think parks, nature preserves, cafés, libraries and bookstores, gyms, beaches, welcoming public spaces—or your own backyard.

- Try journaling—writing, sketching, or just doodling—outdoors as a way to let the natural world infuse your thoughts, your mental and physical processing, and your expression. Tuck a volunteer leaf or flower petal into the pages as a postscript.

- Breathe. Technology pioneer Linda Stone refers to how our hyperalert, always-on state creates an artificial sense of constant crisis, triggering excessive cortisol and norepinephrine. Those ill effects are made worse by what she calls "screen apnea," in which the poor posture and inhalation that accompanies anticipation or surprise leads to poor breathing—temporarily holding one's breath or shallow breathing while in front of a screen. Your breathing is the master control of attention, cognition, imagination, and memory. Pause to replenish.

HUG NATURE

Revitalize Your Roots

Embrace your place in the natural
ecosystem and connect with life's powerful
resources to flourish.

*Deep inside, we still have a longing to be reconnected with
the nature that shaped our imagination, our language,
our song and dance, our sense of the divine.*

—JANINE BENYUS, BIOLOGIST

When I was a kid, a pack of wolves howled at night in the fields and forests and even sometimes on my front lawn. The creek ran clear, but it was
no place to play barefoot even in the summer. That territory belonged to
leeches, crayfish, and the snapping turtles that lumbered up our backyard
to lay their eggs. As far back as I can remember, my dad used to corral my
sister and me and our mom and just go for a drive—with no destination
in mind—and see what we saw. I grew up in a small city of 65,000 people,
and my dad, a dentist, was supercurious about exploring nature and little
towns and walking around places with rivers and lakes. Because we lived
out away from the city, those drives were always around farmers' fields
and into the countryside. We drove down private lanes just to see what
was lurking beyond. We stopped at farm stands to buy fresh fruits or ber-
ries. We also made frequent visits to arts and crafts festivals and various
flea markets where all kinds of different art and handmade contraptions

were being sold. Eventually our family field trips turned into longer road trips, and our favorite destination was a lakeside cabin in the woods.

Those drives were simple stuff—nothing particularly ambitious, no punishing treks, nothing anyone would call an expedition. Yet their ordinariness didn't diminish the impact that a casual, freewheeling relationship with nature can have on a kid. Years later, as I traveled remote roads through unfamiliar countryside in India, Italy, and Great Britain, the sensation of passing through a patch of the planet where the natural world was more present than the man-made one always struck the same deep chord for me. I was, and still am, drawn to this feeling of nature's close presence, the opportunity to just observe and be at ease in it, and the sense of wonder and awe at whatever presents itself.

Nature has always been a sanctuary for the spirit, articulated by poets, songwriters, philosophers, and sacred texts. More recently, scientific research has advanced our understanding of the neural links, or neurocorrelates, between brain function and the beneficial effects of feeling awe, wonder, or what we consider a spiritual or transcendent experience.

When I asked Pandora Thomas, the permaculture activist you'll meet shortly, how literally she meant it when she told me that the trees talk to her, it was because other people have shared with me interesting variations of that experience: an inner voice, a sweeping sound audible to them alone, the sense of a deep emotional presence of a higher guide, a reassuring protective spirit. Something in "the soul's register," one said.

Whether you hear the trees sing or not, and whether you feel you're in conversation with nature or not, you are, by your very existence, always deeply in that dialogue. Listen to it, and let it in.

In the previous chapter, I wrote at length about why pausing, silence, deliberate mindfulness, and other steps are so important to *lit*. It's important to elaborate on one aspect of all that: the ways that we interact with nature and why our interactions can be so meaningful to our mental processes and sense of well-being.

Nature doesn't give us the dramatic dopamine swings or steady drip of stimulation and variable rewards that our digital devices and media do. It won't quench our desires in the same way. But it's unlikely that you'll ever feel awestruck online the way you will when you look up at a star-studded night sky or out across a pond where a blue heron stands poised against the sunrise. Or at the engineering feat of a bird's nest or a beehive—or for that matter the extraordinary creatures who build them. "Nature is orderly," wrote the poet, author, and environmental activist Gary Snyder in his book *The Practice of the Wild*. "That which appears to be chaotic in nature is only a more complex kind of order." Nature's complexity is our own, innate to us, and, however mysterious to us at times, essential to our well-being. "It is," Snyder wrote, "that side of our being which guides our breath and our digestion, and when observed and appreciated is a source of deep intelligence."

For decades, an extensive and still growing body of research has established that nature is good for us; that time we spend in nature makes us healthier, happier, and more physically and mentally resilient—even smarter, considering the neurological benefits that enhance cognitive functioning for both young and old and support healthy growth and development, especially critical for children. "Green time" not only lowers the risk of developing some chronic diseases and has measurable therapeutic effects on anxiety and depression, it supports more robust social and emotional growth and can foster a sense of belonging, a critical aspect of mental health, especially for those who struggle with isolation or illness. Not only that, nature's pharmacy—plants, animals, single-cell organisms, and substances with medicinal and healing properties—has saved our collective skin. Processes in nature that clean and cultivate the planet have enabled us to survive as a species.

Nature invites—more accurately, *enables*—us to shift our mindset, sharpen our focus, slow down to calm our primed stimulus-responsive minds and bring our overwhelmed senses back to a ground state. Do you feel bored in nature? That in itself is something to consider. It shows how far we have drifted from our place in the natural world; useful to know. But we can use it to find the *lit* factor. The stimuli we receive from nature will be different from those we experience in the engineered environment. All that we experience in nature, including boredom, prompts us—nudges us, pings us—to shift our mindset, sharpen our focus, and engage with our natural environment. Give it a chance. Step outside, and find a plant or flower that you have never examined before; listen for the sounds of birds and insects, the rustle of the wind, or the quieter voices of trees and plants, often the muted backdrop of our day. Being present and engaged this way can calm the mind, reducing the urgency to shift attention in search of more sensory stimulation.

Experiment to recognize how nature affects your mood and energy. In various outdoor settings, notice how you feel, both physically and emotionally: bored, calm, peaceful, anxious, engaged in negative rumination, and so on. See what changes as you engage in different ways: standing or sitting quietly immersed in your surroundings, taking a walk, tending a garden. In what way, however slight, does your state of mind shift? Pause to contemplate the feeling of connection; this is embodied intelligence, fully engaged.

> *Adopt the pace of nature: her secret is patience.*
> —RALPH WALDO EMERSON

THERE'S ALWAYS SOMETHING NEW

Think of the time you have spent figuring out a new phone or device or a game. At first, it's a great feeling: sorting through new or unfamiliar features, discovering bugs in the system and workarounds—sometimes spending hours on tech support. I've done it. It seems natural to want new, more, better. The concept of hedonic adaptation, also known as the hedonic treadmill, says that no matter how much we have, we eventually adjust to our standard of living and want something more; we feel we need more to be happy, and we're dissatisfied without it. There's a difference between "get new" and "do new," though, and I'm trying harder to remember it more often. The natural world can help us with that. As consumers, we're immersed in a "get new" environment that unquestioningly cultivates consumption—even though we know that we eventually part ways with material things, even those with purpose and value. But step into nature for a "do new" experience (even if you've done it countless times before), and you step out of the consumer role and into an environment that rewards simple connection. We know that new experiences shape the brain and become an integrated part of who we are. So what better to choose than the natural world to bring into our being?

Pause and step away from screens and tech long enough to engage the natural environment in any way you can. When we are removed even briefly from the human-made stuff that surrounds us, nature has a way of grabbing onto and hugging us. And it is *always* available—it's we who are not! We need to hug back. In nature, there is always something nuanced, something new.

I remember in grade school playing an outdoor challenge called Survival Game (also called Predator/Prey). I think I was an herbivore. The game, with informational support materials that were fun and fact packed (the kind of thing my brain liked), was captivating: running around the woods, shifting from the normal social ecosystem of the classroom to completely different dynamics and hierarchy. It helped me better appreciate the importance, diversity, and balance of ecosystems, the reliance on others—and the sensation of being on the run, with only brief moments of calm and safety. Everyone participating had advantages and limitations. It was a real mind shift for me and *very* exhilarating. The game's description of ecosystems large and small sticks in my memory today, especially in the context of *lit*. Ecosystems had to balance out for life to continue. But what would sustain life? Energy, and the flow of energy through the ecosystem. Each organism in the ecosystem had a certain role based on how it acquired and released energy. Today, the need for us to bring energy—*lit* energy—to our ecosystem is critical.

This multiplayer, multiplatform (woods and classroom) game was compelling, presenting information in a novel and engaging way, exciting the brain, and opening the channels for learning. Nature can't always present its own information so attractively. There are rain, bugs, the nitty-gritty of it all. But if we take the time to learn the "language" of our natural environment, we can access so much that a game can never offer, including a spiritual dimension.

I often think that many of us know we need a dose of nature but avoid seeking it. We defer and deprioritize it as something we'll get around to when there's time—and time never frees itself up. We push ourselves harder and longer until at last we get the signal—sick, exhausted, or burned out—that now is the time. But it's like waiting until you're dehydrated to take a drink of water. Or waiting (indefinitely) for the right time to go to the gym, to ask for help, to schedule that checkup, or—fill in the blank. When we are laser focused on life detached or divorced from nature, no matter how good it may seem, our cognitive processes are too engaged to free up bandwidth for our relationship with nature and with ourselves as part of nature. If you're waiting for a sign from the universe to reconnect, consider that this book could be it.

As I thought about individuals to interview for this chapter, people whose lives and livelihoods are deeply grounded in their relationship with the natural world, three in particular came to mind. You'll meet them shortly. Simply put, they are a farmer, a scientist, and a spiritual guide, each a steward of our planet and visionary in their own realm.

Bioinspiration is as old as the hills, and as I've shared in the stories from lab and life, it's a sophisticated field of science today, the source of innovations that have transformed medicine and saved countless lives. But as the creation stories and traditions of Indigenous cultures remind us, long before science formalized the study, nature was understood as the single most vital source of humankind's best wisdom and most inspired action. However distanced from the elements we may live and work in each day, our lives are defined by our relationship with nature, and our capacity for the *lit* life flourishes in that connection.

> *Walking is the great adventure, the first meditation, a practice of heartiness and soul primary to humankind. Walking is the exact balance of spirit and humility.*
>
> —GARY SNYDER, *THE PRACTICE OF THE WILD*

My walks in the woods and our lab's forays into nature, boots on the ground, have always stimulated fresh thinking that has proved essential to advancing our work. Beyond such anecdotal evidence (which may include your own memorable experiences) research has shown that time in nature provides not only a range of physical and mental health benefits but also self-regulation and spiritual development. Nature in some form is at the core of every LIT tool because, as it's been said, we aren't separate from nature, *we are nature;* our thought processes are embedded and inextricably intertwined: physical, mental, social, emotional, and spiritual. Dismiss any one of those and you lose that energy source and diminish your own potential. Engage them all and that's *lit*!

ELDER DAVE COURCHENE: A VISION, A QUEST

For all the science and philosophy that attempt to explain the deep dynamic of intertwining energies that shape us, to me the most powerful model is that of the vision quest, a wilderness rite of passage and nature immersion experience from Indigenous traditions. The solitary quest, always with the guidance of a mentor, can be a transformational, even transcendent, breakthrough experience of clarity, passion, and purpose.

"Once you're on the land, you cannot help but feel something," the late Elder Courchene said. "You certainly can hear the voice of nature, you can even smell the land itself; there's a lot of things with the senses that we are given as human beings. If you align them to nature itself, you're going to grow and go more toward fulfilling your true purpose as a human being in this world. We were all given a universal collective purpose, and that was to become real stewards of the land, to take care of the land."

It was during his own vision quest, a series of them years ago, that the dream and vision of Turtle Lodge came to him. First, though, he had some healing to do, which his grandmother told him was essential. That was where his journey started, he said—out of frustration and anger.

Growing up in Canada, Elder Courchene witnessed the near-total assimilation of his tribal culture by force, as other Indigenous peoples also experienced. Many of the tribes' traditional ceremonies, languages, and other hallmarks of cultural identity were forcibly removed or had languished under school programs and laws imposed by governments hostile to their presence. Coming of age as a young man, he was angry about what he saw happening to Indigenous people across the country. "I wanted to do something, but I didn't know what to do." So he turned for counsel to the grandmothers of his Nation.

Elders hold an honored role as mentors and spiritual leaders in the community, and grandmothers are a special source of moral and life guidance; the role of grandmothers in Indigenous society has been valued across time and tribes. When he sought advice from the grandmothers about what to do, he was told that the vision quest would become central to his path. The first step wasn't into the woods for a solitary sojourn; a grandmother guided him with this advice: "The first thing we've got to do is get rid of your anger, because anger will not bring anything positive in your life. You're going to harm yourself and harm other people. Anger is like a little black spot that can enter into your heart, and it will spread quite easy."

Elder Courchene took her wisdom to heart. He was fast-tracked into sacred lodge ceremonies from his early twenties. He began to feel a major shift in his life. In the nature-based rituals, and especially the traditional drumming, "I started to feel something that I felt good about," he said. "I found some comfort in the ceremonies I was attending, and I began to become really attracted to the drums of our people. Every time I would hear the drum, I would get very emotional; it would bring me to tears many times. And a lot of these things I didn't understand. So I went and visited more of our elders and began to get more of the teachings that helped influence me to walk a way of life that did give me joy, comfort, and, of course, a lot of challenges."

His deep learning of the Seven Sacred Laws of Indigenous culture began with his mother and the example she set, then grew through his new grounding in ritual and practice. "It wasn't until I went on a series of vision quests to try to feel comfortable that I found what I was looking for," he said. "I had the vision of the Turtle Lodge, which was manifested, a beautiful dream to build this place. . . . With no money, nothing like that, but a dream. And I think that's where my life really, really began to heal."

To me, the vision quest tradition, and Elder Courchene's in particular, embodies the *lit* experience as a process. In Elder Courchene's case, anger was the pain point that first motivated him to seek the counsel of the grandmothers, flipped the switch that led from bothered awareness to action. Through the mentorship of elders, the ceremonies and values of his community, all deeply rooted in nature, his dream of the Turtle Lodge emerged and now has come to fruition: a place for all where people from around the world and various cultures can engage directly with Indigenous knowledge and wisdom, ceremonies, traditions, and education as a sacred path to healing through nature. Perhaps most important, the tradition is rooted in our relationship with nature, rather than disconnected from it as so much of contemporary life is.

> *The simple understanding that our people have always said is "What you do to the land, you do to yourself; you are the land." And we see it more than ever today, that what we have done to the land, we have really done to ourselves.*
>
> —ELDER DAVE COURCHENE, ANISHINAABE NATION

DAVID SUZUKI: FIND YOUR PLACE IN THE WEB OF LIFE

David Suzuki, a Canadian scientist and outspoken environmental activist, put it in blunt terms when we spoke not long after his eighty-fifth birthday. He shared the story of meeting with the CEO of a major oil company who had asked to talk with him about some contentious issues over development. Suzuki agreed to the meeting but insisted on one condition: they would talk first as human to human—no other agendas, not Suzuki's, Big Oil's, or others—and find commonalities of interest, as humans, on which to base a relationship for further conversation. After all, he says, "if we can't agree, what the hell is the point of discussing pipelines, carbon taxes, and carbon emissions?" Thus agreed, the meeting began, and, as Suzuki tells it, he spoke first, referring to the most fundamental human commonality: biology. Could they agree on just four basic biological facts?

First, "if you don't have air for three minutes, you're dead. If you have to breathe polluted air, you're sick. So would you agree with me that clean air is a gift from nature that we accept and have a responsibility to protect, because that air is used by all other terrestrial animals?"

Second, "We're over seventy percent water by weight. We're just a blob of water with enough thickener added so we don't dribble away on the floor, but we leak water out of our skin and our mouth and our nose and our crotch, and if you don't have water for four to six days, you're dead. If you have to drink contaminated water, you're sick. So clean water is like clean air—it's a gift from nature that we have a responsibility to protect."

He went on, "Food is a little different. We'll go a hell of a lot longer without food, but four to six weeks without food, we'll die. And most of our food comes from the soil. So clean food and soil, then, are like clean air, clean water."

And so on. He made the case for photosynthesis as a sacred, vital element of nature. Photosynthesis represents fire, being the process through which plants absorb sunlight (energy), and store it as chemical energy, which transfers to us when we eat plants or animals. We burn plant energy as fuel for ourselves, just as we tap the sun's stored energy from fossil fuels, wood, dung, or peat. "And the miracle of that is that those four things that Indigenous people call earth, air, fire, and water, the very source of our lives, those elements are delivered to us by the web of life," he says. "The miracle of life on this planet to me is that the very things that we need are cleansed, created, and amplified by the web of living things. That is the fundamental basis of our lives and well-being."

The CEO was "a good man," he says, but he bristled when Suzuki mentioned that we are all animals and share these basic needs—though Suzuki remarked dryly to me, "Hey, I'm a biologist. If you're not an animal, you must be a plant." Their conversation was long past as we spoke, but Suzuki has had to continue to explain these unchanging basic facts to CEOs and other power brokers and wider audiences for decades. This helps explain his impatience at the arrogance of our species.

Self-pride only hastens our demise, he says. Without clean air, clean water, safe food, and plants that convert sunlight into energy we can consume, we're dust. Those biological facts of life, the underpinnings of our existence, simply don't change.

"We're so hyped up about how smart we are that we've elevated our own creations above nature itself," he says, referring to manufactured products and systems to support them, which we've created at the expense of vital environmental systems we all need to survive.

Researchers continue to discover new evidence of the complex interconnections of life on this planet, and too often we learn that we are the source of suffering for creatures whose lives we've been oblivious to: spiders, worms, snails, lobsters, octopi, and insects, to name a few. Once we know that they are not immune to pain, how can we make them part of our moral landscape when they haven't been before?

"The challenge of our time is rediscovering what we've known for most of human existence: our place in this web of relationships," says Suzuki. "And then molding our institutions to ensure that we don't destroy the web as we go."

Paying attention to nature, we can move past simply reading or hearing *about* it and how critical it is for our mental health and survival. We can let personal experience and awareness motivate us to action. Although we're on a steep learning curve, as the damage has been mounting for decades, leading to environmental tipping points now, we can do this: shift away from "we humans" and "we" in general seeing the world through the lens of elevated importance.

> *Merely by falling in love with the world, you will begin*
> *to make it better. Human beings will work to their dying*
> *breath to save something they love. Fall in love with the wild*
> *world, and you are taking the first step toward saving it.*
>
> —MARGARET RENKL

PANDORA THOMAS:
PERMACULTURE AS LEGACY AND BLUEPRINT

For most of her life, Pandora Thomas has been "one of those people in variations," she explains, by which she means that she is always listening for cues from the universe for her next steps. So guided, she studied, taught, and was a community builder the first three decades of her life. She designed curricula and taught in more than twelve countries, groups as diverse as Iraqi and Indonesian youths to men serving time in San Quentin and men and women returning home after incarceration. She's studied four languages, been featured in documentary films, and been awarded internships and fellowships to the Institute for the Study of Human Rights at Columbia University, the Bronx Zoo, and Green for All. She worked for six years with Toyota to design and serve as a coalition member of the Toyota Green Initiative. And most recently, she arrived where she started, back home in Berkeley, California, guided by her lifelong practice of ancestral honoring—that is, listening to the voice of legacy in her African American–African Indigenous family. That legacy includes a strong bond with the natural world, she says. "I realized it wasn't just the universe I was asking for direction, it was also kind of all of the things—the human, nonhuman in forms of plants and animals, but also the spirit world."

When she turned twenty-eight, something clicked and she got a clear answer. "I quit my job and became a naturalist. I spent all of my time on it, for very little money, but it was the best thing I've ever done, being a naturalist," she wrote later in an email. "And the trees saved me. They listened, loved, and continued to support me and reflect my beauty without expectations other than that I would keep letting out carbon dioxide for them to consume as food." She added a smiley face emoji to her email text. "With them I could breathe!"

She felt drawn to step into a role that would advance her ancestors' legacy, not only for herself but in a much broader way through the global permaculture movement. Permaculture is an approach to sustainable living, or restorative, regenerative practices in agriculture that view humans, agriculture, and society as part of the natural ecosystem. Instead of a human-centered designed ecosystem, in which most of us live and the majority of actions are intended to support humans and their livestock, in permaculture, humans are just one small part of the ecosystem. Rainwater harvesting from roofs, for instance, becomes a way to live in a more integrated way with nature. All plants and animals are considered to be vital to the community as mutual beneficiaries of one another. Food, energy, and shelter are provided in a sustainable way.

Human survival has always required attunement to nature's systems and rhythms, but as modernization has marginalized nature and Indigenous wisdom, permaculture as an intentional choice saw a revival of interest in the 1970s. Today it has emerged as a global response to climate change, environmental degradation, and social and economic inequities that threaten humankind.

The Earth is our oldest teacher—it birthed us—so how do
we ground our daily practices to honor that?
—PANDORA THOMAS

In college Thomas planned to become a city planner. Today she is in essence a planetary planner. As a teacher and curriculum creator, children's book author, designer, and activist, she brings ecological principles to social design, advancing social permaculture as another way to put sustainability principles into action. In 2020, she founded EARTH-seed Permaculture Center (EPC), a fourteen-acre working permaculture farm and education and retreat center in the heart of California's Sonoma Valley wine country. It is the first Afro-Indigenous and all-Black-owned and -operated permaculture farm, and for Thomas, it makes good on her intention to pass forward the legacy of the Earth wisdom traditions of peoples of African and Indigenous descent in a way that makes them accessible to all. In particular, she explains, she incorporates the ancestral principles of Ma'at (pronounced may-yet), the ancient Egyptian concepts of truth, justice, harmony, and balance. Especially relevant in our relationship with nature: Thou shalt not disrespect sacred places, nor do any harm to human or to animals, nor take more than thy fair share of food, nor pollute the water or the land.

The best remedy for those who are afraid, lonely, or
unhappy is to go outside, somewhere where they can be
quite alone with the heavens, nature and God. . . . I firmly
believe that nature brings solace in all troubles.
—ANNE FRANK, *THE DIARY OF A YOUNG GIRL*

Thomas hears in the permaculture principles the echoes of her own upbringing and family values: "All of us have it, the ancestral legacy piece, but for me, my Afro-Indigenous ancestry, human and nonhuman, set me on this path. I had parents who taught me to *listen*. So with all their other shortcomings, for whatever reason, they taught me to love others, the Earth, and a spirit beyond me, and I've been able to listen instead of kind of always *talking*. I feel I've been able to listen and observe in my life, and then permaculture was introduced to me, and it's interesting because one of the first principles of permaculture is to observe and interact. So I tend to listen, and that includes a level of faith that there are things beyond me that are guiding me—if I listen."

BIOINSPIRATION VERSUS BIOEXPLOITATION: WHAT'S YOUR RELATIONSHIP STYLE WITH NATURE?

In the natural order of things, humans don't take any prizes as predators in the conventional sense. Apex or alpha predators—predators at the top of the food chain that have no natural predators—include lions, killer whales, and their predator peers among the most dominant birds and reptiles. A human, unarmed in those predators' environments, is less a threat, more an appetizer. Yet through a different lens, one of environmental impact, our species shows up quite differently. Armed with an outsized sense of entitlement, profit-driven priorities, and the industrial tools to have our own way, we are a mortal threat to all. (Including ourselves, it turns out; as we have eliminated predators in the communities in which we live, the only ones left are other humans that threaten our health and safety.) We would be more effective, successful, thriving humans if we could shift our relationship with the human and nonhuman world to be less transactional—*What's in it for me?*—and recognize that we are all part of the same natural ecosystem. In that sense we are one, and the often-quoted Indigenous wisdom applies: *What we do to the Earth, we do to ourselves.*

We are, as the Japanese farmer and philosopher Masanobu Fukuoka said, "nature working." We *are* nature. The more clearly we understand that the cycles that drive and sustain all of nature are intrinsic to the planet's dynamic equilibrium, the better we'll be able to create dwellings and communities designed for health, safety, and energy efficiency, raise food with sustainable practices, and manage new challenges based on a deep knowledge of the natural forces at work, rather than fear or greed.

> *In our culture, we never go to the land and take anything from the land until we make an offering—whether it is food, cloth, or tobacco—in a ceremony of gratitude to say, "Thank you, Mother Earth. In spite of what we have done to you, your unconditional love prevails."*
> —ELDER DAVE COURCHENE, ANISHINAABE NATION

David Suzuki remembers when he had just begun his career as a geneticist, in 1962, the same year Rachel Carson's book *Silent Spring* was released. It was a call to arms about the evidence showing the devastating consequences in store due to the indiscriminate use of pesticides, notably DDT. A newly minted geneticist focused on the most minute fragment of a microscopic particle of life, Suzuki was shocked. "I realized that in focusing, we lose all sense of context that makes what we're studying interesting in the first place. We have no idea how it all works. Then I realized when Paul Müller discovered DDT kills insects, won a Nobel Prize for that in 1948, and everyone thought, *Whoa, what a great way to control pests!* I'm surprised the ecologists didn't say, 'Wait a minute, now, you know, maybe one or two species of insects are pests to humans. Why would you use something that kills all insects, which are the most important group of animals on the planet, to get at the one or two that are pests? This is no great innovation.' Geneticists could have said, 'Look, you're going to get on a never-ending treadmill. You start selecting this way, you're going to select for mutants and you're just going to have to keep inventing new kinds of pesticide—it's never ending.' But of course, we didn't pay attention. We were just struck with how powerful DDT was.

"Over and over, we go for what seems to be a great idea," he says. "But we don't see the context within which it has its effect and end up paying an enormous price."

We need to get over the "wow" factor favoring innovations that control nature without thorough consideration of the consequences when those measures ultimately risk destabilizing the ecosystem. We can ask in any setting: What could we learn about this from nature?

Janine Benyus, a cofounder of the Biomimicry Institute, holds that "the answers to our questions are everywhere; we just need to change the lens with which we see the world." As she wrote in her book *Biomimicry*, "The more our world functions like the natural world, the more likely we are to endure on this home that is ours, but not ours alone."

> *Those who contemplate the beauty of the Earth find reserves of strength that will endure as long as life lasts . . . There is something infinitely healing in the repeated refrains of nature—the assurance that dawn comes after night, and spring after winter.*
>
> —RACHEL CARSON, *THE SENSE OF WONDER*

Elder Courchene pointed out that "we have been given the gift of choice. Animals don't have that. You always have a choice each morning you wake up, the choice to live the way you want to live. Everybody has that choice, but I think at some point in time we have to stop and say, 'The way we're living, is that really sustainable?'"

NATURE'S SECRETS HIDING IN PLAIN SIGHT

In the field of bioinspiration, as we look to nature for ideas, strategies, mechanisms, and adaptations that evolved over geological time, we often discover that nature has already answered a question, solved a problem in a way that could help us solve it, too. But usually we can't simply mimic nature to solve problems, and unfortunately we don't always know how to ask and there's no master index to nature's work. The more we experiment and discover those secrets and how to adapt them, the more we contribute to that index for others to use, which is exciting in itself.

For example, the lab set out, with a partner in dermatology, to create a topical cream to help people with the common skin allergy to nickel. Nickel is a metal used in everyday items that easily come into contact with the skin. Just as certain sunscreens apply a layer of nanoparticles to the skin to block the sun, we aimed to develop safe nanoparticles that could coat the skin and bind to and block nickel from being absorbed into the skin. We eventually determined that calcium carbonate, the material found in seashells and chalk, could be formulated to do that in a skin cream. We conducted molecular studies to examine the binding process and identify the right-sized nanoparticle and formulation to maximize efficacy and safety, then rapidly brought the barrier cream to patients as a readily available skin care product. Sometime later, I discovered that nature had already solved for this problem—in phytoplankton, the microscopic plants that are vital to the ocean ecosystem. Certain phytoplankton live in layers of the ocean where they are exposed to naturally occurring heavy metals and have been found to use calcium carbonate to build protective plates on their exterior. Whatever other benefits the protective plates may offer, they likely protect the plankton from absorbing heavy metals.

These kinds of discoveries are happening all the time, though they rarely make headlines and often languish in scientific journals. But nature's genius can inspire persistence. About ten years ago, a colleague and his team developed a way to make filters from the strawlike xylem tissue in coniferous trees to purify water—filter out bacteria—making it safe to drink. Plant xylem has specialized cells that transport water and dissolved minerals from the roots of a tree to the rest of it. Drawing from nature's process, the researchers developed a low-tech filter and created a prototype using the readily available, inexpensive, biodegradable, and disposable material. The filter would have a tremendous impact in parts of the world where contaminated water makes waterborne diseases rampant and the need urgent. Most recently, the team's prototype was successfully tested in India, and they're investigating ways to scale up for broad community use.

*No matter how long I forget to water the garden, or how
cold the winter was, the sprouts keep trying to come up
and the leaves keep trying to come back. Despite all that's
happened to life over the millennia—like an asteroid—the
Earth keeps generating beauty and marvels,
and will continue to.*

—SAMBHAV SANKAR, SENIOR VP OF PROGRAMS, EARTHJUSTICE

In humankind's deep but often distracted dialogue with the nonhuman dimension of the natural world, even as we look to it for solutions,
we ignore the cautionary messages that are there for us. "Nature will
send a message, maybe a mild message, and if you don't get it, it'll come
again, increasing in force or pain," Elder Courchene noted. "Pain is a
really good teacher, the master teacher. If you have pain, you do everything that you can to try to get rid of that pain. Pain from a spiritual
sense is a messenger to say, 'Well, maybe you need to think about something, maybe you need to change.'"

The thing is, nature doesn't wait for us to respond, and we ignore the
messages at our peril. When Covid spoke, it didn't mince words. Nearly
15 million people died as a result of Covid in the first two years of the
pandemic, a dramatic wake-up call for humankind. Scientists across
disciplines—epidemiologists, virologists, public health, and others—
had been voicing concern, increasingly urgently, about the potential for
a pandemic years before Covid erupted. Many of the same conditions
that created a perfect storm for the evolution of antimicrobial-resistant
superbugs, especially conditions at industrial-scale factory farms, were
flagged as conditions ripe to cultivate a pandemic such as Covid. The
science didn't lie; the patterns evident in nature spoke clearly. They still
do. Infections caused by antimicrobial resistant superbugs continue to
rise, and experts are watching, warning that conditions are once again
ripe for the next pandemic.

As a British study reported in 2021, most infectious diseases are
zoonotic, jumping from animals to humans. Though the science is yet

to be fully defined, zoonotic transmissions appear to be a function of close interactions by humans with wildlife and factory farming. These transmissions are inextricably linked to conditions of water insecurity and diminishing biodiversity. Yet the public discussion tends to vilify the organisms themselves, and collective denial ignores established evidence-based information and suggested measures to prevent future pandemics. No matter how far removed we think we are from these problems, they belong to us all to solve.

Even now, one of the most important lessons that Covid is teaching us has been largely overlooked: casting viruses as villains is a bad idea. "We talk about viruses," Thomas says, "and when we do, it's about 'battling' them. For me, that's not what this feels like this moment is about. It's really about understanding the patterns—pattern awareness."

Tony Goldberg, an epidemiologist at the University of Wisconsin—Madison, says the pattern is clear: "If all viruses suddenly disappeared, the world would be a wonderful place for about a day and a half, and then we'd all die—that's the bottom line. All the essential things they do in the world far outweigh the bad things." Some even maintain the health of individual organisms, everything from fungi and plants to insects and humans.

I often refer to evolution being the best problem solver because nature has all the wisdom. We humans comprehend only a fraction of a fraction of it, which we can see only through our limited understanding. Look through a microscope at a drop of creek water or look through a telescope at a flickering dot in the night sky, and you'll glimpse the larger, deeper truth: there is so much that we cannot see or know but that is already present, exerting its influence on the creek and the cosmos—and us. How can we acknowledge that in the way we engage with the natural world to observe it, study it, and listen for fresh insights?

Very much contented am I to lie low, to cling to the soil, to be of kin to the sod. My soul squirms comfortably in the soil and sand and is happy.

—LIN YUTANG, *THE IMPORTANCE OF LIVING*

A STICKY SOLUTION TO A SLIPPERY PROBLEM

Several years ago, I received an email from Pedro J. del Nido, the chief of cardiac surgery at Boston Children's Hospital, who was treating many infants and children who had holes between the chambers of their hearts (septal defects). Closing these holes with sutures tended to tear the delicate heart tissue. He explained that the department had devices that worked well in adults, but they were permanent; they can't simply be downsized, as when a child's heart grows bigger, it eventually outgrows the device.

Could we, he asked, invent something to solve this problem? We envisioned a patch that could be placed inside a beating heart to seal the holes and then degrade as the patient's own heart tissue grew over the hole, allowing the fix to expand as the heart developed.

Back at the lab, we brainstormed possibilities, but we couldn't get anything to work. So eventually we started again—fresh, curious, and excited because we know that nature surrounds us with solutions, *ideas* for solving problems. Evolution provides millions and millions of years of research and development. With that in mind we asked: What creatures exist in nature within wet dynamic environments? These are environments that would mimic where we would be placing the patches.

Maria Pereira, then a graduate student in the lab, led the quest, asking everyone to send her pictures of sticky creatures that lived in wet places. We discovered that snails, slugs, and worms have viscous, honeylike secretions and hydrophobic (water-repelling) agents. We set about using what we learned from those tiny creatures to eventually design a glue that could push blood away from the surface of the heart for intimate contact. Ultimately, achieving strong adhesion to wet tissue required following ivy's path. Ivy crawls up buildings by sending out root hairs that insert into crevices, shrivel up, and then interlock. What if we developed a glue that didn't just stick to heart tissue, like a Band-Aid, but actually infiltrated it, like ivy on a wall, to create a strong bond, like Velcro?

We got to work, and a couple years after launching the project, we developed a flexible, thin, transparent patch that could be coated with glue, applied to the heart, and sealed in place using light to activate the glue. The glue was approved in Europe for vascular reconstruction procedures to seal blood vessels during surgery, and several studies are under way to expand its use beyond Europe.

In years to come, the technology could be used in a variety of surgeries, including sutureless nerve reconstruction and hernia repair (eliminating fixation tacks), to reduce complications and speed recovery in patients around the world. From slugs and snails to ivy, nature's playbook held the winning strategy.

Nature offers many dimensions to help us, and we derive a continuing bounty of benefits from it; we need to consider what Elder Courchene said about making offerings and thanking Mother Earth for what we take. One way to do so is to shift our focus from just taking to more gently taking— and giving back, notes the scientist and author Robin Wall Kimmerer, the recipient of a MacArthur "genius grant." Kimmerer, who interweaves Indigenous wisdom from her Potawatomi roots with her scientific training, describes the "worldview of unbridled exploitation" as "the greatest threat to life that surrounds us." The fundamental shift needed to set right our relationship with Earth begins with changing that worldview, she says. Instead of asking "What more can we take from the Earth?," she says, "Isn't the question we need 'What does the Earth ask of us?'"

Check in with how you feel in nature.
↓
Observe the wondrous web of living things.
↓
Let the interconnected support lift you.
↓
Experience the restorative, regenerative, infinite miracle of life.

We can experience the wonder of nature more by linking common things we take for granted with the intrinsic processes that nature has created. The health-boosting effects of exercising? Nature is behind that. The rich range of our emotions and our social and emotional needs? Nature's also behind that. Our ability to stay alive without needing to think about breathing or the food and drink we consume each day? Nature. Our ability to feel supported and calm? Well, nature is behind that, too. *We are nature.*

The natural world is like a cleanse for our minds, a spa that slows down the pace of things, rehabituates us to our baseline, so that even if we don't immediately experience benefits, just letting go in nature has rejuvenating effects that we might not sense until we shift far enough away from the ping-y human experience we have created—driven by drugs, alcohol, devices, marketing, productization—to step into the natural world and just be. Beyond the basic biological fact of that is also the perhaps surprising implication for self-compassion, which we need yet so often deny ourselves. Anytime we appreciate something in nature, in essence we are simultaneously appreciating something within us. If we see a beautiful sunset, we experience it not only as something external to us (the environment) but also as something internal to us, our physical senses and deeper sensibilities. When we have profound experiences of appreciation of nature, we can try to recognize our own beauty in these moments, appreciate their human dimension, and feel compassion for ourselves and others.

Nature also helps us build patience and perseverance if we let it.

Be inspired by the barely perceptible difference in the behavior of ants that Charles Henry Turner observed. Despite our judgment of ants' being robotic, if we just take time to peer a little closer, as Turner did, and develop an awareness of and curiosity about the nuances, we find that the ants are actually displaying acts of creativity—ant neurodiversity! We never lose our neurodiversity, and it's never too late to learn to express it. Consider the ways in which you feel most naturally attuned to experiences and interpret the world. What resonates for you through your own unique brain chemistry and nervous system, what feels most authentic and true to you in both mind and body? Experiment with engaging that way a bit more every day as a way to embrace nature—your own neurodiversity as part of nature's wild and vital mosaic.

I was walking the dogs through the woods one day and saw a mother and her child crouched over, looking at a rock. The mother lifted the rock and said to her child, "I wonder what creepy-crawlies we'll discover under here today!" What a captivating metaphor to carry with us: What rocks might we turn over today to activate our innate curiosity about nature?

Turning over a rock and seeing what's underneath is an instant flip-the-switch moment—like gazing up at the starry night sky, wonder struck. This is a habit that we can cultivate, a skill we can practice with joy.

Be a Solutionary

"We have to be bold and start to learn about things and the relationships with the systems that give us life," says Pandora Thomas. "We need to be the *solutionaries,* as opposed to depending on other people to come do it. And in terms of nature, we have to be the ones to rebuild those relationships." Here are some simple starters, all low–activation energy options, from Thomas and other bioinspirationalists:

SLOW DOWN. Slow down your day. Slow down your reactions. Slow down to notice, observe, and focus your senses fully in the moment.

KNOW YOUR PLACE. Having a deep knowledge and understanding of the place you inhabit is grounding in every way. People who live or work close to the land have always known this. They learn to read the weather, the soil and plant life, the migration patterns. Urban and suburban dwellers can do their version. Understand your water source and the systems that deliver it to you. Grow a garden to engage in nature's system that nourishes us. "If you're a homeowner, shift to solar and electric power. Your home should not just be technologically smart if you have no idea how it all fits together," Thomas says.

SEE FOR YOURSELF. Notice how much you rely on apps, social media, publications, and other people for information about things that impact your neighborhood or broader community. Engage more directly whenever you can.

FOCUS YOUR ATTENTIONAL PENLIGHT on friends or family members who are connected to nature, and create opportunities to learn from them and experience nature together. This can just be observing how others connect with nature—developing that awareness—and expressing curiosity about it.

TAP LEARNING RESOURCES. Check out informative public tours of recycling, power, and water treatment plants, test gardens, or sustainability projects in your own or other communities.

GET DIRTY. Plant a garden if you can, or, if not, a seed or a bulb in a pot, and tend it. Repot a plant. Rake leaves. Try composting. Study permaculture and other topics that delve into nonhuman structures and intelligence. "Ecological awareness, system awareness is crucial because that's also what will help our communities survive," Thomas says. "We can't just have specialists come help us understand how to create more resilience, because those specialists leave, and what happens then?"

CHANGE THE QUESTIONS. Shift from a transactional relationship with nature—What can you do for me?—to one based on the interconnectedness of our lives and fates with the rest of nature: What can I do to give back to the Earth? What changes can I make in how I live to conserve, protect, and cultivate nature's resources? How can we change the questions to find solutions that will repair and strengthen our relationship with nature? Beyond walks in the woods, how can we incorporate these principles into the bricks and mortar of modern life?

ONE THING AT A TIME. Make it a practice to quiet distractions, sharpen your awareness, and maximize the moment. Recognize when you're multitasking and consciously choose to focus on one thing—one person, one task, one activity—with your full attention. This is a skill that improves with practice. Multitasking makes us inefficient, but worse, as my friend Joshua Flash asserts, it clutters our mind and adds stress, and we give off anxious energy, affecting those around us and shrinking our potential for connection. Practicing one thing at a time can slow us down for a fuller, richer experience and pass that energy on to others.

EMBRACE A CONSCIOUS CADENCE FOR WORLD-MAKING. We can heal our environment by healing ourselves, and healing ourselves begins with living at a humane pace that supports clear thinking to take deliberate actions.

LIGHT THE WORLD

Create a Daring, Caring Culture

Stay present to your deepest desire
for a good life and a world that
empowers all to thrive.

*To me the inquiry is a simple one: If we do not accept
the challenge to improve our world now, who will
accept that challenge and when?*
—REGINALD "REGGIE" SHUFORD, EXECUTIVE DIRECTOR,
NORTH CAROLINA JUSTICE CENTER

The dystopian storyboard could have come from the writers' room at Marvel or Universal Pictures. The Earth is ablaze with forest fires, awash with floods in some places while elsewhere crops succumb to drought. One pandemic has wiped out millions; others loom ahead. Wars and vigilante violence fuel fear, driving millions of people from their homes as they seek refuge in areas where resources are already stretched thin. Vengeful power brokers and ideologues, unchecked, bully the world and threaten mass destruction. So begins what some scientists are calling the Anthropocene epoch, the dawning geological age when the human impact on Earth's geology and ecosystems will drive the planet—or at least human existence—toward extinction.

We all know it's not a movie—we're living it—but we don't know how it will end because we're still writing it. Now is our chance. We have all the tools we need globally: resources, technology, ingenuity, and opportunity. But we need to become *lit* in our response if we want the story to take the promising turn we desire not only for ourselves but for the generations ahead. As I said at the start of this book, the capacity for *lit* thinking and action is hardwired in each of us. It is always accessible, and we can use it with intention, at any time and in any situation. LIT tools ignite the energy to fire up every aspect of our lives. You can use them to energize a moment or strategize your way to creating the life you want.

Take a moment and imagine a world in which our best thinking and most inspired action transform the global disaster scenario and bring us back from the brink; a world in which *lit* energy and action set new forces for good into play around the planet. It's a utopian story line in the Hollywood writers' room, but this is no science fiction. This is our story to write. The visionary work of world making is ours to do. In life as in the movies, world making is a creative act of intention. We are all in this shared creative challenge now; we are world making, and we can make it a *lit* world.

We're not starting from scratch. "Humanity is waking up late to the challenges and opportunities of active planetary stewardship. But we are waking up," said a committee of Nobel Prize laureates and other leading experts who convened a global summit in 2021 and published the statement "Our Planet, Our Future." In it, they issued an urgent call to action to focus on our relationship with nature and align our energies in a new way that will serve the planet.

"We need to reinvent our relationship with planet Earth," they wrote in the statement.

The future of all life on this planet, humans and our societies included, requires us to become effective stewards of the global commons—the climate, ice, land, ocean, freshwater, forests, soils, and rich diversity of life that regulate the state of the planet, and combine to create a unique and harmonious life-support system. There is now an existential need to build economies and societies that support Earth system harmony rather than disrupt it.

*If humanity creates any particular problem, humanity
needs to be the answer to the problem.*

—MONIKA BIELSKYTE, FOUNDER OF

PROTOPIA FUTURES

In his book *Half-Earth: Our Planet's Fight for Life,* the biologist
and naturalist Edward O. Wilson described the present time in terms
of not only the peril to the planet but also unprecedented promise
because we are uniquely positioned to act with impact: "For the first
time in history a conviction has developed among those who can actually think more than a decade ahead that we are playing a global
endgame."

The times call for breakthrough strategies and action—*lit* action—on
all of those fronts if we are to solve the problems that confront us and develop the exciting possibilities that await us. The commitment to not just
try but work persistently to successfully meet the moment begins with
personal action, each of us doing what we can within our own sphere of
influence. We need to ask the high-yield questions in our own lives and
drive the conversation around us each day to create responsible, compassionate action.

That humans can be such inventive problem solvers is encouraging.
After all, there was a time when air travel, space travel, and instant
communication with people around the globe were mere fantasy. But
when the assumption that we can eventually solve problems becomes
the justification for downplaying or ignoring them, we're in trouble.

We have the creativity and problem-solving capacity needed to tackle
the problems that confront us now. The raw energy is there, but it's nothing more than potential until we activate it. You can have the greatest
sound system in the world, but you won't hear a thing till you flip the
power switch on. Those packets of seeds for your garden won't grow unless you plant them. We need a culture that creates conditions for vibrant lives and focuses resources on the most pressing problems. How
can we create it?

There comes a time when humanity is called to shift to a
new level of consciousness. . . . That time is now.
—WANGARI MAATHAI, 2004 NOBEL PEACE PRIZE WINNER

Trying to think about all this at once—problems and potential alike—
can feel daunting. There's a natural resistance to taking the first step to
set the ball in motion. But cultivating awareness is itself a first step.
You can hardly get bothered about something that hasn't first registered
in your mind. Progress isn't always about taking an actionable step forward, which some people can do more easily than others. Awareness
can be motivating; bothered awareness lowers the activation energy to
develop more. Don't disrespect or disqualify yourself if you're not quite
ready to act. It's better to get bothered about the problem and your
inaction, and use that energy to act on intention.

In practical terms, instead of feeling that it's save the world or nothing, we can bring our awareness to ourselves as being in and of the world,
think about what that means, and make one choice each day that will
add to the energy and momentum for a *lit* life. You might start simply
with the way you relate to the ground under your feet, as the permaculturist Pandora Thomas recommends. Reflect on the collective wisdom
and commitment that has guided sustainable life on this Earth for eons,
the legacy of energy, both human and nonhuman, invested in the Earth
and thus ultimately in us. Feel that energy, and let it move you. You don't
have to plant an acre, you can plant a seed. Or tend a plant. Or *observe*
a plant and cultivate an appreciation of its place, and yours, in the natural world. Awaken awareness in others—engage, engage, engage. Voice
what bothers you, what doesn't feel right, the work that isn't being done
but ought to be. Ask "the forbidden question"—the one that feels fundamental to a situation but that no one else has asked. The term was
coined in 1973 after an air force major who would be ordered to activate
a nuclear attack at the president's order asked his superiors, "How can
I know that an order I receive to launch my missiles came from a sane
president?"

Do what you can wherever you are. Be an active opportunist, and look around for inspiration, ideas, and opportunities to engage any way you can. We are surrounded by inspiring models. Or start simply by believing in and supporting others who need support to realize their potential.

> *When you find yourself deeply doubting the goodness of the human race, ask yourself these questions: Who is profiting from your sadness and your anger? Who is getting rich by making you afraid? Someone is.*
>
> —MARGARET RENKL

REGGIE SHUFORD:
START CLOSER TO HOME; DON'T GO IT ALONE

When I interviewed Reginald "Reggie" Shuford, then the executive director of the American Civil Liberties Union of Pennsylvania, whose long career as a civil rights lawyer arose from a lifelong calling to fight for equality and justice for all, he described our time as one of enormous potential "precisely because the challenges are immense" and suggested that "the personal level is exactly the place to start."

"Small acts of kindness and generosity can be meaningful and trigger a domino effect," he said. "There is something to the saying 'Think globally, act locally.' Start closer to home. Start with what you know. Don't go it alone. Connect with local individuals and organizations who share your values. They are out there."

Like so many others who shared their stories in these pages, Shuford, now the executive director of the North Carolina Justice Center, recalled the impact of certain individuals early in his life who shaped his values and, because they showed him they believed in him, shaped his belief in himself, which made all the difference.

As a kid and through his teen years, school was tough terrain. He was bullied, struggled with problems at home, and acted out a lot, particularly in junior high. In seventh grade, he said, he was repeatedly written up for various infractions and referred to the principal's office or guidance counselor. It was one teacher turned guidance counselor, Minnie Williams, who saw something more in him than a troublemaker.

"Ms. Williams was patient with me but often a bit exasperated. She would say, 'I am not quite sure what to do with you. Your grades are excellent, but your attitude and behavior leave a lot to be desired.'" By the end of that school year, she had decided what to do with him. "She said, 'I finally have an idea. I am going to take a chance on you.'" She believed he was bored and unchallenged, which was true, but his behavior distracted most others from seeing that as the underlying problem that might be addressed. The next year, she had him placed in the academically gifted program, wished him well, and added, "Don't let me down."

"Ms. Williams's faith and belief in me caused me to believe in myself," Shuford says. "For the first time, notwithstanding how many times I had heard it before, I really believed I was smart. And because she, a Black woman, had gone out on a limb for me, I was committed to not letting her down. Both my behavior and attitude changed drastically, and even my grades improved. The trajectory toward academic success, once started, never let up. I am forever indebted to Ms. Williams for her significant contribution to whatever success I have enjoyed in my life."

His high school freshman English teacher, Bonnie Daniels, was another indelible influence, recognizing his love of the subject and cultivating his interest in reading and writing. Daniels would take him to see Black-themed plays, he says, "paid for out of her own pocket," and in other ways showed that she understood his potential.

Through it all, Shuford said, his late mother, Barbara Shuford, had the greatest impact on his life. "She was uniquely kind, generous of spirit and, with the few material possessions she had, compassionate, funny, and nonjudgmental," he said. "She had empathy for everyone and never had a harsh word for anyone, notwithstanding how difficult her own life had been. She was my biggest fan and cheerleader and never hesitated to say when I made her proud. A primary source of motivation for me still is to do her legacy proud." As a civil rights litigator, a warrior in the courts, and a mentor, Shuford works to bring that legacy to life and into law. Any of us can assert the power of encouragement, looking at our lives to see who did that for us and considering how we might create that legacy, too, in the way we interact with, recognize, value, and encourage others.

> *It's almost a responsibility to share your story and where*
> *you come from, no matter what that is, to make the people*
> *who come after you, make their journey a little bit easier.*
> *That's, I feel, like the whole point of being on Earth.*
> —ADAM RIPPON, OLYMPIC MEDALIST, FIGURE SKATING

We are far more potent contributors to change than we give ourselves credit for, says Abigail Dillen, a lawyer and the president of Earthjustice, a nonprofit public-interest organization dedicated to litigating environmental issues. "We underestimate the power of contribution—of acting within our own sphere of influence to tackle the piece of the problem that is right in front of us," she wrote in her essay "Litigating in a Time of Crisis" in the powerful and inspiring anthology *All We Can Save: Truth, Courage, and Solutions for the Climate Crisis.*

> *In a few decades, if we look back from a place of relative*
> *comfort and safety, I think we will remember millions of*
> *people who saw the unprecedented danger and didn't look*
> *away, who connected with their power and used it to lead*
> *change from the ground up.*
> —ABIGAIL DILLEN, EARTHJUSTICE

As an activist, Shuford says, he values the lessons learned as touchstones for patience and perseverance of the kind that Martin Luther King, Jr., alluded to when he said, "The arc of the moral universe is long, but it bends towards justice."

"Victory often takes a lot longer than expected," Shuford says, "and there may be some losses in the meantime. And sometimes we have to give that arc a little nudge to ensure it bends in the right direction." He has learned to value the victories that "may look different than what is expected. Rather than changing the world all at once, incremental change can be meaningful, too. If I can help improve one person's life or prospects, that counts for something."

In the cultural norms of the scientific world, we're used to encountering all kinds of resistance and roadblocks. It often takes years for advances to make it from bench to bedside. Delays and setbacks can be discouraging, but looking at the long trajectory of historic advances, most of them share that kind of backstory; just look at any technology you use or see around you. Knowing that, and seeing other long-term goals come to fruition, gives us confidence in the process and a continued sense of purpose and passion for our work.

Nature teaches us that, too. Evolution is the ultimate exercise in delayed gratification, measured in geological time and the slow, painstaking path of survival, while human nature is hardwired for impulse and instant gratification. As we've driven cultural change to match that frantic pace, we've inadvertently accelerated the magnitude and urgency of the planet's crisis. Now, with an intentional mindset, we can choose to pause between impulse and action, override the impulse circuit, and choose the mindful *lit* action.

To be truly visionary, we have to root our imagination in our concrete reality while simultaneously imagining possibilities beyond that reality.
—BELL HOOKS

YOUR POWER OF ONE CAN FLIP THE SWITCH

At the lab, where our work in translational medicine is all about maximizing impact, I am always thinking about how we can develop scalable solutions—the broadest possible applications—for the problems we set out to solve. But the more I spoke with the people you have met in this book, as well as countless others who shared their stories, strategies, and suggestions, the more the power of one stood out: one person choosing to do one thing in a moment can shift the energy and open the space for more. Whether you set out to persuade others or not, by living *lit*, you help bring the *lit* world into being. And if in doing so, you inspire a few people to believe in themselves, to discover and pursue their passions and contribute, then you are in fact changing the world. Think of it as the power of the *interconnected* one, and know that we are all interconnected. That's not just a sticker for the fridge—it's a law of nature. The power of one is the power of a single seed to grow, flourish, and enrich the ecosystem. It's the acorn-to-oak story. Or consider that every one of us began as a single cell! How wild is that! Plant a seed—and tend it.

Similar patterns of energy transfer catalyze change throughout nature, from cells to soil to sea. And in the streets. Bishop Mariann Budde, the cleric and social justice activist, described the "constellation of energies" that generate momentum for change. As those energies begin to mount toward a tipping point, she said, "How do we *act* in such a way that we might move the needle on some of the issues that are surfacing now that as a country, if we're *intentional* enough and if the forces of goodness stay aligned long enough, we might be able to accomplish something that hasn't been able to be accomplished for a while? These social movements kind of spike, depending on forces that are bigger than any of us can fully understand."

The pure, positive, breakthrough energy of *lit* cuts through the inertia in everything and sparks new inspiration and action. We each have the capacity to bring this kind of energy to bear, to transform intention into action. The energy we generate may light our way alone at a particular time or light a larger swath of potential with others; we can't predict how the constellation of energies will coalesce. We can predict that even a single *lit* action will ignite more. So question. Get bothered. Reach out. Pay attention. Get active. Experiment. Be open to fresh insight, new ideas and experiences. Ground yourself in nature. Step out of your comfort zone and do new to invite more surprises and serendipity into your life. The natural world is common ground. Solutions that work for the planet will work for all of us. Look out your window. Step outside. Tend a plant. Gaze at the sky. Make the switch from the human-centric and self-centered system to the ecosystem. The fundamental core of life that we can learn from to survive and thrive is one of adaptability and diversity. Let yourself be inspired by the persistence of even the smallest living things! The simplest reconnection with nature can shift your energy in the moment to tap the greater life force that exists all around you.

What this moment calls for is a mosaic of
voices—the full spectrum of ideas and insights
on how we can turn things around.

—AYANA ELIZABETH JOHNSON AND KATHARINE K. WILKINSON,

ALL WE CAN SAVE: TRUTH, COURAGE, AND SOLUTIONS

FOR THE CLIMATE CRISIS

REPAIR AND REINVIGORATE COMMUNITY

Flip the truism that misery loves company on its head, and the truth is that so do love, joy, excitement, curiosity, and discovery. Sharing amplifies the *lit* experience. But sometimes we need help overcoming the barriers to developing a sense of community within our communities and within ourselves.

Many neighborhoods and cities have stepped up their efforts for people to meet others from outside their familiar social circle. It's been nearly fifty years since the urban sociologist Ray Oldenburg coined the term *third place* to refer to physical spaces other than home or work where people can comfortably hang out, enjoying conversation or the company of others and a feeling of shared community.

"Life without community has produced, for many, a lifestyle consisting mainly of a home-to-work-and-back-again shuttle," he wrote. "Social well-being and psychological health depend upon community." He encouraged "placemaking" as a way to inspire people to collectively reimagine and reinvent public spaces as the heart of every community. "Strengthening the connection between people and the places they share, placemaking refers to a collaborative process by which we can shape our public realm in order to maximize shared value. More than just promoting better urban design, placemaking facilitates creative patterns of use, paying particular attention to the physical, cultural, and social identities that define a place and support its ongoing evolution." A DIY placemaker activity doesn't have to be complicated. Check out the excellent Project for Public Spaces website for ideas, but start simply with an intention to observe, engage, experiment, collaborate, and improvise. You might walk your dog, plan to meet friends, or socialize to meet new people—whatever might make the place one of connection, community, creativity, or even solitude among others.

Outdoor installations, such as concrete chess tables in a park or common areas, draw strangers to share a game. New designs for open spaces include "interactive seating" and other design elements that encourage more community interaction, free outdoor concerts, community garden spaces, and more skateboarding parks where kids can be active outdoors together. Some community and online book clubs have developed more diverse selections for reading and discussion, and other efforts to bring diverse ideas and people together have also gained momentum.

Lisa Sasaki, the Smithsonian Deputy Under Secretary for Special Projects, talked with me about how inclusivity and diversity strengthen us as a nation, but only if we act to cultivate them. Often the opportunities are right in front of us, and with fresh eyes and intention we can craft solutions to the problems that have become obstacles. Sasaki saw that in her previous work with the Oakland Museum of California, where she headed up the museum's community involvement programs. As the museum struggled with low attendance and a weak pulse as part of the community it was supposed to serve, Sasaki led a major initiative that helped double the number of museum visits in four years and transformed the institution and its relationship with the neighborhood.

The museum, a concrete behemoth of brutalist design popular when it was built in the 1960s, claims a prominent spot near the beautiful lakefront of downtown Oakland, but at the time, its presence was hardly inviting. "People didn't realize that behind those big ugly concrete walls was this magical place of gardens and art and natural sciences and history that was built for them, for the people," Sasaki says. The neighborhood around it evolved in the years ahead, becoming increasingly culturally diverse, with growing communities including Chinese, Latino, and other new immigrants from around the globe.

"So this amazing vibrant confluence of cultures was happening all around this museum, but those walls had become a barrier," Sasaki explains, "and as a result of that, if you went into the neighborhoods and had conversations, which we did for our research, the neighbors didn't even recognize that the museum was a resource of value." Why? In their experience, it wasn't. In interviews, the reasons for the museum's isolation became clear: "What I heard over and over and over again, people were saying 'We live in these urban spaces, and there's not really a safe place for us to be able to gather with our families. We're working all the time—we work from nine to five, and the museum's open nine to five. I have time with my family in the evening I want to spend with them, and I don't have any safe place to go.'"

The museum was clearly isolated from the community it was meant to serve. Thus began the problem-solving work by the museum leadership. A new set of questions drove their work: "How do you break down those walls? What are the barriers that are keeping people from coming, that are not allowing us to create that flow and shared space?" In discussion groups with community members, Sasaki says, "we listened very carefully." And the museum launched an initiative to respond to the needs the community had identified.

Friday Nights at OMCA was launched to create space for the community within the museum. The leadership threw open the large gates that close the museum off and put out picnic tables, and it became a hub for food trucks, live music, and free or reduced admission to the museum complex itself. Because that area of downtown Oakland is typically deserted after five o'clock, they addressed concerns about safety by inviting the local fire department and providing free food for the firefighters. They were grateful for the presence of first responders if needed.

In a lot of ways I think at its very best, museums are the kitchen tables and can be the kitchen tables of our country, because we are the place that can contribute to and trigger some thoughtful and important discussions.

—LISA SASAKI

"What ended up happening from that moment of creating that liminal space, that area of overlap between these two very different worlds was something that was really beautiful," Sasaki says. Although Friday Nights at OMCA was suspended during the pandemic, at its height it drew up to four thousand people on Friday nights and "led to the sense of the community really owning the museum," Sasaki says. The revitalized relationship with the community led the museum leadership to change the building's fortresslike structure, eventually overhauling the walls and removing barricades, creating new entrances that allow people to freely flow in from the Lake Merritt grounds and use the space. "It was literally a matter of bringing down the walls," Sasaki says.

On an individual level, we can bring down cultural walls in many different ways. The lessons of the OMCA example are applicable even on a smaller scale in any neighborhood. We can also actively work to lift barriers across all fields that have excluded so many people from full access to participation and marginalized or exploited their valuable contributions.

Just one example: Charles Henry Turner, who pioneered the insect behavior studies mentioned earlier and whose undergraduate thesis on the neuroanatomy of bird brains was published in the journal *Science* in 1891, published more than seventy papers in diverse fields during his career. Despite his distinguished body of work and having earned his Ph.D. from the University of Chicago in 1907, entrenched racism in society and in the sciences sharply limited opportunity and resources for African Americans such as Turner. Only recently has there been a concerted effort to address the legacy of "shameful neglect" of his scientific contributions, as *Nature* contributor Charles I. Abramson wrote in "Henry Turner Remembered." A growing number of others, both in science and beyond, are pressing for something better.

UNPRECEDENTED TIMES, TECHNOLOGY, AND OPPORTUNITIES

On so many fronts—health, education, the environment, human rights—we are on the exciting horizon of nearly limitless potential for a *lit* world. Unlike any other time in history, we are equipped to solve large-scale problems with rapidly developing new technology. Nano-technology, for example, which allows us to manipulate molecules and atoms, is ubiquitous in the research community. All labs have access to it. We also now have global communication platforms in place that enable social media as well as specialized platforms and networks that enable unprecedented scientific, social action, diplomatic, governmen-tal, and other cross-cultural exchanges. We've never had such advanced tools to make communication so swift and accessible.

The initial period of the Covid pandemic brought that home to many in science and medicine. A technologically advanced global society pop-ulated with problem solvers everywhere confronted an acute global challenge that had the potential to impact every single person on Earth in a negative way, mobilizing the global community to positively im-pact civilization as we know it. As a global community, we tackled the emerging challenges and generated significant solutions that in the past would have taken months or years to produce, from vaccines, to masks, to modified ventilators to serve more patients, to new therapies, to test-ing, to ways of tracking the spread, to ways of communicating truths and debunking myths through peer-reviewed research.

When Covid hit, I was asked to colead the N95 respirator work group at the Mass General Brigham Center for COVID Innovation to help de-velop mask backup plans for the hospitals. The work group quickly grew to 320 people, including engineers, basic scientists, students, people from industry, and people from the community who were interested in helping.

One of our many efforts involved addressing the shortage of small-sized N95 masks for frontline hospital workers. (That shortage had also revealed an equity issue in that upward of 90 percent of nurses are female and typically needed the smaller-size mask for the appropriate fit for proper protection.) The supply was quickly running out. Within that larger effort a very specific one arose that involved repairing thousands of elastic bands on a shipment of N95 masks that had been donated after it was discovered that they'd been damaged in storage. The New Balance shoe company volunteered to help, and we were able to quickly increase our manufacturing scale and deliver the repaired masks to the hospitals for immediate use.

The pull of community, purpose, and collective energy was powerful for all of us, amplified by the inspiring commitment we could see all around us—around the world—by so many. The *lit* energy was palpable and, as *lit* energy does, led to more collaborations on other fronts focused on innovations to prevent disease transmission not only for Covid but for future pandemics.

The N95 work group was just one example of how a highly diverse team came together with a deep intention—to respond to the Covid crisis—and swiftly evolved a working structure and a decision and execution process. Energies coalesced in the rapid evolution of process with the potential for immediate impact. All of that required complex collaboration across disciplines, institutions, and organizational systems. Despite the inevitable missteps and setbacks in responding to a crisis that was unfolding in real time, the unprecedented collaborative potential of our time also revealed itself.

> *I don't have the power to dismantle Monsanto. But what I do have is the capacity to change how I live on a daily basis and how I think about the world. I just have to have faith that when we change how we think, we suddenly change how we act and how those around us act, and that's how the world changes. It's by changing hearts and changing minds. And it's contagious.*
>
> —ROBIN WALL KIMMERER

I'm reminded of Steffanie Strathdee's comment about the astonishing collaborative response that saved her husband's life several years ago, when he was near death due to an antibiotic-resistant superbug infection. Strathdee drew on her knowledge and network as a leading infectious disease expert to reach out to researchers and clinicians, most of whom she'd never met, to try to concoct an experimental treatment that might save her husband and hold promise for others. As she shared in *The Perfect Predator: A Scientist's Race to Save Her Husband from a Deadly Superbug*, with very little time and little chance of success, she sent cold-call emails, posted on social media, and searched the internet for possibilities, eventually piecing together suggestions, a strategy, and a tag team of scientists and essential others who created an experimental treatment that eventually saved him.

"I was just the spark," Strathdee says now, explaining that the synergy came from others, often by chance, the result of serendipitous conversations and encounters. "They could see there was something in it for the greater good, that sense of collectivism," she says. "That's what I see happening. And that's what I find incredibly exciting—that even though it's a scary time to be alive, the vulnerability we have as individuals and as human beings is bringing us together to combat a problem."

The same holds true in every facet of human endeavor, from arts and literacy programs to socially responsible business and social and environmental activism. This is part of the unlimited human potential we all have within us that attracts like energy from those around us. When someone defines a problem and shows commitment and passion to solving it, that energy creates massive gravity, and not only in that particular situation. It signals to others that *anyone can do this; we all have the power*—the same power of energy that resonates in the stories from Elder Courchene at Turtle Lodge and Steffanie Strathdee searching for a way to save her husband.

It's human nature that when someone brings their passion forward for a cause, others want to join in and help. That is built into our human DNA. Often the first step is the hardest, and it can be hard to imagine all the help we will be able to recruit. But once we get moving, get the ball rolling, it picks up speed, momentum. So we get to decide: we can focus on either starting something new or joining something already in motion.

Rather than wait for others to act or for collective momentum to build before we jump in, we can use everyday opportunities to generate momentum—seed the conversation and stimulate the energy for action on the issues we feel are most pressing. You never know when something you say or do will be the spark that prompts someone else to reach out, take action, and ignite the energy for needed change. The passion and commitment of a single person, which create the enormous gravity and magically bring people to the table to help solve problems, when they're aimed for good, are grounded in compassion at its core.

"People often think that great leaders are born, not made—that they are somehow destined for greatness," writes environmental activist Lynne Twist in her book *Living a Committed Life: Finding Freedom and Fulfillment in a Purpose Larger Than Yourself.* "I believe, however, it's the opposite—that committing oneself to an inspiring cause is what forges you into a great human being. It's the commitment that shapes you into who you need to be to fulfill it. It's not that you have to be smart enough or talented enough or knowledgeable enough to make commitments. You make the commitment, and then the talent, the knowledge, the passion, the resources start to become visible and move toward you."

JAMES DOTY: COMPASSION AS HUMANITY'S COMMON DENOMINATOR

James Doty, the Stanford neurosurgeon who launched an initiative to study the neurological underpinnings of compassion, explains that even with our innate capacity for compassion, it isn't necessarily a reflexive response, especially with people or in situations that are stressful for us. It can be easy to feel compassion for someone we feel sorry for or someone we can relate to. It can be harder to have compassion for people whose appearance, behavior, or beliefs put us off. But Doty and other compassion activists say that this is especially fertile ground in which to practice and cultivate compassion.

Compassion is a willingness to look at another human being with the most generous eyes that you possibly can. Even if that person has done something that you really disagree with or you've done horribly wrong, to do your very best to think of that person and to look at that person and to try to see them with the eyes of their mother or father or that of their really close friend, or ask yourself: How could I treat this person if they were beloved to me?

—BISHOP MARIANN BUDDE

I consider compassion to be empathy *lit*—empathy in action—to not only see things through someone else's eyes and understand their perspective but actively transform that energy to make a difference. In effect you convert empathy's potential into kinetic energy, kinetic compassion. That might be on an individual level or in your family, workplace, or community.

Doty and other mentors in the emerging compassion movement suggest raising your awareness of compassion as an innate human capacity and a powerful energy source that you can direct. You might start with a practice of self-compassion: accept yourself and your imperfections, and say something kind to yourself. I often try to consume media that highlight stories, research, and practical tips for developing compassion or that connect with me emotionally. Nature itself offers us that when we take a moment to appreciate it and at the same time recognize ourselves as part of it, worthy of compassion. Brené Brown did a study of many of the greats from the past, people who were known for their compassion, and a commonality she found is that they all set strict boundaries for their lives. For example, people who are compassionate tend to uphold their personal boundaries, protecting their own space while protecting a safe space for others as well.

Compassion is not just about having a compassionate mindset; it is about pinching our brain to listen more closely to others with all senses activated; to quiet the impatient yet caring parts of us that rush to problem solve or the reactive pings to push a conversation quickly in a comfortable direction or one that we control.

A calling to care is innate to us as humans. Compassionate communication invites mutuality. In a work setting, in addition to opening the space and listening to others, I find it helps to share aspects of my struggles or my vulnerabilities with others. Being open about my rejections and my failures, being a little more transparent, invites others to do the same. I'll share my thoughts as they evolve, accepting that we don't need to say everything perfectly; life is an iterative process.

In the context of my lab, the tools and compartmentalizations that I developed to maximize rigor and impact in the work over time have become hardwired into my instincts and reactions. But they aren't impervious to change. Personal evolution is the point, after all, a *lit* process. With compassion, you can cultivate *lit* in the simplest ways.

Now when I meet with people, I try to observe my responses to them, and since I'm often reactive and want to change that, I'm working on compassion skill building. Starting with compassion for myself, I mute my inner critic and focus instead on others and their experience in the moment. I pay attention to how they are responding to me. Then I try to adjust as the meeting goes on, experimenting with my words, tone, and body language. This might seem routine to many people, but for those of us who struggle at times to read social cues effectively and to respond as we'd like to if we'd had the presence of mind, this practice of self-compassion and compassionate listening is *lit*—it's a start. Practice makes the habit more natural, less effortful.

TAPPING THE SPIRITUAL SOURCE

Science is behind the curve in explaining our capacity to have transcendent or spiritual experiences. The field has only relatively recently emerged from a long-held silence on the concept of a kind of spiritual intelligence that is as real as cognition or brain-based intelligence. Long considered impossible to quantify and thus impossible to prove scientifically, it could not even be acknowledged as legitimate. That hasn't stopped humans from having such experiences and describing them, from dream states to near-death experiences to flashes of insight or a sense of oneness with a universal presence or higher plane.

The science of spirituality is evolving, too, as MRI brain scan imagery and other methods provide glimpses into the human brain during meditation and other states that we might consider aspects of higher consciousness or transcendence. Spiritual practices and experiences, like any other life experiences, register in the brain. How can they not? As Elder Courchene pointed out, spirituality and science don't invalidate each other; they offer two distinct approaches to understanding the universe we inhabit, two valuable realms of insight into a reality.

> *When an ecosystem is fully functioning, all the*
> *members are present at the assembly. To speak*
> *of wilderness is to speak of wholeness.*
> —GARY SNYDER, POET, AUTHOR, AND ENVIRONMENTAL ACTIVIST

Spirituality offers a particular *lit* factor as an energy source, whatever way you tap it, whether through nature, cultural traditions, or organized religion. The nineteenth-century American Transcendentalist philosophy, expressed in the writings of Ralph Waldo Emerson and Henry David Thoreau, described the fundamental unity of all creation, the basic goodness of humankind, and the superiority of insight and spiritual intelligence over logic. Much of that centered on nature as our spiritual bedrock. Today we talk about global challenges such as climate change and environmental devastation as transcendent issues because the future of life on Earth depends on how we solve those problems. I also see a connection with our spiritual capacities as a unique resource or renewable energy in our lives. Spiritual engagement is a facet of our nature-based, embodied intelligence.

The *lit* response invites us to broaden our exploration of spiritual values and teachings to find new ways to use them in service of the global good. In that quest, cultivating the spiritual space is full of exciting opportunities for discovery and advances for humankind.

Today our very survival depends on our ability to stay awake, to adjust to new ideas, to remain vigilant and to face the challenge of change.
—MARTIN LUTHER KING, JR.

BISHOP MARIANN BUDDE: AN EXAMINED LIFE

"There is a universality to the spiritual path, and the further you are, the more particular you become on that path; if you're open to its teachings and you really are transformed by it, the more universal it becomes," Bishop Mariann Budde told me. "And so Martin Luther King was a Baptist preacher, and who was he most influenced by but Mahatma Gandhi in India, right? Desmond Tutu, the Anglican archbishop of South Africa, who fought his entire life to end apartheid—the Dalai Lama was one of his closest friends, and so you see this connection. There are basic truths that are at the heart of every spiritual tradition that has gravitas and depth to it, and they are universal."

Something about the spiritual path "constantly puts before us a reflective life, the invitation to an examined life, the invitation to see one's own shortcomings, the invitation to live one's life with an orientation that is not focused solely on the self," Budde says. "And if you have that, there's an orientation toward your life that is not simply about your survival or even about the survival of your clan, but of a higher purpose. And part of the spiritual quest is to walk that path, however you find yourself drawn to it."

The path varies for each of us. Some of us will explore through prayer or meditation, formal religious practice or traditions, or in activism in service to others or the planet. Stephen Wilkes, the photographer, finds the transcendent experience in the visual language of photography, and he sets out to open that sensory space for those who view his works. In his Ellis Island project, for example, he says he set out to capture the rich visual texture of the rooms in "the gorgeous paint, the Renaissance-looking color in these rooms, and the very simple, elegant composition."

But there is more in those photographs, he explains, that is not apparent to the eye. "It is the history of the people who lived in those rooms, who died in those rooms," he says. "The immigrant experience lives in my photographs. I became very keenly aware of it as I was photographing on the island. As I got certain images back, I would have this feeling, the feeling I had in the room, the feeling that I have on the street. The 'Yes, you can take my picture, no, you can't take my picture,' except there were no people in the rooms at Ellis Island. I was feeling this palpable sense of humanity in an empty room. It was as if the light was reenergizing the history that was in that room."

As he began to explore the experience more deeply, he says, "I saw that there was this tremendous power—what looked like an empty room in architectural photographs were literally overflowing with emotion." As he edited down the thousands of images to create the final gallery of seventy-six images, he says, "every one had that feeling in it, the subtext of the humanity that was in this room. There was something else that happened in this room."

We are always in a state of evolution. We are evolving constantly, and we are in a very important moment of our evolution right now, to evolve to a greater understanding of how we should live and behave as human beings. What has always been neglected is the spiritual understanding.
—ELDER DAVE COURCHENE, ANISHINAABE NATION

To cultivate a *lit* spiritual connection, imagine your heart and soul (instead of your logic-driven brain) in the driver's seat at different points in your day. Especially when you feel stressed or impatient, give spirit a chance to slow you down so you can engage, listen, and respond.

DINNER TABLE WISDOM FOR A *LIT* WORLD

In our family, we don't always gather around the kitchen table for dinner, but we aim for one time a day that brings us together in that spirit to share a meal and conversation or time for reflection. It isn't always cheerful. Sometimes it's definitely contentious. Regardless, the one thing we've come to know is that it's important to be able to bring up what's on our minds, and sometimes in our hearts, for some open-mic time—a time when we give one another the benefit of the doubt and try to engage with curiosity, practice nonjudgment and compassion, and really listen to understand a different point of view. Kids, especially, need to be heard. But we all gain from the opportunity to reflect on how we may have handled something the day before, or some time past, with the awareness that we have it in our power to recalibrate our thinking and behavior moving forward. Each day brings new possibilities, and each of us brings fresh potential to every moment. How will we use it? The idea is to bring the big issues and universal messages down to the everyday challenges we face, the choices we make, and the values that guide us.

Togetherness raises optimism and creativity. When people feel they belong to one another, their lives are stronger, richer, and more joyful.
—VIVEK MURTHY, *TOGETHER: THE HEALING POWER OF HUMAN CONNECTION IN A SOMETIMES LONELY WORLD*

So whether the question is about where to devote attention and resources for our immediate family or the global one, we can practice stepping outside the worn grooves of conversation and engage in some *lit* thinking, some visioning, some world making. Even in our family's relatively small sphere of action, brainstorming can energize our attention and commitment to choices we can make that will be truly beneficial to us and to the planet.

I like to imagine some kitchen table wisdom applied to the redesign of Walt Disney's Carousel of Progress concept for the *lit* age. It's not a stretch to envision it. We can replace the unquestioned awe of technological progress with a more thoughtful, more thorough view of the costs and benefits associated with innovation. We can take the natural world into account, and treat the living planet as our home and family, not as a backdrop. We can recognize complexity as a fact and turn to it with our best problem-solving skills and *lit* engagement. In the process we will see challenges to be met, not excuses for inaction.

LIGHT THE WORLD: STAY PROXIMATE, AND YOUR PASSION WILL FIND A PURPOSE

We spend so much time cocooned in our own worlds, seeming to gravitate inward. Perhaps it is a survival mechanism, a way to deal with all the noise and nonstop stimuli. But to maximize survival and thriving, we need to embrace the interconnections, the diversity of thoughts and frames of mind in this textured world of ours. For example, wearing ear pods while we are out and about on subways or buses, while in line at the grocery store or a coffee shop, means we lose the opportunity for chance encounters to connect, to observe or reflect on the lives of others. Sometimes we need that solitude from interaction, especially if we feel vulnerable to the negative energy of other people. But it's important to be aware of what more we are blocking when we tune out. Part of developing compassion is our inner work: spending time thinking about others and letting chance interactions randomly and frequently ping our attention and emotions. These are opportunities to shift from our narrow mindset and nurture our personal evolution.

We can't always be around the same dinner table, or even in the same community garden, but we can step up our efforts, knowing the potential that proximity opens up for us. Keeping our eye on the prize can boost our motivation and lower the activation energy of taking the first step. If physical proximity isn't an option, then boost the *lit* value of social media and other platforms that enable you to participate in conversations or shared presence remotely. The point is to bridge distances, lift barriers, and cultivate relationships with genuine caring.

As diverse and sometimes distant as global concerns may feel, it is possible to stay proximate to the source of well-being by embracing nature as who and what we are, seeing inspiration all around us as a means of cultivating compassionate connection.

Opportunities to create a *lit* world are all around us. To cultivate is to nurture something, to tend it with special attention and with the intention to help it grow. A farmer cultivates crops. Gardeners talk about feeding the soil, cultivating it to create the optimal growth environment for their plants. In the lab we culture cells, cultivate them to gain insight into biological processes we can tap for therapeutic innovations. In the larger world, we cultivate all kinds of things: ideas, interests, relationships, and connections. We can cultivate a *lit* life and a *lit* world the same way, with care and intention, using the tools we have to activate energy for good and use it to light the world.

Renew the Spark:
Life Ignition Tools (LIT) Questions

What constellation of energies creates the conditions that infuse fresh energy into your day: work, family, time outdoors, social settings, rest and relaxation? What maximizes your curiosity, compassion, and intention? There's no need for a quick answer. This and the other questions below are meant for reflection that can hone your intentions. Whether a thought comes to mind or you're stumped and can't think of an answer, reflect on it, explore a memory or whatever comes to mind, look to the natural world for ideas and inspiration, and let that be a start as you engage *lit* and ask: What's next?

FLIP THE SWITCH. What is an example of a time you intercepted your routine patterns to make simple changes that set the ball in motion? This could be an opinion or belief that you once had about yourself but have changed. For things in your life about which you want to be more intentional, what is holding you back?

LIVE FOR THE QUESTIONS. What is an example of a time you asked an intentional question that energized your mind? How do you "think about how you think"? How do you understand yourself as a problem solver, a learner, or an observer of others and the world around you?

GET BOTHERED. What is an example of a time something incentivized you to care and channel your energy into something? What is one "Why?" that motivates you?

BE AN ACTIVE OPPORTUNIST. Opportunism *lit* is grounded in contribution, cultivating connections and relationships for action that serves a greater good. What is an example of a time you actively recognized and responded to this kind of opportunity? How do you actively create these opportunities?

PINCH YOUR BRAIN. What is an example of a time you resisted the pulls that cause unintentional mind drift to focus your attention on what you wish? In this very moment, what is something wondrous you'd like to let your mind wander with?

GET HOOKED ON MOVEMENT. What is an example of a small step you have taken that made you feel energized for more? What single thing can you easily do to bring more movement into your life?

FALL IN LOVE WITH PRACTICE. What experiences have you had with practicing a skill that gives you joy? What motivates you to be persistent with your practice?

DO NEW, DO DIFFERENT. What is an example of a time you confronted what typically holds you back to do something new and interesting or invigorating? How do you typically encounter surprises or unexpected experiences? What is something new you've thought of doing but have been hesitant to try?

FOCUS BEYOND FAILURE. What setback have you encountered in which a fresh insight completely changed your mindset moving forward? What is your go-to response for dealing with setbacks, both emotionally and tactically?

BE HUMAN. BE HUMBLE. What is an example of a time you responded to something someone said or did with your heart instead of a reflexive reaction? What are steps you could take to be a little more compassionate toward yourself?

PRESS "PAUSE." What is an example of a time you've been able to step away from the hustle and bustle of your life to refresh and recharge your energy? What are the challenges you experience in setting boundaries to protect your downtime?

HUG NATURE. What is an example of an encounter with something in the natural world that calmed your mind or soothed your soul? How would you define your relationship with nature, and how has it evolved (if at all) over time?

AFTERWORD

The Answers Are in Questions

From my travels and from watching documentaries about various cultures, for me, the question that arises as a north star illuminating the limits of a fixed perspective is: How much of what we think is ordinary and "normal" is different in other cultures? In other words, "normal" is malleable, a cultural construct, and much as we can look to nature for inspiration, we can look to other cultures for ideas—both traditions and innovations—to seed new idea generation in our own lives and work. As Peter Drucker, the management consultant, educator, and author, has said, "The important and difficult job is never to find the right answers. It is to find the right question."

I work with this truth in the lab every day and included it as a LIT tool because I've seen how questions can unlock unimaginable insights and innovation. As Hal B. Gregersen, the author of *Questions Are the Answer: A Breakthrough Approach to Your Most Vexing Problems at Work and in Life*, has said, "Questions have a curious power to unlock new insights and positive behavior change in every part of our lives. They can get people unstuck and open new directions for progress no matter what they are struggling with."

Here's a question I've mentioned before but feel is so fundamental that it bears repeating: *How do we define the village to encompass nature and all of humanity, embrace diversity of all kinds, and expand our sense of connection rather than close the borders of belonging to those we don't yet know or understand?*

The following questions from conversations and research for this book can also be helpful starters.

*What impact can I have, no matter how small, to improve
the life of one person each day?*

JAMES DOTY

What is enough?

DAVID SUZUKI

*How can you deepen your connection to the nonhuman
world today?
How are you treating others?*

PANDORA THOMAS

*How can we find a way to unite as humanity to have a
stronger voice of how we should be living and treating each
other as human beings?*

ELDER DAVE COURCHENE, ANISHINAABE NATION

*We're awake now, and the question is: How do we stay
awake to the living world? How do we make the act of asking
nature's advice a normal part of everyday inventing?*

JANINE BENYUS

How could I treat this person if they were beloved to me?

BISHOP MARIANN BUDDE

*What is your strategy to achieve clarity in your life? What
can you do or what have you found that brings you clarity?*

JESSICA SIMONETTI

I encourage you to live for the questions in your own way, step into
the space they open for conversation, reflection, and eventually action.
Create your own *lit* life!

ACKNOWLEDGMENTS

I have received incredible support throughout my life and have deep appreciation for the limitless patience, understanding, and brilliant enlightenment and love of my wife. Thank you.

To my mother, Suzie Vanston; my father, Mel Karp; and my sister, Jen Karp, too: without you I'd have succumbed to my learning challenges and been isolated and downright blue! Thank you, Mom, for holding my hand as I struggled with school. Thank you, Dad, for getting me curious about nature. It was totally my fuel!

To my incredible teachers Lyle Couch, Ed McAuley, and Glen McMullen and mentors, including Robert Langer, John Davies, Molly Shoichet, and Jaro Sodek: you saw my potential, sparking curiosity and igniting passion and my interest in medical innovation.

My children, Jordyn and Josh, bring me so much joy and inspire me every day. My love for them, and for our Cavaliers, Ryder and Ginger, is more than words can say! Back to my wife, Jessica Simonetti, whose boundless wisdom and spiritual connection have helped me evolve and learn about myself; her inspiring compassion and ability to change my perspective and mindset are gifts. And my gratitude for the support from my wife's family, and friends, including Mike, Gil, Jason, Ryan, Dan, Ben, Michael, Koen, and Josh, as well as those no longer with us, including Angela Haynes and Dick Butterfield.

To my wonderful collaborator, Teresa Barker, whose deep commitment to world making and with whom I have a magical synergy, thank you for your brilliance, kindness, support, mentorship, and energy—I have learned so much about purposeful communication and the wonders of life from you. You have helped me define and redefine what is most important.

To Mariska van Aalst, Alisa Bowman, Elaine St. Peter, Steve Weiner, Rebecca Barker, Sue Shellenbarger, Aaron and Lauren Weiner, and Dolly Joern: thank you.

I'm so grateful to Cassie Jones, Jill Zimmerman, and all the wonderful and helpful people who have contributed at William Morrow.

A big shout-out to my agent, Heather Jackson, for her salient advice along the way and for helping me find a wonderful home for *LIT*. And to Teresa's agent, Madeleine Morel, for her enthusiastic support.

I appreciate the generosity of all those I interviewed for the book, whose stories, insights, and passions inspired me and can now carry that *lit* spark forward to a broader audience. This includes those I met through chance encounters and everyday interactions, from Uber drivers to coffee shop commuters. Thank you, students and collaborators; my extended family and friends; and the staff and administrators at Brigham and Women's Hospital, Harvard Medical School, Harvard Stem Cell Institute, Broad Institute of Harvard and MIT, and Harvard-MIT Division of Health Sciences and Technology.

A final shout-out to those whose limitless potential has evaded others and who at times have felt as though they didn't fit in or who, like me, have been told, "No, set your sights lower," "You're doing it the wrong way," "You can't do it," and so on. Just know that nature never judges and you are a critical part of the natural ecosystem of life. Nature is always on your side when you engage it with kindness and integrity.

NOTES

Introduction: One Boy's Journey to LIT

ix   *"The universe is full of magical things"*: Eden Phillpotts, *A Shadow Passes* (New York: The Macmillan Company, 1919), 17.

ix   *Anxiety and depression:* Megan Brenan, "Americans' Reported Mental Health at New Low; More Seek Help," Gallup, December 21, 2022, https://news.gallup.com/poll/467303/americans-reported -mental-health-new-low-seek-help.aspx; Joan P. A. Zolot, "Depression Diagnoses Surge Nationwide," *American Journal of Nursing* 118, no. 8 (2018): 18.

xiii   *I didn't know it:* Shriram Ramanathan, "Nickel Oxide Is a Material That Can 'Learn' like Animals and Could Help Further Artificial Intelligence Research," The Conversation, December 21, 2021, https://theconversation.com/nickel-oxide-is-a-material-that-can -learn-like-animals-and-could-help-further-artificial-intelligence -research-173048.

xiv   *Emerging science shows:* Krista Tippett, "The Thrilling New Science of Awe," February 2, 2023, *On Being,* podcast, https://onbeing.org /programs/dacher-keltner-the-thrilling-new-science-of-awe.

xvii   *Thomas Edison was "addled":* Library of Congress, "Life of Thomas Alva Edison," https://www.loc.gov/collections/edison-company -motion-pictures-and-sound-recordings/articles-and-essays /biography/life-of-thomas-alva-edison/.

xviii   *it takes as little:* David S. Yeager et al., "A National Experiment Reveals Where a Growth Mindset Improves Achievement," *Nature* 573, no. 7774 (2019): 364–69.

xviii   *National Study of Learning Mindsets:* David S. Yeager, *The National Study of Learning Mindsets, [United States], 2015–2016* (Ann Arbor, MI: Inter-university Consortium for Political and Social Research, 2021).

xviii   *schools are a lightning rod:* National Center for Education Statistics, "Students with Disabilities," U.S. Department of Education, May 2022, https://nces.ed.gov/programs/coe/indicator/cgg/students-with -disabilities.

xix   *"Today, we want":* Temple Grandin, "Temple Grandin: Society Is Failing Visual Thinkers, and That Hurts Us All," *New York Times,* January 9, 2023, https://www.nytimes.com/2023/01/09/opinion /temple-grandin-visual-thinking-autism.html.

xix   *"All children start":* Jessica Shepherd, "Fertile Minds Need Feeding," *Guardian,* February 10, 2009, https://www.theguardian.com /education/2009/feb/10/teaching-sats.

xix   *"The key is not to standardize":* Ken Robinson, *The Element: How Finding Your Passion Changes Everything* (New York: Penguin, 2009), 238.

xix   *"Human resources are":* Ken Robinson, "Bring On the Learning Revolution!" TED Talk, 2010, https://www.ted.com/talks/sir_ken _robinson_bring_on_the_learning_revolution.

xix   *In our conversation:* Temple Grandin, scientist, author, autism education advocate, in discussion with Jeff Karp and Mariska van Aalst, July 6, 2018; discussion with Jeff Karp and Teresa Barker, July 19, 2021.

xxi   *"Everything in life is vibration":* Arthur Austen Douglas, *1955 Quotes of Albert Einstein*, ebook (UB Tech, 2016), 60.

xxii   *we are late in recognizing:* Ed Yong, *An Immense World: How Animal Senses Reveal the Hidden Realms Around Us* (New York: Random House, 2022).

xxii   *"planetary intelligence":* James Bridle, *Ways of Being: Animals, Plants, Machines: The Search for a Planetary Intelligence* (New York: Farrar, Straus, and Giroux, 2022), 10.

xxii   *"Microscopic parts of your neurons":* Lisa Feldman Barrett, "People's Words and Actions Can Actually Shape Your Brain—A Neuroscientist Explains How," ideas.TED.com, November 17, 2020, https://ideas.ted .com/peoples-words-and-actions-can-actually-shape-your-brain-a -neuroscientist-explains-how/.

xxvi   *an "energy-saving" mode:* Zahid Padamsey et al., "Neocortex Saves Energy by Reducing Coding Precision During Food Scarcity," *Neuron* 110, no. 2 (2022): 280–96.

xxvi   *Spend too much time:* Baowen Xue et al., "Effect of Retirement on Cognitive Function: The Whitehall II Cohort Study," *European Journal of Epidemiology* 33, no. 10 (2018): 989–1001.

xxvii   *"What you're getting":* Allison Whitten, "The Brain Has a 'Low-Power Mode' That Blunts Our Senses," Quanta Magazine, June 14, 2022, https://www.quantamagazine.org/the-brain-has-a-low-power-mode -that-blunts-our-senses-20220614/.

xxix   *"The old brain is selfishness":* Rudolph Tanzi, neuroscientist at Harvard Medical School, leading Alzheimer's researcher, author, keyboardist, in discussion with Jeff Karp and Mariska van Aalst, September 20, 2018; discussion with Jeff Karp and Teresa Barker, June 26, 2020, and June 18, 2021.

Get the Ball Rolling! Lower the Activation Energy

xxxvi   *"willingness of the mind":* Robin Wall Kimmerer, *Gathering Moss: A Natural and Cultural History of Mosses* (Corvallis: Oregon State University Press, 2003), 8.

xxxix   *Ask someone to join you:* Mingdi Xu et al., "Two-in-One System and Behavior-Specific Brain Synchrony During Goal-Free Cooperative Creation: An Analytical Approach Combining Automated Behavioral Classification and the Event-Related Generalized Linear Model," *Neurophotonics* 10, no. 1 (2023): 013511-1.

xxxix *chemical and electrical signaling:* Lydia Denworth, "Brain Waves Synchronize When People Interact," *Scientific American* (July 1, 2023), https://www.scientificamerican.com/article/brain-waves -synchronize-when-people-interact/.

xxxix *Our genes are programmed:* Annaëlle Charrier et al., "Clock Genes and Altered Sleep-Wake Rhythms: Their Role in the Development of Psychiatric Disorders," *International Journal of Molecular Sciences* 18, no. 5 (2017): 938.

Flip the Switch: What's Holding You Back?

1 *"We have to be willing":* Lynne Twist, cofounder Pachamama Alliance, in discussion with Teresa Barker, May 3, 2022.

6 *"When you become comfortable":* Eckhart Tolle, *A New Earth: Create a Better Life* (New York: Penguin, 2009), 274–75.

10 *"What stands in the way":* Marcus Aurelius, *Meditations,* Book 5.20, trans. George Long, http://classics.mit.edu/Antoninus/meditations .html.

12 *"The inner critic doesn't exist":* James Shaheen interview with Jan Chozen Bays, "How to Break Free of the Inner Critic," *Tricycle: The Buddhist Review,* August 7, 2022, https://tricycle.org/article/jan -chozen-bays-burnout/.

13 *"Show up for life":* Joyce Roché, in discussion with Jeff Karp and Teresa Barker, May 26, 2021.

15 *"Oscar Wilde famously said":* Reggie Shuford, executive director, North Carolina Justice Center, in email discussion with Jeff Karp and Teresa Barker, May 10, 2022.

19 *"There's magic in beginning":* Diana Nyad, author, motivational speaker, long-distance swimmer, in discussion with Jeff Karp and Mariska van Aalst, May 30, 2018.

20 *"People have several times":* Tom Rath, *StrengthsFinder 2.0* (New York: Gallup Press, 2007).

Live for the Questions: Swap Caution for Curiosity and the Deeper Dig

22 *"Those moments in our lives":* Krista Tippett, "Foundations 2: Living the Questions," October 20, 2022, *On Being,* podcast, https:// www.ivoox.com/foundations-2-living-the-questions-audios-mp3 _rf_94396875_1.html.

22 *One of the answers:* Frequency Therapeutics, April 8, 2023, www .frequencytx.com.

25 *"Questioning takes the familiar":* Julia Brodsky, "Why Questioning

Is the Ultimate Learning Skill," *Forbes*, December 29, 2020, https://www.forbes.com/sites/juliabrodsky/2021/12/29/why-questioning-is-the-ultimate-learning-skill/?sh=7ff9bc2c399f.

29 *"If you never question things"*: jamesclear.com, https://jamesclear.com/quotes/if-you-never-question-things-your-life-ends-up-being-limited-by-other-peoples-imaginations.

29 *discovery of split genes:* Michael Blanding, "The Man Who Helped Launch Biotech," *MIT Technology Review*, August 18, 2015, https://www.technologyreview.com/2015/08/18/166642/the-man-who-helped-launch-biotech/.

31 *the "seductive lure of curiosity":* Lily FitzGibbon, Johnny King L. Lau, and Kou Murayama, "The Seductive Lure of Curiosity: Information as a Motivationally Salient Reward," *Current Opinion in Behavioral Sciences* 35 (2020): 21–27, https://doi.org/10.1016/j.cobeha.2020.05.014.

31 *"The Future Belongs to the Curious":* Behnaz Nojavanasghari et al., "The Future Belongs to the Curious: Towards Automatic Understanding and Recognition of Curiosity in Children," *Proceedings of the 5th Workshop on Child Computer Interaction*, 2016, 16–22.

31 *"created stronger associations":* Pierre-Yves Oudeyer, Jacqueline Gottlieb, and Manuel Lopes, "Intrinsic Motivation, Curiosity and Learning: Theory and Applications in Educational Technologies," *Progress in Brain Research* 229 (July 2016): 257–84.

32 *"To find enchantment":* Margaret Ables and Amy Wilson, "Fresh Take: Katherine May on 'Enchantment,'" March 17, 2023, *What Fresh Hell: Laughing in the Face of Motherhood*, podcast, https://www.whatfreshhellpodcast.com/fresh-take-katherine-may-on-enchantment/#show-notes.

33 *"You have to really be courageous":* https://achievement.org/achiever/francis-ford-coppola/.

33 *Long attentive to mental health:* Vivek Murthy, "Protecting Youth Mental Health," *The U.S. Surgeon General's Advisory*, 2021, https://www.hhs.gov/sites/default/files/surgeon-general-youth-mental-health-advisory.pdf.

34 *In subsequent reports:* Clay Skipper, "Surgeon General Vivek Murthy Sees Polarization as a Public Health Issue," *GQ*, March 11, 2022, https://www.gq.com/story/surgeon-general-vivek-murthy-interview.

34 *"In return for these":* Karen Heller, "'Braiding Sweetgrass' Has Gone from Surprise Hit to Juggernaut Bestseller," *Washington Post*, October 12, 2022, https://www.washingtonpost.com/books/2022/10/12/braiding-sweetgrass-robin-wall-kimmerer/.

35 *"the consumption habits":* Natasha Gilbert, "Funding Battles Stymie

Ambitious Plan to Protect Global Biodiversity," *Nature*, March 31, 2022, https://www.nature.com/articles/d41586-022-00916-8.

36 *"I think the first question"*: Dave Asprey, "Use Atomic Habits to Upgrade Your Decisions," *The Human Upgrade*, https://daveasprey .com/wp-content/uploads/2019/11/Use-Atomic-Habits-to-Upgrade -Your-Decisions-%E2%80%93-James-Clear-%E2%80%93-645.pdf.

37 *"Could a greater miracle"*: Henry David Thoreau, *Walden; or, Life in the Woods* (Boston: Ticknor and Fields, 1854), 6, http://www .literaturepage.com/read.php?titleid=walden&abspage=6& bookmark=1.

37 *"When you're a student"*: Trisha Gura, "Robert Langer: Creating Things That Could Change the World," *Science*, November 18, 2014, https://www.science.org/content/article/robert-langer-creating -things-could-change-world.

38 *Preferences and inclinations:* Steven D. Goodman, "The Spiritual Work of a Worldly Life: Buddhist Teachings Offer More than an Escape from the Samsaric World," *Tricycle: The Buddhist Review*, August 14, 2020, https://tricycle.org/article/buddhist-attitudes -worldly-life/.

Get Bothered: Wake Up to What You Want

41 *"The best thing we can do"*: Diana Nyad, in discussion with Jeff Karp and Mariska van Aalst, May 30, 2018.

45 *"Nature will send a message"*: David Courchene, Anishinaabe Nation elder and founder of the Turtle Lodge Centre of Excellence in Indigenous Education and Wellness, in discussion with Jeff Karp, August 8, 2021.

46 *"Sometimes a moment"*: Reggie Shuford, executive director, North Carolina Justice Center, in email discussion with Jeff Karp and Teresa Barker, May 10, 2022.

53 *"The greater the contrast"*: Carl Jung, *Psychological Reflections*, edited by Jolande Jacobi and R. F. Hull (New York: Bollington, 1953).

Be an Active Opportunist: Scout Ideas, Insight, and Inspiration Everywhere

57 *"No wonder people"*: Lisa Feldman Barrett, "People's Words and Actions Can Actually Shape Your Brain—A Neuroscientist Explains How," ideas.TED.com, November 17, 2020, https://ideas.ted.com /peoples-words-and-actions-can-actually-shape-your-brain-a -neuroscientist-explains-how/.

57 *"The neuron changes constantly"*: Daniel Câmara, *Bio-inspired Networking* (Washington, D.C.: ISTE Press, 2015), 50–51.

58 *A recent study:* Hanne K. Collins et al., "Relational Diversity in Social Portfolios Predicts Well-Being," *Proceedings of the National*

Academy of Sciences of the United States of America 119, no. 43 (2022): e2120668119.

58   *"a person who exploits"*: Google English Dictionary. Google's English dictionary is provided by Oxford Languages. Oxford Languages is the world's leading dictionary publisher, with more than 150 years of experience creating and delivering authoritative dictionaries globally in more than fifty languages.

59   *For neurons, it can be:* Michael Fricker et al., "Neuronal Cell Death," *Physiological Reviews* 98, no. 2 (2018): 813–80.

59   *Swarm behavior:* Câmara, *Bio-inspired Networking*, 81–102.

59   *"presents an intelligence":* Câmara, *Bio-inspired Networking*, 81.

60   *"the extended mind":* Annie Murphy Paul, *The Extended Mind: The Power of Thinking Outside the Brain* (Boston: Mariner Books, 2021).

60   *"The mind extends":* "Thinking Outside the Brain, Interview and Q&A with Annie Murphy Paul," youtube.com, February 16, 2023. https://www.youtube.com/watch?v=Y6zgaSiDcFk.

60   *"to look beyond":* James Bridle, *Ways of Being: Animals, Plants, Machines: The Search for a Planetary Intelligence* (New York: Farrar, Straus and Giroux, 2022), 10.

61   *As Sharp described it:* "Phillip A. Sharp—Interview," Nobel Prize, April 7, 2023, https://www.nobelprize.org/prizes/medicine/1993/sharp/interview/; Infinite History Project MIT, "Phillip Sharp," YouTube, March 8, 2016, https://www.youtube.com/watch?v=1ihodN7hiO0&t=214s.

61   *"as you enter that community":* "Phillip A. Sharp—Interview."

62   *He saw an opportunity:* Michael Blanding, "The Man Who Helped Launch Biotech," *MIT Technology Review*, August 18, 2015, https://www.technologyreview.com/2015/08/18/166642/the-man-who-helped-launch-biotech/.

62   *"The thing that entrepreneurship":* Phillip Sharp, in discussion with Jeff Karp and Mariska van Aalst, June 1, 2018.

62   *"Someone standing in front":* Becky Ham, "Phillip A. Sharp: Supporting Science and Engineering as Innovative Forces," American Association for the Advancement of Science, February 20, 2013, https://www.aaas.org/news/phillip-sharp-supporting-science-and-engineering-innovative-forces.

62   *"Children are the living messages":* Neil Postman, *The Disappearance of Childhood* (New York: Vintage, 1994), xi.

63   *"If your knowledge":* Chris Hadfield, astronaut, engineer, fighter pilot, musician, in discussion with Jeff Karp, June 22, 2021.

66   *"We are drowning":* Edward O. Wilson, *Consilience: The Unity of Knowledge* (New York: Vintage, 1994), 294.

68   *A hole in one is:* "What Are the Odds of Making a Hole in One?," American Hole 'n One's Blog, https://www.ahno.com/americanhno -blog/odds-of-making-a-hole-in-one.

71   *"It's been a fascinating journey":* Stephen Wilkes, visionary landscape photographer, in discussion with Jeff Karp and Mariska van Aalst, July 5, 2018.

72   *other workplace settings:* Max Nathan and Neil Lee, "Cultural Diversity, Innovation, and Entrepreneurship: Firm-Level Evidence from London," *Economic Geography* 89, no. 4 (2013): 367–94.

73   *Temple Grandin has made:* Temple Grandin, "Temple Grandin: Society Is Failing Visual Thinkers, and That Hurts Us All," *New York Times,* January 9, 2023, https://www.nytimes.com/2023/01/09 /opinion/temple-grandin-visual-thinking-autism.html.

74   *"Our environments, our world":* Lisa Sasaki, Smithsonian Deputy Under Secretary for Special Projects, in discussion with Jeff Karp and Teresa Barker, July 15, 2021.

74   *The impulse for altruism:* Graham J. Thompson, Peter L. Hurd, and Bernard J. Crespi, "Genes Underlying Altruism," *Biology Letters* 9, no. 6 (2013); Jennifer E. Stellar and Dacher Keltner, "The Role of the Vagus Nerve," in *Compassion: Concepts, Research and Applications,* edited by Paul Gilber (London: Routledge, 2017), 120–34.

75   *"Our mammalian and hominid evolution":* Dacher Keltner and David DiSalvo, "Forget Survival of the Fittest: It Is Kindness That Counts," *Scientific American,* February 26, 2009, https://www .scientificamerican.com/article/kindness-emotions-psychology/.

75   *"You cannot dig a hole":* Edward de Bono, *Serious Creativity: Using the Power of Lateral Thinking to Create New Ideas* (London: HarperBusiness, 1992), 52–53.

75   *"don't dig deeper":* Mark A. Runco, "Enhancement and the Fulfillment of Potential," in *Creativity: Theories and Themes; Research, Development, and Practice,* 2nd ed. (Burlington, MA: Elsevier Academic Press, 2007), 335–87.

76   *Volunteer:* Michael J. Poulin et al., "Giving to Others and the Association Between Stress and Mortality," *American Journal of Public Health* 103, no. 9 (2013): 1649–55.

Pinch Your Brain: Attention Is Your Superpower

77   *"The capacity to attend":* Alexandra Horowitz, *On Looking: A Walker's Guide to the Art of Observation* (New York: Scribner, 2014), 3.

79   *a physical skin pinch:* Medical College of Georgia at Augusta University, "Scientists Explore Blood Flow Bump That Happens When Our Neurons Are Significantly Activated," ScienceDaily, July 15, 2019, www.sciencedaily.com/releases/2019/07/190715094611.htm; Amy R.

Nippert et al., "Mechanisms Mediating Functional Hyperemia in the Brain," *Neuroscientist* 24, no. 1 (2018): 73–83.

79 *Angelo Mosso:* Marcus E. Raichle and Gordon M. Shepherd, eds., *Angelo Mosso's Circulation of Blood in the Human Brain* (New York: Oxford University Press, 2014).

79 *"Hence a wealth":* Herbert A. Simon, "Designing Organizations for an Information-Rich World," in *Computers, Communications, and the Public Interest,* edited by Martin Greenberger (Baltimore: Johns Hopkins Press, 1971), 37–72.

82 *"Attention is the most powerful tool":* https://lindastone.net/.

83 *In a study:* Athanasia M. Mowinckel et al., "Increased Default-Mode Variability Is Related to Reduced Task-Performance and Is Evident in Adults with ADHD," *Neuroimage: Clinical* 16 (2017): 369–82; Luke J. Normal et al., "Evidence from 'Big Data' for the Default-Mode Hypothesis of ADHD: A Mega-analysis of Multiple Large Samples," *Neuropsychopharmacology* 48, no. 2 (2023): 281–89.

84 *Studies suggest:* See, e.g., Melissa-Ann Mackie, Nicholas T. Van Dam, and Jin Fan, "Cognitive Control and Attentional Functions," *Brain and Cognition* 82, no. 3 (2013): 301–12; Marcus E. Raichle et al., "A Default Mode of Brain Function," *Proceedings of the National Academy of Sciences of the United States of America* 98, no. 2 (2001): 676–82.

84 *cognitive control:* Mackie, Van Dam, and Fan, "Cognitive Control and Attentional Functions."

84 *In studies that measure:* Richard B. Stein, E. Roderich Gossen, and Kelvin E. Jones, "Neuronal Variability: Noise or Part of the Signal?," *Nature Reviews Neuroscience* 6, no. 5 (2005): 389–97.

84 *because of neural variability:* Ayelet Arazi, Yaffa Yeshurun, and Ilan Dinstein, "Neural Variability Is Quenched by Attention," *Journal of Neuroscience* 39, no. 30 (2019): 5975–85; Ilan Dinstein, David J. Heeger, and Marlene Behrmann, "Neural Variability: Friend or Foe?," *Trends in Cognitive Sciences* 19, no. 6 (2015): 322–28; Mark M. Churchland et al., "Stimulus Onset Quenches Neural Variability: A Widespread Cortical Phenomenon," *Nature Neuroscience* 13, no. 3 (2010): 369–78.

85 *If focused attention calms:* Arazi, Yeshurun, and Dinstein, "Neural Variability Is Quenched by Attention."

85 *"Focus like a laser":* Paul Buyer, *Working Toward Excellence: 8 Values for Achieving Uncommon Success in Work and Life,* ebook (Morgan James Publishing, 2012).

89 *"Let yourself be silently drawn":* Akşapāda, *The Analects of Rumi,* ebook, 2019.

90 *Research shows that pausing:* Sapna Maheshwari, "TikTok Claims

It's Limiting Teen Screen Time. Teens Say It Isn't," *New York Times*, March 23, 2023, https://www.nytimes.com/2023/03/23/business/tiktok-screen-time.html.

90 *"You can put frictions in place":* Jonathan Bastian, "How Habits Get Formed," October 15, 2022, *Life Examined,* podcast, https://www.kcrw.com/culture/shows/life-examined/stoics-self-discipline-philosophy-habits-behavior-science/katy-milkman-how-to-change-science-behavior-habits.

90 *mind-body-spirit interconnectedness:* Michelle L. Dossett, Gregory L. Fricchione, and Herbert Benson, "A New Era for Mind-Body Medicine," *New England Journal of Medicine* 382, no. 1 (2020): 1390–91.

91 *In studies of motivation:* Vrinda Kalia et al., "Staying Alert? Neural Correlates of the Association Between Grit and Attention Networks," *Frontiers in Psychology* 9 (2018): 1377; Angelica Moe et al., "Displayed Enthusiasm Attracts Attention and Improves Recall," *British Journal of Educational Psychology* 91, no. 3 (2021): 911–27.

95 *Focus your attention:* Patrick L. Hill and Nicholas A. Turiano, "Purpose in Life as a Predictor of Mortality Across Adulthood," *Psychological Science* 25, no. 7 (2014): 1482–86.

Get Hooked on Movement: It's the Key to Evolutionary Success

97 *"The longest journey":* Turtle Lodge Staff, "Indigenous Knowledge Keepers and Scientists Unite at Turtle Lodge," *Cultural Survival,* December 5, 2017, https://www.culturalsurvival.org/publications/cultural-survival-quarterly/indigenous-knowledge-keepers-and-scientists-unite-turtle.

97 *"Movement of individual organisms":* Ran Nathan, "An Emerging Movement Ecology Paradigm," *Proceedings of the National Academy of Sciences* 105, no. 49 (December 9, 2008): 19050–51, https://www.pnas.org/doi/full/10.1073/pnas.0808918105.

98 *"Mind creates the abyss":* Nisargadatta Maharaj, *I Am That: Talks with Sri Nisargadatta Maharaj,* 3rd ed. (Durham, NC: Acorn Press, 2012), 8.

99 *"People who are physically active":* Kelly McGonigal, *The Joy of Movement: How Exercise Helps Us Find Happiness, Hope, Connection, and Courage* (New York: Avery, 2019), 3.

100 *"The walking of which I speak":* Henry David Thoreau, "Walking," thoreau-online.org, Henry David Thoreau Online, https://www.thoreau-online.org/walking-page3.html.

100 *"We forget that the body":* Ellen Gamerman, "New Books on Better Workouts That Include Brain as well as Body," *Wall Street Journal,* January 11, 2022, https://www.wsj.com/articles/best-books-2022-workout-fitness-11641905831.

101 *"connectedness to nature"*: Valerie F. Gladwell et al., "The Great Outdoors: How a Green Exercise Environment Can Benefit All," *Extreme Physiology & Medicine* 2, no. 1 (2013): 3.

101 *"They calm us down"*: Krista Tippett, "The Thrilling New Science of Awe," February 2, 2023, *On Being*, podcast, https://onbeing.org /programs/dacher-keltner-the-thrilling-new-science-of-awe/.

102 *"Humans have"*: Juan Siliezar, "Why Run Unless Something Is Chasing You?" *Harvard Gazette*, January 4, 2021, https://news .harvard.edu/gazette/story/2021/01/daniel-lieberman-busts -exercising-myths.

102 *"Take that activity away"*: John J. Ratey, *Spark: The Revolutionary New Science of Exercise and the Brain* (New York: Little, Brown, 2008); "Physical Inactivity," National Center for Chronic Disease Prevention and Health Promotion, September 8, 2022, https://www .cdc.gov/chronicdisease/resources/publications/factsheets/physical -activity.htm.

102 *a complex pattern of moves*: Steven Brown and Lawrence M. Parsons, "So You Think You Can Dance? PET Scans Reveal Your Brain's Inner Choreography," *Scientific American*, July 1, 2008, https://www .scientificamerican.com/article/the-neuroscience-of-dance/.

102 *One study of grandmothers*: Einat Shuper Engelhard, "Free-Form Dance as an Alternative Interaction for Adult Grandchildren and Their Grandparents," *Frontiers in Psychology* 11 (2020): 542.

103 *"Every time you work out"*: Dana Foundation, "The Astonishing Effects of Exercise on Your Brain with Wendy Suzuki, PhD," YouTube, November 23, 2020, https://www.youtube.com/watch?v=Y0cI6uxSnuc &ab_channel=DanaFoundation.

103 *In a review of studies*: Julia C. Basso and Wendy A. Suzuki, "The Effects of Acute Exercise on Mood, Cognition, Neurophysiology, and Neurochemical Pathways: A Review," *Brain Plasticity* 2, no. 2 (2017): 127–52, https://doi.org/10.3233/BPL-160040.

103 *even a single workout*: Basso and Suzuki, "The Effects of Acute Exercise on Mood, Cognition, Neurophysiology, and Neurochemical Pathways."

103 *Every bit helps*: Yannis Y. Liang et al., "Joint Association of Physical Activity and Sleep Duration with Risk of All-Cause and Cause-Specific Mortality: A Population-Based Cohort Study Using Accelerometry," *European Journal of Preventive Cardiology*, March 29, 2023.

104 *"Nothing happens until"*: Arthur Austen Douglas, *1955 Quotes of Albert Einstein*, ebook (UB Tech, 2016), 60.

109 *"Cultural evolution is now"*: Daniel Lieberman, *The Story of the Human Body: Evolution, Health, and Disease* (New York: Knopf Doubleday, 2014), 20.

110   *"As runners, we were able"*: "Run as One: The Journey of the Front Runners," CBC, February 6, 2018, https://www.cbc.ca/shortdocs /shorts/run-as-one-the-journey-of-the-front-runners.

113   *"With time"*: Jill Satterfield, "Mindfulness at Knifepoint," *Tricycle: The Buddhist Review,* March 21, 2019, https://tricycle.org/article /mindfulness-knifepoint/.

114   *"hunter-gatherer societies"*: Bettina Elias Siegel, "Michael Moss on How Big Food Gets Us Hooked," Civil Eats, April 9, 2021, https:// civileats.com/2021/04/09/michael-moss-on-how-big-food-gets-us -hooked/.

115   *"Circadian rhythms are"*: Satchin Panda, "How Optimizing Circadian Rhythms Can Increase Health Years to Our Lives," TED Talk, 2021, https://www.ted.com/talks/satchin_panda_how_optimizing _circadian_rhythms_can_increase_healthy_years_to_our_lives /transcript?language=en.

117   *Stanford researchers found:* May Wong, "Stanford Study Finds Walking Improves Creativity," Stanford News, April 24, 2014, https://news.stanford.edu/2014/04/24/walking-vs-sitting-042414/.

Fall in Love with Practice: Savor the Joys of the Brawny Brain

119   *"I never practice"*: Nat Shapiro, ed., *An Encyclopedia of Quotations About Music* (New York: Springer, 2012), 98, https://www.google .com/books/edition/An_Encyclopedia_of_Quotations_About_Musi /rqThBwAAQBAJ?hl=en&gbpv=0.

121   *"how it twists and turns"*: Justin von Bujdoss, "Tilopa's Six Nails," *Tricycle: The Buddhist Review,* February 6, 2018, https://tricycle.org /magazine/tilopas-six-nails/.

125   *"Practice puts brains"*: K. Anders Ericsson, Michael J. Prietula, and Edward T. Cokely, "The Making of an Expert," *Harvard Business Review* (July–August 2007), https://hbr.org/2007/07/the-making-of -an-expert.

125   *says JoAnn Deak:* See JoAnn Deak, *The Owner's Manual for Driving Your Adolescent Brain: A Growth Mindset and Brain Development Book for Young Teens and Their Parents* (San Francisco: Little Pickle Press, 2013); JoAnn Deak and Terrence Deak, *Good Night to Your Fantastic Elastic Brain: A Growth Mindset Bedtime Book for Kids* (Naperville, IL: Sourcebooks Explore, 2022).

127   *"It is possible"*: Molly Gebrian, "Rethinking Viola Pedagogy: Preparing Violists for the Challenges of Twentieth-Century Music," doctoral dissertation, Rice University, July 24, 2013, https://scholarship.rice .edu/bitstream/handle/1911/71651/GEBRIAN-THESIS.pdf?sequence =1&isAllowed=y, 31, 32.

131   *I also learned:* Mark E. Bouton, "Context, Attention, and the Switch

Between Habit and Goal-Direction in Behavior," *Learning & Behavior* 49, no. 4 (2021): 349–62.

132 "I think I am making progress": Leonard Lyons, "The Lyons Den," *Daily Defender,* November 4, 1958, 5; E. J. Masicampo, F. Luebber, and R. F. Baumeister, "The Influence of Conscious Thought Is Best Observed over Time," *Psychology of Consciousness: Theory, Research, and Practice* 7, no. 1 (2020): 87–102, https://doi.org/10.1037 /cns0000205.

132 *In his 1907 dissertation:* C. H. Turner, "The Homing of Ants: An Experimental Study of Ant Behavior," *Journal of Comparative Neurology and Psychology* 17, no. 5 (1907): 367–434.

133 *Try these* lit *boosters:* See Jim Dethmer, Diana Chapman, and Kaley Warner Klemp, *The 15 Commitments of Conscious Leadership: A New Paradigm for Sustainable Success* (The Conscious Leadership Group, 2015).

134 Running the Sahara: *Running the Sahara,* directed by James Moll, NEHST Out, 2010.

Do New, Do Different: Invite Surprise and Serendipity

136 *"I left the woods":* "The Dog-Eared Page, Excerpted from *Walden* by Henry David Thoreau," *The Sun,* February 2013, https://www .thesunmagazine.org/issues/446/from-walden.

136 *A 2022 study:* Ariana Anderson et al., "Big-C Creativity in Artists and Scientists Is Associated with More Random Global but Less Random Local fMRI Functional Connectivity," *Psychology of Aesthetics, Creativity, and the Arts,* 2022, https://psycnet.apa.org/record/2022 -45679-001?doi=1. See also "How Practice Changes the Brain," Australian Academy of Science, https://www.science.org.au/curious /people-medicine/how-practice-changes-brain.

137 *Known as the Troxler effect:* Brandon Specktor, "This 'Disappearing' Optical Illusion Proves Your Brain Is Too Smart for Its Own Good," Live Science, April 11, 2018, https://www.livescience.com/62274 -disappearing-optical-illusion-troxler-explained.html.

140 *"You must do the thing":* Eleanor Roosevelt, *You Learn by Living; Eleven Keys for a More Fulfilling Life* (New York: Harper Perennial Modern Classics, 2011).

142 *"Neuroplasticity is better":* Deepak Chopra and Rudolph E. Tanzi, *Super Brain: Unleashing the Explosive Power of Your Mind to Maximize Health, Happiness, and Spiritual Well-Being* (New York: Harmony Books, 2012), 22.

143 *attempting something new:* Judith Schomaker, Valentin Baumann, and Marit F. L. Ruitenberg, "Effects of Exploring a Novel Environment on Memory Across the Lifespan," *Scientific Reports* 12 (2022): article 16631.

143   *"Any activity that uses"*: Francesca Rosenberg, Amir Parsa, Laurel
      Humble, and Carrie McGee, "Conversation with Gene Cohen of
      the Center on Aging, Health & Humanities and Gay Hanna of
      the National Center for Creative Aging," in *Meet Me: Making Art
      Accessible to People with Dementia* (New York: The Museum of
      Modern Art, 2009), https://www.moma.org/momaorg/shared/pdfs
      /docs/meetme/Perspectives_GCohen-GHanna.pdf.

143   *"At one hundred"*: Jon Schiller, *Life Style to Extend Life Span*
      (Charleston, SC: Booksurge, 2009), 180, https://www.google.com
      /books/edition/Life_Style_to_Extend_Life_Span/E92Kijnr9tQC?hl
      =en&gbpv=0p.

143   *In the 2014 study:* Denise C. Park et al., "The Impact of Sustained
      Engagement on Cognitive Function in Older Adults," *Psychological
      Science* 25, no. 1 (2014): 103–12.

144   *"Defamiliarization is one"*: Pádraig Ó Tuama, "*On Being* Newsletter,"
      The *On Being* Project, May 22, 2021, https://engage.onbeing.org
      /20210522_the_pause.

145   *"Substituting nuance for novelty"*: Peter High, "The Secret Ingredient
      of Successful People and Organizations: Grit," Forbes.com,
      May 23, 2016, https://www.forbes.com/sites/peterhigh/2016/05/23
      /the-secret-ingredient-of-successful-people-and-organizations
      -grit/?sh=6e79fe1862ef.

Focus Beyond Failure: Tee Up Energy for Renewed Action

151   *"I've missed more than"*: "Michael Jordan 'Failure' Commercial HD
      1080p," YouTube, December 8, 2012, https://www.youtube.com
      /watch?v=JA7G7AV-LT8.

152   *"never, ever give up"*: Matt Sloane, Jason Hanna, and Dana Ford, "'Never,
      Ever Give Up:' Diana Nyad Completes Historic Cuba-to-Florida Swim,"
      CNN.com, September 3, 2013, https://edition.cnn.com/2013/09/02
      /world/americas/diana-nyad-cuba-florida-swim/index.html.

153   *"If you have a growth mindset"*: Peter Bregman, "Why You Need to
      Fail," *Harvard Business Review*, July 6, 2009, https://hbr.org
      /2009/07/why-you-need-to-fail.

155   *"It became more and more apparent"*: Megan Thompson, "The Quirky
      'Museum of Failure' Celebrates Creativity and Innovation," *PBS
      NewsHour Weekend*, November 20, 2021.

155   *This silence costs us:* Allison S. Catalano et al., "Black Swans,
      Cognition, and the Power of Learning from Failure," *Conservation
      Biology* 32, no. 3 (2018): 584–96.

157   *"When we started the project"*: National Science Foundation, "Scientist
      Who Helped Discover the Expansion of the Universe Is Accelerating,"
      NSF.gov, February 3, 2015, https://new.nsf.gov/news/scientist-who
      -helped-discover-expansion-universe.

157   *"science isn't a matter of trying"*: Zoë Corbyn, "Saul Perlmutter: 'Science Is About Figuring Out Your Mistakes,'" *Guardian*, July 6, 2013, https://www.theguardian.com/science/2013/jul/07/rational -heroes-saul-perlmutter-astrophysics-universe.

160   *"To learn to succeed"*: R. J. Bear, "To Learn to Succeed, You Must First Learn to Fail," The Shortform, June 14, 2022, https://medium .com/the-shortform/to-learn-to-succeed-you-must-first-learn-to-fail -34338ac87c92#.

160   *"It's not a failure"*: Nico Martinez, "NBA Insider Exposes Major Problem for the Milwaukee Bucks: 'There's a Thundercloud on the Horizon,'" Fadeaway World, May 5, https://fadeawayworld.net/nba -insider-exposes-major-problem-for-the-milwaukee-bucks-theres-a -thundercloud-on-the-horizon.

160   *My most memorable failure:* Nanomole, "I Forgot My Lines During a TED Talk (and Survived)!!!!," YouTube, October 13, 2020, https:// www.youtube.com/watch?v=1PfpQlRrqHg&ab_channel=nanomole.

162   *"a challenge"*: Stuart Firestein, *Failure: Why Science Is So Successful* (Hong Kong: Oxford University Press, 2016), 47.

163   *"There's nothing wrong"*: James Doty, neurosurgeon, professor at Stanford, in discussion with Jeff Karp and Teresa Barker, January 22, 2021.

Be Human: Be Humble

166   *"Have the humility"*: John C. Maxwell, "'Have the Humility to Learn from Those Around You'–John C. Maxwell," LinkedIn, https://www .linkedin.com/posts/officialjohnmaxwell_have-the-humility-to-learn -from-those-around-activity-6785592172545617921-aIHB/.

166   *humble people handle stress better:* Mark R. Leary, "Cognitive and Interpersonal Features of Intellectual Humility," *Personality and Social Psychology Bulletin* 43, no. 6 (2017): 793–813.

168   *"Humble people see value"*: Christoph Seckler, "Is Humility the New Smart?" The Choice, January 11, 2022, https://thechoice.escp.eu /choose-to-lead/is-humility-the-new-smart/.

170   *"Errors of human judgment"*: Robert J. Shiller, *Irrational Exuberance* (Princeton, NJ: Princeton University Press, 2000), xxi.

170   *"I believe that"*: Henry David Thoreau, "Walking," *The Atlantic* (June 1862), https://www.theatlantic.com/magazine/archive/1862/06 /walking/304674/.

171   *"we are part of an ecosystem"*: Krista Tippett, "The Thrilling New Science of Awe," February 2, 2023, *On Being*, podcast, https://onbeing .org/programs/dacher-keltner-the-thrilling-new-science-of-awe.

172   *"Search for the Sacred"*: Sarah Ban Breathnach, *Simple Abundance: A Daybook of Comfort of Joy* (New York: Grand Central Publishing, 2008).

172   *Turtle Lodge is now:* Grounded, "Why Protecting Indigenous
       Communities Can Also Help Save the Earth," *Guardian*, October 12,
       2020, https://www.theguardian.com/climate-academy/2020/oct
       /12/indigenous-communities-protect-biodiversity-curb-climate
       -crisis.

173   *Despite systematic efforts:* Gleb Raygorodetsky, "Indigenous Peoples
       Defend Earth's Biodiversity—But They're in Danger," *National
       Geographic*, November 16, 2018, https://www.nationalgeographic
       .com/environment/article/can-indigenous-land-stewardship-protect
       -biodiversity-.

173   *"In Indigenous ways of knowing":* Robin Wall Kimmerer, *Gathering
       Moss: A Natural and Cultural History of Mosses* (Corvallis: Oregon
       State University Press, 2003), 100.

176   *"moral beauty":* Tippett, "The Thrilling New Science of Awe."

177   *"Time and time again":* Tippett, "The Thrilling New Science of Awe."

177   *"Awe tells us to go out":* Tippett, "The Thrilling New Science of Awe."

179   *"The humble are those":* Nicole Winfield, "Pope Demands Humility
       in New Zinger-Filled Christmas Speech," Associated Press,
       December 23, 2021, https://apnews.com/article/pope-francis-lifestyle
       -religion-christmas-a04d3c12674a14127f8efbdaafd3ae97.

Press "Pause": Protect Time to Be and Behold

183   *"We all need to be reminded":* Arianna Huffington, "Introducing
       HuffPost Endeavor: Less Stress, More Fulfillment," Huffington Post,
       January 25, 2017, https://www.huffpost.com/entry/introducing
       -huffpost-ende_b_9069016. Paraphrased quotation approved by
       Arianna Huffington in communication with author.

183   *unusual meditation practice:* Vivek Ramakrishnan, "Rewiring the
       Brain for Happiness," The Awakening of Impermanence, February 27,
       2022, https://www.awakeningofimpermanence.com/blog/rewiring
       thebrain.

185   *All life depends:* "Circadian Rhythms," National Institute of General
       Medical Sciences, May 5, 2022, https://nigms.nih.gov/education/fact
       -sheets/Pages/circadian-rhythms.aspx.

185   *The cues are still coming:* Erin C. Westgate et al., "What Makes
       Thinking for Pleasure Pleasureable?," *Emotion* 21, no. 5 (2021):
       981–89.

186   *found that even microbreaks:* Sooyeol Kim, Seonghee Cho, and
       YoungAh Park, "Daily Microbreaks in a Self-Regulatory Resources
       Lens: Perceived Health Climate as a Contextual Moderator via
       Microbreak Autonomy," *Journal of Applied Psychology* 107, no. 1
       (2022): 60–77.

186   *Music resonates:* Luciano Bernardi, C. Porta, and P. Sleight,
       "Cardiovascular, Cerebrovascular, and Respiratory Changes Induced

by Different Types of Music in Musicians and Non-musicians: The Importance of Silence," *Heart* 92, no. 4 (2005): 445–52.

187 *"Mindfulness is a pause":* Tara Brach, *True Refuge*, ebook (New York: Random House, 2016), 61.

187 *You can train your brain:* See Vivek Ramakrishnan, "Default Mode Network & Meditation," *The Awakening of Impermanence* (blog), April 10, 2022, https://www.awakeningofimpermanence.com/blog /defaultmodenetwork.

188 *"A life well lived":* Diana Nyad, in discussion with Jeff Karp and Mariska van Aalst, May 30, 2018.

189 *"People have come to value":* Susan L. Worley, "The Extraordinary Importance of Sleep: The Detrimental Effects of Inadequate Sleep on Health and Public Safety Drive an Explosion of Sleep Research," *Pharmacy and Therapeutics* 43, no. 12 (December 2018): 758–63.

190 *Jenny Odell:* Jenny Odell, *How to Do Nothing: Resisting the Attention Economy* (Brooklyn, NY: Melville House, 2020).

190 *"We say peace of mind":* Naval Ravikant, "Finding Peace from Mind," Naval, March 3, 2020, https://nav.al/peace.

191 *"Whether or not":* Jill Suttie, "How Mind-Wandering May Be Good for You," *Greater Good Magazine*, February 14, 2018, https://greatergood .berkeley.edu/article/item/how_mind_wandering_may_be_good _for_you.

192 *"It is now clear":* Matthew P. Walker and Robert Stickgold, "Sleep, Memory, and Plasticity," *Annual Review of Psychology* 57 (2006): 139–66, https://doi.org/10.1146/annurev.psych.56.091103.070307.

192 *Gene Cohen:* See, e.g., Gene D. Cohen, *The Creative Age: Awakening Human Potential in the Second Half of Life* (New York: William Morrow, 2000), 34–35.

193 *The researchers found:* Thomas Andrillon et al., "Predicting Lapses of Attention with Sleep-like Slow Waves," *Nature Communications* 12, no. 1 (December 2021), https://doi.org/10.1038/s41467-021-23890-7.

193 *All the world's:* Patrick McNamara and Kelly Bulkeley, "Dreams as a Source of Supernatural Agent Concepts," *Frontiers in Psychology*, no. 6 (2015): https://www.frontiersin.org/articles/10.3389/fpsyg .2015.00283.

194 *"Each person deserves":* Maya Angelou, *Wouldn't Take Nothing for My Journey Now* (New York: Bantam, 1994), 139.

195 *"Almost everything will work":* Anne Lamott, "12 Truths I Learned from Life and Writing," TED Talk, 2017, https://www.ted.com/talks/anne _lamott_12_truths_i_learned_from_life_and_writing/transcript.

197 *"When I say listen":* Pandora Thomas, permaculturist, environmental justice activist, in discussion with Jeff Karp and Teresa Barker, May 18, 2021.

197　*"What's required is the white space"*: Vivek Murthy, *Together: The Healing Power of Human Connection in a Sometimes Lonely World* (New York: Harper Wave, 2020), 206.

197　*"Continuity of mindfulness"*: Kathy Cherry, "A Reminder to Pause," *Tricycle: The Buddhist Review*, December 30, 2022, https://tricycle .org/article/pause-practices/.

Hug Nature: Revitalize Your Roots

203　*"Deep inside, we still"*: Janine Benyus, *Biomimicry: Innovation Inspired by Nature*, ebook (Boston: Mariner Books, 2009), 298.

205　*"Nature is orderly"*: Gary Snyder, *The Practice of the Wild* (San Francisco: North Point Press, 1990), 93.

205　*has saved our collective skin:* Nikita Ali, "Forests Are Nature's Pharmacy: To Conserve Them Is to Replenish Our Supply," Caribois Environmental News Network, March 3, 2021, https://www.caribois .org/2021/03/forests-are-natures-pharmacy-to-conserve-them-is-to -replenish-our-supply/.

208　*"Walking is the great adventure"*: Snyder, *The Practice of the Wild*, 18.

213　*Researchers continue to discover:* See, e.g., Frans B. M. de Waal and Kristin Andrews, "The Question of Animal Emotions," *Science*, March 24, 2022, https://www.science.org/doi/abs/10.1126/science .abo2378?doi=10.1126/science.abo2378.

213　*the damage has been mounting:* See, e.g., Melissa R. Marselle et al., "Pathways Linking Biodiversity to Human Health: A Conceptual Framework," *Environment International* 150, no.1 (2021): 106420.

213　*"Merely by falling"*: Margaret Renkl, "Graduates, My Generation Wrecked So Much That's Precious: How Can I Offer You Advice?" *New York Times*, May 15, 2023, https://www.nytimes.com/2023/05/15 /opinion/letter-to-graduates-hope-despair.html.

214　*she got a clear answer:* Pandora Thomas, in discussion with Jeff Karp and Teresa Barker, May 18, 2021.

214　*Permaculture is an approach:* Sami Grover, "How Simple Mills Is Supporting Regenerative Agriculture," Treehugger, July 29, 2021, https://www.treehugger.com/simple-mills-supporting-regenerative -agriculture-5194744.

215　*"The Earth is our oldest teacher"*: Thomas, in discussion with Karp and Barker.

218　*"the answers to our questions"*: Janine Benyus, "Biomimicry's Surprising Lessons from Nature's Engineers," TED Talk, 2005, https://www.ted.com/talks/janine_benyus_biomimicry_s_surprising _lessons_from_nature_s_engineers/transcript?language=en.

218　*"The more our world functions"*: Janine Benyus, *Biomimicry: Innovation Inspired by Nature* (New York: Harper Perennial, 2002), 3.

218 *"Those who contemplate"*: Rachel Carson, *The Sense of Wonder* (New York: Harper, 1998), 98.

219 *Plant xylem has specialized cells:* Jennifer Chu, "MIT Engineers Make Filters from Tree Branches to Purify Drinking Water," MIT News, March 25, 2021, https://news.mit.edu/2021/filters-sapwood-purify -water-0325.

220 *"No matter how long"*: Sambhav Sankar and Alison Cagle, "How an Environmental Lawyer Stays Motivated to Fight the Climate Crisis," Earthjustice, November 17, 2021, https://earthjustice.org/article/how -an-environmental-lawyer-stays-motivated-to-fight-the-climate -crisis.

220 *Nearly 15 million people died:* Helen Branswell, "WHO: Nearly 15 Million Died as a Result of Covid-19 in First Two Years of Pandemic," STAT, May 5, 2022, https://www.statnews.com/2022/05/05/who -nearly-15-million-died-as-a-result-of-covid-19-in-first-two-years-of -pandemic/.

221 *"Very much contented am I"*: Lin Yutang, *The Importance of Living* (New York: William Morrow Paperbacks, 1998), v.

223 *Kimmerer, who interweaves:* Karen Heller, "'Braiding Sweetgrass' Has Gone from Surprise Hit to Juggernaut Bestseller," *Washington Post*, October 12, 2022, https://www.washingtonpost.com/books /2022/10/12/braiding-sweetgrass-robin-wall-kimmerer/.

Light the World: Create a Daring, Caring Culture

228 *"Humanity is waking up late"*: Statement signed by 126 Nobel Prize laureates delivered to world leaders ahead of G-7 Summit; "Our Planet, Our Future," Nobel Prize Summit, June 3, 2021, https://www .nobelprize.org/uploads/2021/05/Statement-3-June-DC.pdf.

229 *"If humanity creates"*: Joshua Needelman, "Forget Utopia. Ignore Dystopia. Embrace Protopia!" *New York Times*, March 14, 2023, https://www.nytimes.com/2023/03/14/special-series/protopia -movement.html.

229 *"For the first time"*: Edward O. Wilson, *Half-Earth: Our Planet's Fight for Life* (New York: Liveright, 2016), 1.

230 *"There comes a time"*: Wangari Maathai, Nobel Lecture, Oslo, December 10, 2004, https://www.nobelprize.org/prizes/peace/2004 /maathai/lecture/.

230 *"How can I know"*: Michael Rosenwald, "What If the President Ordering a Nuclear Attack Isn't Sane? An Air Force Major Lost His Job for Asking," *Washington Post*, April 10, 2017, https://www .washingtonpost.com/news/retropolis/wp/2017/08/09/what-if-the -president-ordering-a-nuclear-attack-isnt-sane-a-major-lost-his-job -for-asking/.

231 *"When you find yourself"*: Margaret Renkl, "Graduates, My Generation Wrecked So Much That's Precious. How Can I Offer You Advice?" *New York Times,* May 15, 2023, https://www.nytimes .com/2023/05/15/opinion/letter-to-graduates-hope-despair.html ?smtyp=cur&smid=tw-nytopinion.

233 *"We underestimate the power"*: Ayana Elizabeth Johnson and Katharine K. Wilkinson, eds., *All We Can Save: Truth, Courage, and Solutions for the Climate Crisis* (New York: One World, 2021), 58.

234 *"To be truly visionary"*: Needelman, "Forget Utopia."

236 *"What this moment"*: Johnson and Wilkinson, eds., *All We Can Save,* xxi.

236 *coined the term* third place*:* "What Is Placemaking?," Project for Public Spaces, https://www.pps.org/category/placemaking. See also Lowai Alkawarit, "Ray Oldenburg, Author of The Great Good Place," YouTube, September 20, 2018, https://www.youtube.com/watch?v =5h5YFimOOlU&ab_channel=LowaiAlkawarit.

236 *"Life without community"*: Ray Oldenburg, "Our Vanishing Third Places," *Planning Commissioners Journal* 25 (1997): 6–10.

239 *Charles Henry Turner:* Charles I. Abramson, "Charles Henry Turner Remembered," *Nature* 542, no. 31 (2017), https://doi.org/10.1038 /542031d.

239 *"shameful neglect"*: Abramson, "Charles Henry Turner Remembered."

241 *"I don't have"*: James Yeh, "Robin Wall Kimmerer: 'People Can't Understand the World as a Gift Unless Someone Shows Them How,'" *Guardian,* May 23, 2020, https://www.theguardian.com/books/2020 /may/23/robin-wall-kimmerer-people-cant-understand-the-world-as -a-gift-unless-someone-shows-them-how.

243 *"People often think"*: Lynne Twist, *Living a Committed Life: Finding Freedom and Fulfillment in a Purpose Larger Than Yourself* (Oakland, CA: Berrett-Koehler Publishers, 2022), 18.

244 *"Compassion is a willingness"*: Mariann Budde, diocesan bishop, social justice activist, in discussion with Jeff Karp and Teresa Barker, June 11, 2021.

245 *Science is behind the curve:* Jack Fraser, "How the Human Body Creates Electromagnetic Field," *Forbes,* November 3, 2017, https:// www.forbes.com/sites/quora/2017/11/03/how-the-human-body -creates-electromagnetic-fields/.

247 *"Today our very survival"*: Martin Luther King, Jr., *Where Do We Go from Here: Chaos or Community?* (Boston: Beacon Press, 2010), 181–83.

249 *"Togetherness raises optimism"*: Vivek Murthy, *Together: The Healing Power of Human Connection in a Sometimes Lonely World* (New York: Harper Wave, 2020), xxi.

Afterword: The Answers Are in Questions

255   *"The important and difficult job":* Peter F. Drucker, *The Practice of Management* (Bengaluru, Karnataka, India: Allied Publishers, 1975), 353.

255   *"Questions have a curious power":* Hal B. Gregersen, Clayton M. Christensen, and Jeffrey H. Dyer, "The Innovator's DNA," *Harvard Business Review* 87, no. 12 (December 2009): 4.

BIBLIOGRAPHY

Banaji, Mahzarin, and Anthony Greenwald. *Blindspot: Hidden Biases of Good People*. New York: Random House, 2016.

Barrett, Lisa Feldman. *Seven and a Half Lessons About the Brain*. Boston: Mariner Books, 2020.

Bridle, James. *Ways of Being: Animals, Plants, Machines: The Search for a Planetary Intelligence*. New York: Farrar, Straus and Giroux, 2022.

Brown, Brené. *Atlas of the Heart: Mapping Meaningful Connection and the Language of Human Experience*. New York: Random House, 2021.

———. *The Gifts of Imperfection*, Anniversary Edition. Center City, MN: Hazelden Publishing, 2022.

Carson, Rachel. *Silent Spring*. New York: Houghton Mifflin, 1962.

Chopra, Deepak, and Rudolph Tanzi. *The Healing Self: A Revolutionary New Plan to Supercharge Your Immunity and Stay Well for Life*. New York: Harmony Books, 2018.

———. *Super Brain: Unleashing the Explosive Power of Your Mind to Maximize Health, Happiness, and Spiritual Well-Being*. New York: Harmony Books, 2013.

———. *Super Genes: Unlock the Astonishing Power of Your DNA for Optimum Health and Well-Being*. New York: Harmony Books, 2017.

Csikszentmihalyi, Mihaly. *Flow: The Psychology of Optimal Experience*. New York: Harper Perennial, 1991.

David, Susan. *Emotional Agility: Get Unstuck, Embrace Change, and Thrive in Work and Life*. New York: Avery, 2016.

Deak, JoAnn. *Your Fantastic Elastic Brain: A Growth Mindset Book for Kids to Stretch and Shape Their Brains*. Napierville, IL: Little Pickle Press, 2010.

Deak, JoAnn, and Terrence Deak. *Good Night to Your Fantastic Elastic Brain: A Growth Mindset Bedtime Book for Kids*. Naperville, IL: Sourcebooks Explore, 2022.

———. *The Owner's Manual for Driving Your Adolescent Brain: A Growth Mindset and Brain Development Book for Young Teens and Their Parents*. San Francisco: Little Pickle Press, 2013.

Dolan, Paul, and Daniel Kahneman. *Happiness by Design: Change What You Do, Not How You Think*. New York: Plume, 2015.

Doty, James. *Into the Magic Shop: A Neurosurgeon's Quest to Discover the Mysteries of the Brain and the Secrets of the Heart*. New York: Avery, 2017.

Duhigg, Charles. *The Power of Habit: Why We Do What We Do in Life and Business*. New York: Random House, 2014.

Epstein, David. *Range: Why Generalists Triumph in a Specialized World*. New York: Penguin, 2021.

Ferriss, Tim. *Tribe of Mentors: Short Life Advice from the Best in the World*. New York: Harper Business, 2017.

Ferriss, Tim, and Arnold Schwarzenegger. *Tools of Titans: The Tactics, Routines, and Habits of Billionaires, Icons, and World-Class Performers*. New York: Harper Business, 2016.

Fogg, B. J. *Tiny Habits: The Small Changes That Change Everything*. New York: HarperCollins, 2020.

Frankl, Viktor. *Yes to Life: In Spite of Everything*. Boston: Beacon Press, 2021.

Gibbs, Daniel. *A Tattoo on My Brain: A Neurologist's Personal Battle Against Alzheimer's Disease*. London: Cambridge University Press, 2021.

Gilbert, Elizabeth. *Big Magic: Creative Living Beyond Fear*. New York: Riverhead Books, 2015.

Gladwell, Malcolm. *Outliers: The Story of Success*. New York: Little, Brown and Company, 2008.

Goleman, Daniel. *Altered Traits: Science Reveals How Meditation Changes Your Mind, Brain, and Body*. New York: Avery, 2017.

Grant, Adam. *Think Again: The Power of Knowing What You Don't Know*. New York: Viking, 2021.

Gregersen, Hal. *Questions Are the Answer: A Breakthrough Approach to Your Most Vexing Problems at Work and in Life*. New York: Harper Business, 2018.

Hadfield, Chris. *An Astronaut's Guide to Life on Earth: What Going to Space Taught Me About Ingenuity, Determination, and Being Prepared for Anything*. New York: Back Bay Books, 2015.

Hanson, Rick. *Neurodharma: New Science, Ancient Wisdom, and Seven Practices of the Highest Happiness*. New York: Harmony Books, 2020.

Horowitz, Alexandra. *On Looking: A Walker's Guide to the Art of Observation*. New York: Scribner, 2014.

Hwang, Victor W., and Greg Horowitt. *The Rainforest: The Secret to Building the Next Silicon Valley*. Los Altos Hills, CA: Regenwald, 2012.

Iyer, Pico. *The Art of Stillness: Adventures in Going Nowhere*. New York: Simon & Schuster/TED Books, 2014.

Kabat-Zinn, Jon. *Full Catastrophe Living: Using the Wisdom of Your Body and Mind to Face Stress, Pain, and Illness*. New York: Delacorte Press, 1990.

Keltner, Dacher. *Awe: The New Science of Everyday Wonder and How It Can Transform Your Life*. New York: Penguin, 2023.

———. *Born to Be Good: The Science of a Meaningful Life*. New York: W. W. Norton, 2009.

Kimmerer, Robin Wall. *Braiding Sweetgrass: Indigenous Wisdom, Scientific Knowledge, and the Teachings of Plants*. Minneapolis: Milkweed Edition, 2015.

———. *Gathering Moss: A Natural and Cultural History of Mosses*. Corvallis: Oregon State University Press, 2003.

Kwik, Jim. *Limitless: Upgrade Your Brain, Learn Anything Faster, and Unlock Your Exceptional Life*. Carlsbad, CA: Hay House, 2020.

Lieberman, Daniel. *Exercised: Why Something We Never Evolved to Do Is Healthy and Rewarding*. New York: Pantheon, 2021.

Louv, Richard. *Last Child in the Woods: Saving Our Children from Nature-Deficit Disorder*. Chapel Hill, NC: Algonquin Books, 2005.

McGonigal, Kelly. *The Joy of Movement: How Exercise Helps Us Find Happiness, Hope, Connection, and Courage*. New York: Avery, 2019.

Moss, Michael. *Hooked: Food, Free Will, and How the Food Giants Exploit Our Addictions*. New York: Random House, 2021.

Murthy, Vivek. *Together: The Healing Power of Human Connection in a Sometimes Lonely World:* New York: Harper Wave, 2020.

Niebauer, Chris. *No Self, No Problem: How Neuropsychology Is Catching Up to Buddhism.* San Antonio, TX: Hierophant Publishing, 2019.

Odell, Jenny. *How to Do Nothing: Resisting the Attention Economy.* Brooklyn, NY: Melville House, 2020.

Panda, Satchin. *The Circadian Code: Lose Weight, Supercharge Your Energy, and Transform Your Health from Morning to Midnight.* Emmaus, PA: Rodale Books, 2020.

Prévot, Franck. *Wangari Maathai: The Woman Who Planted Millions of Trees.* Watertown, MA: Charlesbridge; reprint, 2017.

Roché, Joyce, with Alexander Kopelman. *The Empress Has No Clothes: Conquering Self-Doubt to Embrace Success.* San Francisco: Berrett-Koehler, 2013.

Saunt, Claudio. *Unworthy Republic: The Dispossession of Native Americans and the Road to Indian Territory.* New York: W. W. Norton, 2020.

Simard, Suzanne. *Finding the Mother Tree: Discovering the Wisdom of the Forest.* New York: Vintage, 2022.

Snyder, Gary. *The Practice of the Wild.* San Francisco: North Point Press, 1990.

Strathdee, Steffanie, and Thomas Patterson. *The Perfect Predator: A Scientist's Race to Save Her Husband from a Deadly Superbug.* New York: Hachette, 2020.

Suzuki, Wendy, and Billie Fitzpatrick. *Healthy Brain, Happy Life: A Personal Program to Activate Your Brain and Do Everything Better.* New York: Dey Street Books, 2016.

Twist, Lynne. *Living a Committed Life: Finding Freedom and Fulfillment in a Purpose Larger Than Yourself.* Oakland, CA: Berrett-Koehler Publishers, 2022.

Tyson, Neil deGrasse. *Astrophysics for People in a Hurry.* New York: W. W. Norton, 2017.

Wahl, Erik. *Unthink: Rediscover Your Creative Genius.* New York: Crown Business, 2013.

Wilkerson, Isabel. *Caste: The Origins of Our Discontents.* New York: Random House, 2020.

Williams, Caroline. *Move: How the New Science of Body Movement Can Set Your Mind Free.* New York: Hanover Square Press, 2022.

Wilson. Edward O. *Half-Earth: Our Planet's Fight for Life.* New York: Liveright, 2016.

Wolf, Maryanne. *Reader, Come Home: The Reading Brain in a Digital World.* New York: Harper Paperbacks, 2019.

Yong, Ed. *An Immense World: How Animal Senses Reveal the Hidden Realms Around Us.* New York: Random House, 2022.

INDEX

Abramson, Charles I., 239–40
activation energy, xxxv–xlii, *xxxviii*, 18, 39, 52–53, 90, 95, 126–27
active opportunism, 57–76, 252; contagious altruism, 74–75; LIT tools, 75–76; maximizing potential to get lucky, 68–70; outgoing, 63–66; Sharp's story, 61–62; Stone's story, 68–70; synergizing superpowers, 72–73; talking with people who know something different, 61–62; traveling for inspiration, 70–72; use of term, 58–59; Vemula's story, 66–68; Wilkes's story, 70–72
adaptability, 28, 84, 141, 148, 218–19, 236
addiction, 33, 114
ADHD/ADD, xxxiii; author's story, x–xiv, 34–35, 51, 77–79, 82–83, 90–91, 169–70; default mode variability and, 83; norepinephrine processing in, 81
adversity, 117, 143, 182
aha moments, 2
alcohol, 115–16
All We Can Save (Johnson and Wilkinson, ed.), 233, 236
altruism, 74–75
Alzheimer's disease, xxvi, 46, 103, 107, 122
Amazon, xxviii
Amazon rain forest, 174
American Civil Liberties Union, 231
Ammendolia, Dustin, 177
amygdala, 140
amyotrophic lateral sclerosis (ALS), 179
Angelou, Maya, 194
anger, 12, 209–11
Animal Farm (Orwell), 144
Anishinaabe Nation, 171–72, 217

Ankrum, James, 41–43, 54–55
answers: questions vs., 23, 37, 255. *See also* living for the questions
Antetokounmpo, Giannis, 160
ants, 59, 101, 132–33, 224
anxiety, ix, 103, 113, 205, 226
Apex predators, 216
Apple, xxviii, 48, 70
asking questions. *See* living for the questions
assumptions, xxxiv, 9, 26, 27, 37, 85–86
Atomic Habits (Clear), 29, 36
attentional penlight, 80, 225
attentional "pulls," 89–90, 96
attentional "pushes," 89–90, 96
attention pinch, 77–96, 252; author's story, 77–79, 82–83, 90–91, 92–95; brain static and white noise, 83–85; distractions and, 79–83; motivation and, 91–92; nudges and nuances, 88–89; partnership and parenthood, 92–95; pushing past limits of perception, 85–88; three steps for, 81–82
Auden, W. H., 24
Australian National University, 157
authenticity, 5, 7, 14–16
autism, xviii–xix, xxxiii, 125
autopilot, interrupting, 38–39
Avon Products, 1, 2
awe, 166, 170–71, 176–77
Awe (Keltner), 101

bariatric surgery, 9–10
Barrett, Lisa Feldman, xxii, 57
basic biological facts, 211–13
Bays, Jan Chozen, 12
belief perseverance, 4–5
Benyus, Janine, 203, 218, 256
Bielskyte, Monika, 229
"Big C" creativity, 136–37

biodiversity, xix, xxiii–xxiv, 221
bioexploitation, 216–18
Biogen, 62
bioinspiration, 85, 86, 101, 176, 208, 216–19, 222, 225
Bio-inspired Networking (Câmara), 57–58, 59
biomedicine, 48
biometrics, 50, 51
Biomimicry (Benyus), 218
Biomimicry Institute, 218
bipedalism, 97
blind spots, 40, 76, 137, 156–57, 165
Bob, Darrell, 97
body language, 12, 245
boredom, 53, 145, 189, 205–6
Born to Be Good (Keltner), 75
Bosch, Hieronymus, 71
Boston Children's Hospital, 222
boundaries, 5, 6, 38–39
"bounded awareness," 156
Brach, Tara, 187
brain, xiii–xiv, xxii–xxiii; activation energy and, xxxviii–xxxix; attention and, 79–81; breaks and pauses, 184; curiosity and, 30–31; default mode network (DMN), 83–84, 148, 183–84, 187, 189; energy, xx–xxi, xxvi; going against cognitive grain, 142–44; hijacking, xiv, xxvi, xxviii, xxx, 80, 114–15; low-energy brain (LEB), xxvi–xxx, 6–7, 126, 189; mind-wandering mode, 191–92; movement and, 100–101, 103; neural networks, x, xxii, xxiv, xxvii, 60, 91, 120, 137, 139–42, 166; outward bound for, 63–66; pinching (*see* pinching your brain); plasticity (*see* neuroplasticity); reward system, xxvi, xxviii, 4, 31, 80, 114, 130–34, 143; sleep and, 192–93; variability in, 83–84, 85, 147
"brain bound," 60
brain-derived neurotrophic factor (BDNF), 102

brain imaging. *See* neuroimaging
brain static, 83–85
brainstorming, xxxi, 85–86, 87, 117, 149–50, 164, 180, 199, 222, 249
brawny brain, 125–27
breaks, xxxi, 184–85, 189–90, 202; author's story, 52; microbreaks, 186, 201; movement and, 117–18; from practice, 127–29. *See also* "pause"
Breathnach, Sarah Ban, 172
Bregman, Peter, 153–54
Bridle, James, xxii, 60
Briefs, Nancy, 64–65
Brigham and Women's Hospital, 9, 147–48, 154
Brodsky, Julia, 25
Brown, Brené, 244
Bruegel, Pieter, the Elder, 71
Budde, Mariann, 46, 235, 244, 247–48, 256
Bujdoss, Justin von, 121
burnout, 189–90, 208
button batteries, 44–45

cadence, 112–16
call to action, 37, 55–56, 228
call to service, 14–16
Câmara, Daniel, 57–58, 59
Cambridge University, 41
cancer, xxxi, 30, 46, 50, 101, 169, 176
card mechanics, 119–20
caring culture, 227–53; Budde's story, 247–48; compassion as humanity's common denominator, 243–45; Doty's story, 243–45; power of one flipping the switch, 234–36; repairing and reinvigorating community, 236–40; Shuford's story, 231–34; spirituality, 245–48; unprecedented times, technology, and opportunities, 240–43
Carson, Rachel, 217, 218
Casals, Pablo, 132
Catalano, Allison S., 155–56
Center for Compassion and Altruism Research and Education, 3

chance encounters, 147–48
Cherry, Kathy, 197
chess puzzles, 52
Cho, Seonghee, 186
Chopra, Deepak, 142
Circadian Code, The (Panda), 115
circadian rhythms, xl, 105, 115, 185–86
Civil Eats, 115
clarity, 121–23
Clear, James, 29, 36
climate change, 172, 215, 228, 233
cognition, xxxix, 84, 103, 107, 120, 123
cognitive biases, 156–57, 158
cognitive grain, 142–44
Cohen, Gene D., 143, 192–93
cold water showers, 150
collaboration, xxxix, 64–66, 73, 76, 165, 236–37, 240–42
Collins, Hanne, 58
Columbia and *Challenger* disasters, 153
Columbia University, 214
comfort zone, 85, 140, 141, 144, 148–50, 235. *See also* new and different
"communications disabled," xiii
community, repairing and reinvigorating, 236–40
compassion, 11–14; as humanity's common denominator, 243–45
composting, 226
Computers, Communications, and the Public Interest (Simon), 79
confirmation bias, 156–57
conscious cadence, 16–19, 112–16
constructive failure, 158–60, 165
contagious altruism, 74–75
Coppola, Francis Ford, 33
cortisol, 195, 202
cosmological constant, 157–58
Couch, Lyle, xiii
Courchene, Dave, 45, 110, 171–73, 209–11, 217, 218, 220, 223, 242, 246, 248, 256
Covid pandemic, 33–35, 220–21; author's story, 34–35, 94, 183–84;

Karp Lab research, 94, 146–47, 240–41; mRNA vaccines, 29–30, 178; N95 masks, 240–41; youth and mental health, 33–34
creativity, xvii–xviii, 136–37, 229; failure and, 159–60, 164–65; movement and, 99, 117–18; new, different, or surprising stimuli and, 136–37, 143, 148, 149; togetherness and, 249
criticism, 182
cross-pollination, 59, 60
curiosity, 8, 25, 26, 47–48, 76; igniting inquiry and discovery, 29–33; talking with people who know something different, 61–62. *See also* living for the questions; new and different

Dalai Lama, 247
dance, 99, 102–3, 150
Daniels, Bonnie, 232
dark energy, 157–58
daydreaming, 83, 84, 193
DDT, 217
Deak, JoAnn, 125–26, 130, 143–44, 145, 233
de Bono, Edward, 59–60, 75
defamiliarization, 144–47
default mode network (DMN), 83–84, 148, 183–84, 187, 189
Dellis, Nelson, 121–23, 129–30
dementia, 103. *See also* Alzheimer's disease
dendrites, xxii, 126
depression, ix, 99, 103, 116, 189, 205
DeRita, Gabe, 18–19, 20, 100
De Sena, Joe, 110–11, 117, 143, 148
diabetes, 9, 65, 101, 198
diet, 102, 114–15
different. *See* new and different
Dillen, Abigail, 233
Dinges, David F., 189
dinner table conversations, 248–49, 250
dinosaurs, 163

Disappearance of Childhood, The
 (Postman), 62
Disney, Walt, xvii
distractions, 77, 79–83, 113–14
diversity, 237. *See also* biodiversity;
 neurodiversity
Djembe drumming, 135
"do new," 206–7. *See also* new and
 different
"do nothing," 19, 190
dopamine, xxxviii–xxxix, 103, 130,
 131–32, 143, 150, 204
Doty, James, xxv–xxvi, 3, 11–12, 163,
 195, 243–45, 256
downtime, 190, 192–93, 200–201.
 See also "pause"
dreams (dreaming), xxxii, 5–7, 193.
 See also daydreaming
Drucker, Peter, 255
Duckworth, Angela, 145
Duhigg, Charles, 38
Dweck, Carol, 153

Earthjustice, 220, 233
EARTHseed Permaculture Center
 (EPC), 215
Edison, Thomas, xvii
egalitarianism, 168
Einstein, Albert, xvii, xxi, 104
Element, The (Robinson), xix
Elizabeth, Tracy, 90
embodied intelligence, xl, 206, 246
Emerson, Ralph Waldo, 206, 246
Empress Has No Clothes, The
 (Roché), 14
endocannabinoids, 100
endorphins, xxxviii, 100, 112, 150
endurance, 109–12
energy transfer, xx–xxi, 235
epidural anesthesia, 65
epigenetics, xxiv, 20
Evergreen State College, 68–69
evolution, x, 19–20, 21, 23, 132, 136,
 163, 165, 221, 234; accelerating
 innovation, xxxi–xxxii; movement
 and, 97–98, 102, 104; survival of
 the *LIT*-est, xxi–xxvi

exercise, 50, 95, 99; benefits of,
 98–103. *See also* movement
Exercised (Lieberman), 102, 104, 109
expectations, 96, 135
"extended mind," 60
Extended Mind, The (Paul), 60

Facebook, xxviii
"fail fast," 165
failure, 9, 39, 42–43, 151–65, 252;
 aiming for constructive, 158–60,
 165; author's story, 159, 160–62;
 bias against, 155–57; getting lost
 in, 153–55; giving yourself credit
 for, 163–64; Langer's story, 153–55;
 LIT tools, 164–65; managing,
 155–57, 165; nowhere to hide,
 160–63; Nyad's story, 151–53;
 successfully proving something
 doesn't work, 157–58
Failure (Firestein), 162
familiarity, 137
Farokhzad, Omid, 65
fast food, 114–15
FDA's Generally Recognized as Safe
 (GRAS), 67
fear, 64, 72, 140–42
feedback, 105–6
fight-or-flight response, xxix, 162
Firestein, Stuart, 162
fitness trackers, 105, 107, 109
fixed mindset, 153–54
flipping the switch, 1–21, 251;
 accepting barriers vs. building
 bridges, 3–5; answering call to
 service, 14–16; author's story,
 3–4, 7–8, 16–17; compassion
 transforming roots of resistance,
 11–14; conscious cadence vs.
 urgency of now, 16–19; Doty's
 story, 11–12; Hockfield's story,
 14–15; letting dreams inspire, 5–7;
 LIT tools, 19–22; Rippon's story,
 5–7; Roché's story, 1–2, 7, 13–14,
 17–18; thought processes, 7–11
focused attention, 78, 80–81, 84–85,
 88–89, 95

"follow your passion," 47–49
forward motion, 24, 30, 56, 82–83, 134–35, 159, 182
frames of reference, 4, 9
Francis, Pope, 179
Frank, Anne, 215
Fukuoka, Masanobu, 216
functional hyperemia, 79
"fundamental attribution error," 156

Gale, Michael, 198–99
Gandhi, Mahatma, 247
gardening, 226
gastric bypass surgery, 9–10
Gebrian, Molly, 127–29, 186
Gehrig, Lou, 179
generosity, 75, 231
genetics, xxxix–xl, 20, 64, 72, 74, 147, 164
"get new," 206–7
getting bothered, 41–56, 252; Ankrum's story, 41–43, 54–55; author's story, 48–49; learning what moves the needle, 49–53; LIT tools, 55–56; pain points as traction for action, 43–46; purpose finding passion, 47–49; sharing a call to action, 55–56; wrong fit, 53–55
Gibbs, Daniel, 107
Girls Inc., 2, 13, 14
glass ceiling, 2
Goldberg, Tony, 221
Goleman, Daniel, 79
Grandin, Temple, xviii–xx, 13, 73
Great Depression, 178
greater good, 74, 166, 242, 252
Greater Good Science Center, 170
"green time," 205
Gregersen, Hal B., 255
growth mindset, 153–54
Gründer, Gerhard, 34
"gut feeling," 100, 184

habits, 38, 139–40, 149–50
habituation, xiii–xiv

Hadfield, Chris, 63, 123–25, 162
Half-Earth (Wilson), 229
happiness, 31, 58, 200–201
Harvard Business Review, 153–54
Harvard Business School, 58
Harvard Medical School, x, 192
Healthy Brain, Happy Life (Suzuki), 103
heart rate variability (HRV), 107–8, 193, 195
hedonic adaptation, 206–7
high-energy brain (HEB), xxiv, xxviii–xxix, 60, 75
Hockfield, Susan, 14–15, 73
holon, 145
homeostasis, 16
hook-and-hold strategies, 104
Hooked (Moss), 114–15
hooked on movement. *See* movement
hooks, bell, 234
hormetic stress, 150
Horowitz, Alexandra, 77
household chores, 120, 150
How Do We Want to Live? (Gründer), 34
How to Change (Milkman), 90
How to Do Nothing (Odell), 190
hubris, 169, 172
Huffington, Arianna, 183
hugging nature. *See* nature
humility, 166–82, 252–53; author's story, 169–70, 179–81; bringing it home, 179–82; Elder Courchene's story, 171–73; Langer's story, 178–79; LIT tools, 182; Moser's story, 167–68; transforming premise and potential, 173–75; Twist's story, 173–75
humor, 124–25
Hunte, Chad, 111–12
hunter-gatherers, 102, 114–15
hydrogels, 67, 147

ikigai, 18–19
imagination, 20–21
immune system, 26, 101, 115, 195
Imperial College London, 155–56

impermanence, 88, 108, 169, 184, 187–88, 195

imposter syndrome, 2–3, 13, 14, 54

inattentiveness, 80–81

inclusivity, 237

incoming opportunities, 65–66

Indigenous wisdom, 100, 171–73, 174–75, 209–11, 223

inertia, 18, 103–4, 112

inflammatory bowel disease (IBD), 68

inquiry: role of curiosity, 29–33. *See also* living for the questions; scientific inquiry; self-inquiry

insecurities, 1–3; Roché's story, 1–2, 7, 13–14, 17–18

insights, 58, 61, 75, 133, 159–60, 164, 184, 235, 236, 246, 255

inspiration, 21, 70–72, 87, 103, 134

Instagram, xxviii, 114, 177

intelligence, xxii, 60, 171

intention, 9, 56; energy activating, xxx–xxxi

Into the Magic Shop, 12

introversion, 58–59

intuition, 123–24

iteration, 66, 106, 153, 155, 158, 160, 164, 180, 245

jellyfish, xxxi, 152, 169, 176

Johns Hopkins University, 157

Johnson, Ayana Elizabeth, 236

Jordan, Michael, 85, 151, 160

journaling, 13, 20, 198–99, 202

joy, 47–49, 99; of persistence, 129–33

Joy of Movement, The (McGonigal), 99

Jung, Carl, 53

junk food, 114–15

Kandel, Eric, xiii

Karp Lab, xvi, xxxi–xxxii, 245; active opportunism, 63–67; chance encounters, 147–48; contagious altruism, 74; Covid research, 94, 146, 240–41; failure and, 154–55, 164; humility and, 169–70, 175–77; living for the questions,

22–28; medical problem solving, xxxi–xxxii, 8–10, 22–25, 85–88, 138, 219, 222–23; pain point and, 43–44; pinching in, 85–88; Wednesday presentations, 145–47, 177

Katzschmann, Grace (Teo), 137–42

Kavli Institute for Systems Neuroscience, 32, 168

Keltner, Dacher, 75, 101, 170–71, 176–77

Kennedy Center for the Performing Arts, 161

Keshavarzian, Tina, 106

Kim, Sooyeol, 186

Kimmerer, Robin Wall, xxxvi, 34, 173, 223, 241

kindness, 75, 166, 176, 178, 182, 231

King, Martin Luther, Jr., 233, 247

Lamott, Anne, 195

Landowska, Wanda Aleksandra, 119

Langer, Robert, 22, 28, 37, 63, 65, 153–55, 178–79, 200–201

lateral thinking, 59–60, 75

Laulicht, Bryan, 44–45

Lawrence Berkeley National Laboratory, 157

learning disabilities. *See* ADHD/ADD

Levin, Richard, 14–15

Lieberman, Daniel, 102, 104, 109

Life (magazine), 200

Life Ignition Tools (LIT), 251–53

lighting the world, 227–53; Budde's story, 247–48; compassion as humanity's common denominator, 243–45; Doty's story, 243–45; power of one flipping the switch, 234–36; repairing and reinvigorating community, 236–40; Shuford's story, 231–34; spirituality, 245–48; unprecedented times, technology, and opportunities, 240–43

limbic system, xxix

linear thinking, 9

LinkedIn, 74
LIT: author's story, xiv–xvii; energy transfer, xx–xxi; survival of the *LIT*-est, xxi–xxvi; use of term, xiv–xv
LIT (Life Ignition Tools), xv–xvii; active opportunism, 75–76; failure, 164–65; flipping the switch, 19–22; getting bothered, 55–56; humility, 182; living for the questions, 40; lowering activation energy, xxxv–xlii; movement, 116–18; nature, 225–26; new and different, 149–50; "pause," 201–2; pinching your brain, 95–96; practice, 133–35
Living a Committed Life (Twist), 243
living for the questions, 22–40, 251–52; asking the big questions, 19, 30, 34–37; bridge from asking to acting, 33–34; curiosity igniting inquiry and discovery, 29–33; interrupting autopilot on inclinations and boundaries, 38–39; LIT tools, 40; questioning own processes, 26–28; self-inquiry, 28–29
local sleep, 193
locus coeruleus, 80–81
loneliness, 59, 99, 215
"loss aversion," 156
lost in failures, 153–55
Lou Gehrig's disease, 179
low-energy brain (LEB), xxvi–xxx, xxxiv, 4, 6–7, 126, 189
luck, 47, 68–70

Ma'at, 215–16
Maathai, Wangari, 230
Maharaj, Sri Nisargadatta, 98
managing failure, 155–57, 165
Marcus Aurelius, 10
Mass General Brigham Center for COVID Innovation, 240–41
mastery, xxvii, xxix
Max Planck Institute for Human Development, 84–85

Maxwell, John C., 166
May, Katherine, 32
McCauley, Ed, 109–10
McGill University, 160–61
McGonigal, Kelly, 99
medical adhesives, xxxi, 23, 42, 86–88, 162–63, 222–23
meditation, 98–99, 112–14, 187–88, 194–95; author's experience, 35, 112–13, 183–84, 188, 194–95; default mode network and, 183–84, 187; feedback and, 105, 106–7; impermanence and, 187–88; walking, 106–7, 195
Meditations (Marcus Aurelius), 10
meetings, 91, 139, 245; Karp Lab, 62, 73, 146–47, 177; movement for, 117–18
melanin, 81
memorization, 38–39, 129–30; author's story, xii–xiii, 38, 160–61; Dellis's story, 121–23, 129–30
Miami Heat, 160
microbreaks, 186, 201
Microsoft, 48, 68, 70
Milkman, Katy, 90
Milwaukee Bucks, 160
mind-body-spirit interconnectedness, xl, 35, 90–91, 99–100
mind drifts, 77, 195, 252
mindfulness. *See* meditation
Mindset (Dweck), 153
mind-wandering, 79, 187, 191–92, 193
MIT, x, 14, 41, 66, 73, 92–93, 139, 147, 154
MIT Infinite History Project, 61
MIT Koch Institute for Integrative Cancer Research, 61
MIT Media Lab, 69
momentum, xxxvii, 44, 99, 116–17, 135
monkey mind, 84
mood, xl, 52, 102–3, 117, 120, 206
"moral beauty," 176–77, 182
morning routine, 117
Moser, May-Britt, 32, 167–68
Moss, Michael, 114–15

Mosso, Angelo, 79

motivation, xxxvii, 126–27, 133; attention and, 91–92; pain points and, 44–45; passion and inspiration, 50, 51, 134; practice and, 123, 126–27, 130, 133

Mount Everest, 122–23

Move (Williams), 100

movement, 97–118, 252; author's story, 105–6, 107–8, 111, 116, 126, 130–32, 133; benefits of, 98–103; conscious cadence for, 112–16; endurance and, 109–12; inertia and, 103–4, 121; Langer's story, 200–201; LIT tools, 116–18; methodology for experimentation, 104–9; nature and, 97–99, 101, 102–3

mRNA technology, 29–30, 178

Müller, Paul, 217

multiple sclerosis (MS), 22–23

Murthy, Vivek, 33–34, 197, 249

muscular dystrophy (MD), 138–39

music, 127–28, 132, 150, 186

myelin, 128

"naive realism," 156

nanotechnology, 67–68, 240

Nanyang Technological University, 138

"narrative fallacy," 156

nasal sprays, 146–47

Nathan, Ran, 97–98

National Center for Chronic Disease Prevention and Health Promotion, 101

National Institutes for Health, 154

National Study of Learning Mindsets, xviii

National University of Singapore, 186

nature (natural world), xxxiii, 21, 96, 202, 203–26, 230, 251, 253; author's story, 77–78, 203–4, 207; Elder Courchene's story, 209–11; failure and, 165; homeostasis, 16; LIT tools, 225–26; movement and, 97–99, 101, 102–3; pauses in, 185–86, 191–92, 201, 207; place in web of life, 211–13; relationship style with, 216–18; secrets hiding in plain sight, 218–21; Suzuki's story, 211–13; Thomas's story, 213–16; walking in (nature walks), 77–78, 191–92, 203, 223–25

negative thoughts or beliefs, 11–12, 31, 140–42, 206

networking, 59–60, 64–65, 70. *See also* active opportunism

neural networks, x, xxii, xxiv, xxvii, 60, 91, 120, 137, 139–42, 166

neural synchrony, xxxix–xl

neurochemicals, xxxviii–xxxix, 4, 81, 100, 103

neurodiversity, xvii–xx, 72–73, 76, 224

neuroimaging, xiv, xxvii, 79, 102–3, 136

neurons, xiii, 6, 38, 57–58, 59, 79, 102, 126, 141, 184, 185, 192

neuroplasticity, xxii–xxiii, 6, 20, 102, 120, 141, 142, 191, 192

neuroscience, x, xxi, xxvi, 4, 31, 60, 79, 80, 83, 191; habituation and sensitization, xiii–xiv. *See also* brain

new and different, 136–50, 252; fear factor and, 140–42; "get new" vs. "do new," 206–7; going against cognitive grain, 142–44; LIT tools, 149–50; Sharp's story, 61–62; synergizing superpowers, 72–73; taking a chance on chance encounters, 147–48; using defamiliarization to transform perspective, 144–47

New Year's resolutions, 103

New York Times, xix

New York University, 103

New York Yankees, 179

Nido, Pedro J. del, 222

Nobel Prize, 29, 30, 32, 61, 79, 139, 143, 157, 167, 217, 228, 230

nonverbal communication, 12

noradrenaline, 81, 103
norepinephrine, 81, 150, 202
"normal," 255
North Carolina Justice Center, 231
North Carolina State University, 186
Northwestern University, xxviii
Norwegian culture, 168
"no-upmanship," 168
novelty, 39, 80, 84, 137, 143–44, 145
nuances, 88–89, 121, 136, 145, 224
nudges, 88–89
Nyad, Diana, 19, 41, 47, 151–53, 188

Oakland Museum of California, 237–39
obesity, 9, 101, 105
obstacle courses, 110–11
obstacles, xxxvii, 2–3, 7, 10–11, 155, 182
Odell, Jenny, 190
O'Keefe, John, 167
Oldenburg, Ray, 236–37
Open Style Lab, 139
opioid addiction crisis, 33
opportunism: use of term, 58–59.
    See also active opportunism
Orwell, George, 144
Ó Tuama, Pádraig, 144
"Our Planet, Our Future" (statement), 228–29
outgoing active opportunism, 63–66
outward bound, 63–66
"overlearning," 128
overview effect, 145

pace (pacing), xxxvii, 112, 113, 191, 206, 224
Pachamama Alliance, 174–75
Padamsey, Zahid, xxvii
pain points, 43–48, 53–54, 55
Panda, Satchin, 115
Papert, Seymour, 69
Park, YoungAh, 186
Parsons School of Design, 139
passion, xxxii, 47–49, 61–62; learning what moves your needle, 49–53
pass it forward, 56
patience, 21, 131, 206

patterns (pattern recognition), 21, 39, 55–56, 139–40, 141, 142, 221
Paul, Annie Murphy, 60
"pause," xli, 183–202, 253; borrowing from winter's wisdom, 185–86; burnout and, 189–90; doing what makes you happy, 200–201; impermanence and, 187–88; Langer's story, 200–201; LIT Tools, 201–2; meditation (see meditation); mind-wandering, 187, 191–92; with music, 186; in nature, 185–86, 191–92, 201, 202, 207; pinching your brain and, 88, 89–90; Ramakrishnan's story, 183–84, 187, 195; silence vs. stimulation, 196–97; sleep and, 192–93; unintended, 198–200
"peak states" (flow), xiv
perception, pushing past limits of, 85–88
Pereira, Maria, 162–63, 222–23
Perfect Predator, The (Strathdee), 242
Perlmutter, Saul, 157–58
permaculture, 213–16, 230
Perry, Joe, xxxiii
persistence, 129–33, 182, 219
personal motivators, 91–92
pesticides, 217
philanthropy, 173–75
Phillpotts, Eden, ix
photosynthesis, xx, 212
phytoplankton, 219
Pilates, 90–91
pinching your brain, 77–96, 252; author's story, 77–79, 82–83, 90–91, 92–95; brain static and white noise, 83–85; distractions, 79–83; LIT tools, 95–96; motivation and, 91–92; nudges and nuances, 88–89; partnership and parenthood, 92–95; pushing past limits of perception, 85–88; resisting the pulls and going for the pushes, 89–90; three steps for, 81–82
"placemaking," 236–37

play, 52, 75, 84, 94, 119, 183, 189. *See also* "pause"
porcupine quills, 23, 87–88
Postman, Neil, 62
Power of Habit, The (Duhigg), 38
practice, 119–35, 137, 252; author's story, 126, 130–32, 133, 135; breaks from, 127–29; building brawny brain, 125–27; clarity in a crisis, 121–23; Deak's story, 125–26, 130; Dellis's story, 121–23, 129–30; frequent and shorter sessions, 127–29; Gebrian's story, 127–29; Hadfield's story, 123–25; joy of persistence, 129–33; LIT tools, 133–35; Turner's story, 119–20, 121; for the unpredictable, 123–25
Practice of the Wild, The (Snyder), 205, 208
praise, 182
priorities, 52, 78, 183; meeting new contacts, 149; play, solitude, and silence, 183. *See also* "pause"
problem definition, 180
problem-solving, xxxi–xxxii, 8–10, 22–25, 44–45, 85–88, 180, 229
procrastination, 18, 51
Project for Public Spaces, 237
pruning, xxvii, 141
purpose, xxxii, 47–49, 95, 123, 209, 243, 250–51

questions: answers vs., 23, 37, 255. *See also* living for the questions
Questions Are the Answer (Gregersen), 255
quick dips, 150

racism, 36–37, 239–40
rainwater harvesting, 214
Ramakrishnan, Vivek, 88, 183–84, 187, 195
Ratey, John J., 102
Rath, Tom, 20
Ravikant, Naval, 190
rebounds, 164

recycling, 226
reinforcement learning, 131–32
relationships: happiness and, 58; with nature, 167, 216–18 (*see also* nature); repairing and reinvigorating community, 236–40; social (*see* social interactions)
Renkl, Margaret, 213, 231
repetition, 95, 119, 120, 121, 126, 140, 194. *See also* practice
resistance and compassion, 11–14
Rice University, 127
Riess, Adam G., 157
Rippon, Adam, 5–7, 143–44, 233
Roberts, Richard J., 30
Robinson, Ken, xvii–xviii, xix
Roché, Joyce, 1–2, 7, 13–14, 17–18
Röntgen, Wilhelm Conrad, 157
Roosevelt, Eleanor, 140
Rumi, 89
rumination, 11–12, 83, 84, 89, 206
running, xxxvi, 99, 105–6, 109–10, 134, 207
Running the Sahara (documentary), 134
Russia invasion of Ukraine, 74

Salk Institute, 115
Sankar, Sambhav, 220
Sasaki, Lisa, 36–37, 55, 74, 237–39
Satterfield, Jill, 113
"sauntering," 191
saying "yes," 149, 198–99
scarlet fever, 120
Schmidt, Brian P., 157
scientific inquiry, 22–24, 26–28
scientific inspiration, 61–62, 87
sea slugs, xiii
Seckler, Christoph, 168
sedentary habits, 101, 102, 114, 115, 117–18
Seinfeld, Jerry, 194–95
self-absorption, 159, 166, 167
self-affirmation, 11–12
self-awareness, 2, 7–8, 49–52, 55–56, 76, 81
self-confidence, 134

self-discipline, 121

self-doubt, 1–3; imposter syndrome, 2–3, 13, 14, 54; Roché's story, 1–2, 7, 13–14, 17–18

self-empowerment, 5, 13, 56

self-inquiry, 24, 28–29; curiosity igniting, 29–33

self-inventory, 13, 51, 95

selfless gene, 74

sensitization, xiii–xiv

"separate self," 171

serendipity, 65, 69, 70, 72, 136, 148, 198, 235, 242. *See also* new and different

serotonin, xxxviii, 103, 130

Seven Sacred Laws, 210

sexism, 2–3, 5, 37

"shadow self," 11–12

shame, xxxvi, xli, 31, 39, 76, 93, 95, 104, 118, 163

Sharp, Phillip, 29–30, 61–62, 63, 139

Shiller, Robert J., 170

short practice sessions, 127–28

Shuford, Barbara, 232–33

Shuford, Reginald "Reggie," 15–16, 46, 175, 227, 231–34

silence, 196–97, 201, 204

Silent Spring (Carson), 217

Simon, Herbert A., 79

skin contact allergies, 67–68, 219

sleep, 52, 101, 115, 185–86, 189, 192–93

slowing down, 17, 113, 184, 188, 205, 225, 226

small talk, 40, 64

Snapchat, xxviii

Snead, Sam, 125

Snyder, Gary, 205, 208, 246

"social brain," 133–34

social interactions, 58, 59–60, 82, 117; chance encounters, 147–48; practice and, 133–34; "third places," 202

social media, xxviii, 4, 52, 89–90, 108–9, 114, 204–5

solitary quests, 209–11

solitude, 183, 197

Spark (Ratey), 102

Spartan Race, 110–11

speed bumps, 89–90

spider webs, 23, 175

spirituality, xxi, 172–73, 245–48

Stanford University, xxvi, 3, 153, 190, 195, 243

"stay proximate," 46, 250–51

Stevenson, Bryan, 46

Stickgold, Robert, 192–93

stimulation, 196–97

Stone, Linda, 47–48, 54, 68–70, 82, 202

storytelling, xi, xxiii

Strathdee, Steffanie, 124–25, 242

stress, xxvi, 102, 103, 150, 166, 185, 189, 190, 248

stretches (stretching), 106, 133

structural inequality, 34, 35, 36–37, 215

"stupid" questions, 31–32

Stutz, Phil, 59

sun exposure, 100–101

supercommunicators, 67

superpowers, xi–xii, 72–73; attention as (*see* attention pinch)

surprises, 76, 136–37, 145, 157, 158, 162, 235, 252. *See also* new and different

Survival Game, 207

survival of the *LIT*-est, xxi–xxvi

Suttie, Jill, 191

Suzuki, David, 211–13, 256

Suzuki, Wendy, 103

swarm behavior, 59

Swiss Army knife, 25

Synapse Project, The, 143

synapses, xiii–xiv, xxvi–xxvii, 127–28, 139, 186

Synectics, 69–70

synergizing superpowers, 72–73

Tanzi, Rudolph, xxix–xxx, xxxiii, 132, 139–40, 141–42

taste receptors, 114

Tattoo on My Brain, A (Gibbs), 107

Tauber, Alan, 135

Tavakkoli, Ali, 9–10, 20, 65
termites, 59
"thinking hats," 60
third place, 202, 236–37
Thomas, Pandora, 197, 213–16, 221, 225, 226, 230, 256
Thoreau, Henry David, 37, 100, 136, 170, 191, 246
thought processes, 7–11, 26–28
thumb exercise, 145
TikTok, xxviii, 90
time management, 78, 82
Tippett, Krista, 22
tiredness, 52–53, 76, 116, 185
Tissium, 162–63
Together (Murthy), 33, 197, 249
Tolle, Eckhart, 6
Toyota Green Initiative, 214
Transcendentalism, 246
Transcendental Meditation (TM), 194–95
transparency, 56, 245
trees, xx, 101, 201, 204, 206, 214, 219
tune in, 52, 83, 134–35, 182, 201
Turner, Charles Henry, 132–33, 224, 239–40
Turner, Richard, 119–20, 121
Turtle Lodge, 172, 209–11, 242
Tutu, Desmond, 247
Twist, Lynne, 1, 173–75, 243

uncertainty, 6, 54, 141
unintended pauses, 198–200
University College London, 167
University of California, Berkeley, 170
University of California San Diego School of Medicine, 124
University of Chicago, 239
University of Illinois, 186
University of Pennsylvania, 90, 189
University of Wisconsin, 221
urgency of now, 16–19
USA Memory Champions, 122, 123

Vemula, Praveen Kumar, 66–68
vigilance, 79–80, 98, 187, 189, 195, 227

vision quests, 209–11
visualization, 20–21, 141–42
vitamin D, 100–101
volunteerism, 76, 150

Walden (Thoreau), 136
Walker, Matthew, 192–93
walking, 95, 97, 99, 100, 117–18, 191–92, 208; in nature, 77–78, 191–92, 203, 223–25
walking meditations, 106–7, 195
Wallace H. Coulter Foundation, 65
Walt Disney's Carousel of Progress, xxiv–xxv, 116, 249–50
Walter, Nathan, xxviii
wandering mind, 79, 187, 191–92, 193
Warhol, Andy, 144
Ways of Being (Bridle), xxii, 60
"weak ties," 58
web of life, 211–13
weightlifting, 103–4
weight loss, 105–6
West, Samuel, 155
white noise, 83–85
"Why?," 3–4, 10, 26, 30, 38–39; identifying the, 41 (*see also* getting bothered)
Wilde, Oscar, 15
Wilkes, Stephen, 70–72, 247–48
Wilkinson, Katharine K., 236
Williams, Caroline, 100
Williams, Minnie, 232
Wilson, Edward O., 66, 229
Winfrey, Oprah, xvii
wonder, 80
World War II, 178

X-rays, 157
xylem, 219

Yale University, 14, 73, 170
Yin, Xiaolei, 22
Yong, Ed, xxii
Yutang, Lin, 221

zoonotic diseases, 220–21